AN URGENCY (

An Urgency of Teachers

the Work of Critical Digital Pedagogy

Sean Michael Morris and Jesse Stommel

Hybrid Pedagogy Inc.

CONTENTS

Learning Online

Writing and Reading

ACKNOWLEDGEMENTS

This volume is a collection of our own writing over the last seven years, but it is made possible by a wide network of collaborators and contributors to our educations, thoughts, understanding, and insights. Sean and Jesse would like to acknowledge the ongoing, persistent, and brilliant contributions of a few of our closest friends and colleagues: Audrey Watters, Bonnie Stewart, Cathy Davidson, Howard Rheingold, Martha Burtis, and Christopher R. Friend. Your work inspires and inhabits so many of the sentences here.

We'd also like to thank every writer and editor who has contributed to *Hybrid Pedagogy*. You are the drum beat thrumming beneath this collection. And the educators who've taught, presented, gathered at *Digital Pedagogy Lab*. You are the community pushing us to more deeply realize the stakes of this work.

Sean would like to thank Jesse Stommel, for being a hard-ass and never letting me quit; Amy Collier, who has remained a valued colleague through thick and thin; and all the students who have been my teachers. I would especially like to thank my family: my husband, Matthew Morris, who supported and continues to support the emotional labor of pedagogy, running a journal, and directing an international event; Fio Law, whose insights into social justice, and identity formation and politics has challenged me to keep learning; Ingrid Law, for always staying interested and for caring for the dogs when England calls; and my mother, Linda Bolsen, who was the first person to teach me that imagination had intellectual value and credibility.

Jesse would like to thank the four teachers who most helped as I found my way to the work of teaching, Sean Michael Morris, R L Widmann, Martin Bickman, and Marian Keane. My first moments as a teacher in a classroom were with the four of you. So much of the teacher I've become turns upon those moments. I would also like to thank my family, particularly my mom and dad, Chris De Bruin and Joe Stommel. Your work in the world, and the empowering and compassionate way you approach it, lives inside my pedagogy. Thanks (and adoration) to my husband and best friend, Joshua Lee. And my daughter, Hazel Mae Stommel-Lee, a world-champion snuggler who kicks the ass of the world every single day. Finally, every bit of this is dedicated to the amazing students and teachers I've worked with throughout my career.

We both acknowledge that this work comes to life most fully in dialogue, so we offer a final nod to those who've read, watched, listened, engaged, responded as this work has unfolded. Thank you.

FOREWORD

AUDREY WATTERS

For at least a century now, we've been told stories that machines are poised to "revolutionize" education. The rationale for this revolution has remained largely unchanged: machines will make education more efficient. Machines will make education more streamlined. They will make it cheaper and faster. As education psychologist Sidney Pressey, inventor of one of the very first "teaching machines," wrote in 1933,

> There must be an 'industrial revolution' in education, in which educational science and the ingenuity of educational technology combine to modernize the grossly inefficient and clumsy procedures of conventional education. Work in the schools of the school will be marvelously though simply organized, so as to adjust almost automatically to individual differences and the characteristics of the learning process. There will be many labor-saving schemes and devices, and even machines — not at all for the mechanizing of education but for the freeing of teacher and pupil from the educational drudgery and incompetence.

Machines will automate education, making it more responsive, more engaging. Or so we're told. "The average teacher is woefully burdened by such routine of drill and information-fixing," Pressey had observed. "It would seem highly desirable to lift from her shoulders as much of this burden and make her freer for those inspirational and thought-stimulating activities which are, presumably, the real function of the teacher."

One hundred years into this so-called "industrial revolution" in education, it's hard to see how teaching machines have accomplished much of this promise — Pressey's or otherwise. Nevertheless, technologists still clamor for more machines in classrooms, insisting that these will "personalize education," somehow making it more human by involving teachers less.

But rather than saving labor as Pressey and others have envisioned, these devices have created new kinds of work — work for both the teacher and the pupil. And with efficiency as the goal, machines enable more schoolwork, not less. The school day extends into the nights and weekend and into the holidays as everyone is expected to be within reach of and responsive to their digital devices; the school day extends into retirement as everyone is expected to participate in what's now called "lifelong learning" — homework has become inescapable.

Contrary to Pressey's predictions, much of this work remains drudgery. Even with the advances in education technology, the kinds of tasks that have been automated and digitized — the assessment of multiple choice questions, for example — still require a great deal of repetition and monotony.

We all spend much of our day now clicking on things, a gesture that is far too often confused with "engagement." ("Engagement" — a word that has come to mean "measurable" and "marketable.") And because students now spend much of their time clicking on things — and in turn, generating incredible amounts of data — teachers and administrators are told they must pour through these machine-generated signals, an action that is far too often confused with "care."

It's not clear that Sidney Pressey envisioned "care" as one of the things he considered "the real function of the teacher." There's little evidence that "care" was one of the things his teaching machines were ever intended to facilitate. (It's worth noting perhaps that he did refer to teachers in most of his writing with female pronouns; the students, on the other hand, are gendered male. Indeed, there was unease among other education psychologists that teachers were too subjective, too emotional, too untrained — hence the need for more scientific and objective technologies such as the multiple-choice tests.) Pressey was, with his machines, committed to enhancing the intellectual and administrative labor of teachers. But it seems unlikely that he even recognized their affective labor. He was much more interested in measuring the intellectual activities of students than with caring for their minds, their bodies, their lives.

Education technology has followed his lead.

Some people will insist that technology is neutral — "it's just a tool," they'll say. "What matters is how you use it." But a technology always has a history, and it has a politics. A technology likely has a pedagogical bent as well — how it trains people to use it, if nothing else — and even if one tries to use a tool for a radically different task than it was built for, there are always remnants of those political and historical and pedagogical designs. Technologies are never "just tools." They are, to borrow from the physicist Ursula Franklin, practices. Technologies are systems. Technology "entails far more than its individual material components," Franklin wrote in *The Real World of Technology*. "Technology involves organizations, procedures, symbols, new words, equations, and, most of all, a mindset."

Educational technologies are thus embedded in educational institutions; they're intertwined with the histories and the practices of schooling. Even the technologies that are imagined to "disrupt" institutions and revolutionize teaching and learning are inescapably bound to cultural expectations about what school looks like (or should look like), what teachers and students do (or should do) — to the grammar and "the work" of education. This isn't to say that technologies do not restructure our relationships — they do; they have. But often, when there is an urgency to the adoption of new technologies in the classroom, it's because that work has been deemed inefficient or outmoded, because the workers — students and teachers alike — need to be controlled.

Working on computers is necessary, or so we're told, because the future of work itself demands it.

Sean Michael Morris and Jesse Stommel teach towards a different future — one in which dignity is prioritized over efficiency, one in which agency and freedom are prioritized over compliance and control. It's a future of education not enclosed by teaching machines but unfolded by teaching humans. It is a future of meaningful inquiry — and not because machines have somehow hidden the labor trying to convince us they'll eventually eradicate the drudgery of work. As the title of this collection of writing makes clear, in the face of stories insisting the future will be automated — that is, in the face of the urgency of machines — Morris and Stommel want us to agitate instead for *An Urgency of Teachers*. In positing pedagogy — critical pedagogy specifically — as a lever for change, they ask us to join them in resisting the stories that machines have wants and needs and that their logic dictates the shape of the future. Instead they urge us to center care and justice in our practices — to center humans — knowing that this will require a radical re-ordering of the priorities of our institutions and ideologies as well.

INTRODUCTION

SEAN MICHAEL MORRIS AND JESSE STOMMEL

Education is, in the words of Paulo Freire, an "inescapable concern." The work of teaching is activism. There are many models for this, but ours comes from a concern for the raising of critical consciousness on the part of students and teachers, but also within the minds, hearts, and policies of the administrators, governments, corporations, and other stakeholders (including, increasingly, technologists) who control the environments for learning at institutions of higher education and schools at all levels. No one can be left out of the work of critical pedagogy, or critical *digital* pedagogy, both the effort of it and its ends.

It wouldn't be appropriate to kick this book off with a linear history or neat and tidy map of the trajectory we've taken across our work. The ideas here developed as a series of nodes more than a connected set of thinking on a single subject. Our own definitions for critical digital pedagogy arrived through conversations, moments of intersection between our work as academics, teachers, and students, in the development of *Hybrid Pedagogy* and Digital Pedagogy Lab, and in the long thread of ongoing discussion on Twitter, in synchronous moments at conferences, in late evening text messages, on airplanes, on long walks through parking lots, and in classrooms upon several continents across multiple hemispheres. Critical pedagogy is as a philosophy and educational approach slippery enough to find its way into almost every conversation. And so this book includes tangents towards digital humanities, educational technology, digital writing, social justice, plagiarism and academic integrity, instructional design, and more.

It is in the slipperiness of critical digital pedagogy that we find its most valuable application, and have found throughout two decades working that praxis through. We've traced within this volume, and within the history of our work together, an exercise of pedagogy that pushes past the walls of the classroom and into the complicated practice of being human. This is work increasingly difficult in a world where the possibility of "being human" is not equally distributed — a world where who we can be, the education available to us, the resources which may support our curiosity, our intelligence, our imaginations, has become more and more dependent on the technologies our institutions employ. It is this unevenness, this inequity, that critical digital pedagogy seeks to rout. Our work (across this book and within its pieces) begins from a place of hope but recognizes the hard paths we must tread — the hard paths we must continue to tread—toward action.

And thus, our title "an urgency of teachers" describes the necessary shift we must make toward valuing more the work — affective, flawed, nuanced, unfolding—that teachers (all of them) do online and in classrooms, and also the important work wrought upon the heart and mind by an education that is concerned with the human. It is urgent we have teachers, it is urgent we employ them, pay them, support them with adequate resources; but it is also urgency which defines the project of teaching. In a political climate increasingly defined by its obstinacy, lack of criticality, and deflection of fact and care; in a society still divided across lines of race, nationality, religion, gender, sexuality, income, ability, and privilege; in a digital culture shaped by algorithms that neither know nor accurately portray truth, teaching has an important (*urgent*) role to play.

This book is a somewhat messy assemblage of the public writing we've done over the last 6 and a half years. There are nearly 50 individual pieces here, and yet they represent less than a third of our Web-published work. The choice of what to include and not to include was instinctual more than overtly intentional, a looking back to surface the hows and wheres of the emergence of our idea of critical digital pedagogy. These are the jumping off points we continue looking to as inspiration. Some of these pieces reflect a very distinct moment in time, and while we've edited and re-imagined many of them, we've decidedly left the rough bits that show the wear and tear on our own thinking. There are moments of contradiction we haven't carefully smoothed over, because even after years of circling around this work, we still don't always agree with ourselves.

At various points in the evolution of this volume, we weren't sure whether we'd each end up with separate books or if we'd end up with a single book, co-authored together. In the end, we decided to leave our voices alongside one another (but also distinct), because that's how these ideas were born. When we write together, we don't always know where one voice ends and the other begins. And when we write separately on these topics, we still find ourselves inhabiting one another's sentences.

This book is not meant to be read in any particular order, but it certainly could be read from start to finish, cover to cover. While we haven't assembled the pieces chronologically, they do track a sort of narrative from one to the next, making meaning through friction and metonymy.

When we set out to gather these pieces, our idea was to bring some amount of closure to what has been an extraordinary time for us and our work in education. Our hope is that marking this moment will help create space (in our lives and work) for new projects we find ourselves turning to — new projects that are decidedly not included here (even if the work subtly hints at them). That's also how we hope this work will be read, as a set of calls to dialogue and points of departure, not as a static repository of content. The words here were never meant to just sit on a page. They were always designed to pose questions. They were always designed to do work in the world.

PRAXIS

Educators and students alike have found themselves more and more flummoxed by a system that values assessment over engagement, learning management over discovery, content over community, outcomes over epiphanies.

CRITICAL DIGITAL PEDAGOGY: A DEFINITION

SEAN MICHAEL MORRIS AND JESSE STOMMEL

Over the last several years, we've watched the discussion of pedagogy in higher education shift. The year of the MOOC, the death of the MOOC, the incessant move toward the digital, the welfare of our contingent colleagues, and an imperative to confront directly issues of gender, race, class, ability, and sexuality — both within the university and outside its walls — have us asking more and more critical questions about how we should teach, where we should teach, and why.

WHAT IS PEDAGOGY?

Pedagogy is not ideologically neutral. This line has been for us almost a mantra over the last several years. We've circled around this phrase, across projects like *Hybrid Pedagogy* and Digital Pedagogy Lab, because we feel increasingly certain that the word "pedagogy" has been misread — that the project of education has been misdirected — that educators and students alike have found themselves more and more flummoxed by a system that values assessment over engagement, learning management over discovery, content over community, outcomes over epiphanies. Education has misrepresented itself as objective, quantifiable, apolitical.

Higher education teaching is particularly uncritical and under-theorized. Most college educators (at both traditional and non-traditional institutions) do little direct pedagogical work to prepare themselves as teachers. A commitment to teaching often goes unrewarded, and pedagogical writing (in most fields) is not counted as "research."

The entire enterprise of education is too often engaged in teaching that is not pedagogical. There are a whole host of other words we'd use to describe this work: instruction, classroom management, training, outcomes-driven, standards-based, content delivery. Pedagogy, on the other hand, starts with learning as its center, not students or teachers, and the work of pedagogues is necessarily political, subjective, and humane.

WHAT IS CRITICAL PEDAGOGY?

Critical Pedagogy is an approach to teaching and learning predicated on fostering agency and empowering learners (implicitly and explicitly critiquing oppressive power structures). The word "critical" in Critical Pedagogy functions in several registers:

- Critical, as in mission-critical, essential;
- Critical, as in literary criticism and critique, providing definitions and interpretation;
- Critical, as in reflective and nuanced thinking about a subject;
- Critical, as in criticizing institutional, corporate, or societal impediments to learning;
- Critical Pedagogy, as a disciplinary approach, which inflects (and is inflected by) each of these other meanings.

Each of these registers distinguishes Critical Pedagogy from pedagogy; however, the current educational climate has made the terms, for us, increasingly coterminous (i.e. an ethical pedagogy *must* be a critical one). Pedagogy is praxis, insistently perched at the intersection between the philosophy and the practice of teaching. When teachers talk about teaching, we are not necessarily doing pedagogical work, and not every teaching method constitutes a pedagogy. Rather, pedagogy necessarily involves recursive, second-order, meta-level work. Teachers teach; pedagogues teach *while* also actively investigating teaching and learning. Critical Pedagogy suggests a specific kind of anti-capitalist, liberatory praxis. This is deeply personal and political work, through which pedagogues cannot and do not remain objective. Rather, pedagogy, and particularly Critical Pedagogy, is work to which we must bring our full selves, and work to which every learner must come with full agency.

In *Pedagogy of the Oppressed,* Paulo Freire argues against the banking model, in which education "becomes an act of depositing, in which the students are the depositories and the teacher is the depositor." This model emphasizes a one-sided transactional relationship, in which teachers are seen as content experts and students are positioned as sub-human receptacles. The use here of "sub-human" is intentional and not exaggeration; for in the tenets set out in Freire's work (and the work of other Critical Pedagogues, including bell hooks and Henry Giroux), the banking model of education is part and parcel with efforts most clearly summed up in the term *dehumanization.* The banking model of education is efficient in that it maintains order and is bureaucratically neat and tidy. But efficiency, when it comes to teaching and learning, is not worth valorizing. Schools are not factories, nor are learning or learners products of the mill.

We are made deeply skeptical when we hear the word "content" in discussions about education, particularly when it is accompanied by the word "packaged." It is not that education is without content altogether, but that its content is co-constructed as part of and *not in advance* of the learning.

Critical Pedagogy is concerned less with knowing and more with a voracious not-knowing. It is an on-going and recursive process of discovery. For Freire, "Knowledge emerges only through invention and re-invention, through the restless, impatient, continuing, hopeful inquiry human beings pursue in the world, with the world, and with each other." Here, the language echoes the sort of learning Freire describes. With a flurry of adjectives and clauses separated by commas, his sentence circles around its subject, wandering, pushing restlessly at the edges of how words make meaning — not directly through literal translation into concepts, but in the way words rub curiously against one another, making meaning through a kind of friction. Knowledge emerges in the interplay between multiple people in conversation — brushing against one another in a mutual and charged exchange or dialogue. Freire writes, "Authentic education is not carried on by 'A' for 'B' or by 'A' about 'B,' but rather by 'A' with 'B'." It is through this impatient dialogue, and the implicit collaboration within it, that Critical Pedagogy finds its impetus toward change.

In place of the banking model, Freire advocates for "problem-posing education," in which a classroom or learning environment becomes a space for asking questions — a space of cognition not information. Vertical (or hierarchical) relationships give way to more playful ones, in which students and teachers co-author together the parameters for their individual and collective learning. Problem-posing education offers a space of mutual creation not consumption. In *Teaching to Transgress,* bell hooks writes, "As a classroom community, our capacity to generate excitement is deeply affected by our interest in one another, in hearing one another's voices, in recognizing one another's presence." This is a lively and intimate space of creativity and inquiry — a space of listening as much as speaking.

WHAT IS DIGITAL PEDAGOGY?

Seymour Papert writes in *Mindstorms: Children, Computers, and Powerful Ideas,* "The understanding of learning must be genetic. It must refer to the genesis of knowledge ... Thus the 'laws of learning' must be about how intellectual structures grow out of one another and about how, in the process, they acquire both logical and emotional form." As Utopians go, Papert is a very different sort than those currently running rampant in educational technology. He did, in 1980, advocate that every child should have access to a computer, but he also said quite definitively that "the child should program the computer," instead of the computer being allowed to program the child. Computer aided instruction (CAI), where much of human-computer learning has its roots (not to mention instructional design and the worst-intentioned strategies of most LMSs), "consisted of a learner seated in front of a dumb terminal. The basic computing program presented piecemeal bits of information to the learner. After, the learner was asked to complete a number of questions written specifically to determine if she had learned the content" (Kruger-Ross).

Because computer-aided instruction was more invested in the relationship between the human and the machine, and not at all designed by pedagogues or teachers, the imaginative aspects of the experiment were primarily technological. Instead of embracing the multivalent ways that the human mind works, CAI looked to find ways that the computer could create delimited learning experiences for the user.

We cannot replace agency with response to stimuli.

In "Travels in Troy with Freire: Technology as an Agent of Emancipation," Paulo Blikstein explicitly connects the work of Freire and Papert. He writes specifically, "the rapid penetration of computers into learning environments constitutes an unprecedented opportunity to advance and disseminate a Freirean aesthetic." Papert articulates a move from constructivism to constructionism — from a consideration of the relationship between the human and knowing to a consideration of the relationship between the human and the material, the product of learning and not just the systems of learning. He says that computers are "carriers of powerful ideas and of the seeds of cultural change ... they can help people form new relationships with knowledge that cut across traditional lines." Thus, the material — the product — of learning becomes the connections made manifest by the computer. We would go one step further to say that what is built inside this kind of learning are relationships, meaningful connections between learners. The computer is a mere intermediary, not a tool as much as a vessel, a transport, a "carrier" as Papert describes it.

This isn't to say that the use of computers isn't political, for Papert, for Blikstein, for Critical Pedagogues, for us. Rather, we acknowledge that computers manifest human politics and human politics are made manifest in our technologies. We must ruminate at these intersections and demand that we build better tools and use them more thoughtfully and toward ends that don't merely legitimize the existence of the tools. This is the work of digital pedagogy.

WHAT IS CRITICAL DIGITAL PEDAGOGY?

Our work has wondered at the extent to which Critical Pedagogy translates into digital space. Can the necessary reflective dialogue flourish within Web-based tools, within social media platforms, within learning management systems, within MOOCs? What is digital agency? To what extent can social media function as a space of democratic participation? How can we build platforms that support learning across age, race, culture, ability, geography? What are the specific affordances and limitations of technology toward these ends? If, indeed, all learning is necessarily hybrid, as we've argued, to what extent are Critical Pedagogy and digital pedagogy becoming also coterminous?

The wondering at these questions is, in fact, not particularly new. In his forward to Freire's *Pedagogy of the Oppressed*, Richard Shaull writes, "Our advanced technological society is rapidly making objects of most of us and subtly programming us into conformity to the logic of its system [...] The paradox is that the same technology that does this to us also creates a new sensitivity to what is happening." And, John and Evelyn Dewey write in *Schools of To-Morrow*, published decades earlier, "Unless the mass of workers are to be blind cogs and pinions in the apparatus they employ, they must have some understanding of the physical and social facts behind and ahead of the material and appliances with which they are dealing." If we are to keep every educative endeavor from becoming mill-work — from becoming only a reflection of oppressive labor practices and uneven power relationships — we must engage deeply with its reality.

Increasingly, the Web is a space of politics, a social space, a professional space, a space of community. And, for better or worse, more and more of our learning is happening there. For many of us, it is becoming increasingly difficult to distinguish between our real selves and our virtual selves, and in fact, these distinctions are being altogether unsettled. In "The New Learning is Ancient," Kathi Inman Berens writes, "It doesn't matter to me if my classroom is a little rectangle in a building or a little rectangle above my keyboard. Doors are rectangles; rectangles are portals. We walk through." When we learn online, our feet are usually still quite literally on ground. When we interact with a group of students via streaming video, the interaction is nevertheless face-to-face. The Web is asking us to reconsider how we think about space, how and where we engage, and upon which platforms the bulk of our learning happens.

In *Small Pieces Loosely Joined: a Unified Theory of the Web,* David Weinberger writes, "We are the true 'small pieces' of the Web, and we are loosely joining ourselves in ways that we're still inventing." Ten years ago, following the publication of Weinberger's book, we wouldn't have imagined the learning networks we've now built with colleagues working together (sometimes simultaneously in real time) in places as seemingly remote as Portland, Madison, England, Prince Edward Island, Sydney, Cairo, Vancouver, and Hong Kong.

This is not to say, however, that there aren't challenges to this sort of work. In *On Critical Pedagogy,* Henry Giroux argues,

> Intellectuals have a responsibility to analyze how language, information, and meaning work to organize, legitimate, and circulate values, structure reality, and offer up particular notions of agency

> and identity. For public intellectuals, the latter challenge demands a new kind of literacy and critical understanding with respect to the emergence of the new media and electronic technologies, and the new and powerful role they play as instruments of public pedagogy.

Digital technologies, like social media or collaborative writing platforms or MOOCs, have values coded into them in advance. Many tools are *good* only insofar as they are used. And tools and platforms that do dictate too strongly how we might use them, or ones that remove our agency by too covertly reducing us and our work to commodified data, should be rooted out by a Critical Digital Pedagogy. Far too much work in educational technology starts with tools, when what we need to start with is humans.

We are better users of technology when we are thinking critically about the nature and effects of that technology. What we must do is work to encourage students and ourselves to think critically about new tools (and, more importantly, the tools we already use). And when we're looking for solutions, what we most need to change is our thinking and not our tools.

In short, Critical Digital Pedagogy:

- centers its practice on community and collaboration;
- must remain open to diverse, international voices, and thus requires invention to reimagine the ways that communication and collaboration happen across cultural and political boundaries;
- will not, cannot, be defined by a single voice but must gather together a cacophony of voices;
- must have use and application outside traditional institutions of education.

A Critical Digital Pedagogy demands that open and networked educational environments not be merely repositories of content; rather, they must create dialogues in which both students and teachers participate as full agents. There is a clear irony in our proposing here a neat and tidy definition for Critical Digital Pedagogy. This defining work can not be done by us alone.

Critical Digital Pedagogy asks more questions than it answers:

- How can digital technologies and cultures interrogate and/or deconstruct the roles of student and teacher?
- How does critical pedagogy change the way we see teachers and students as socially, economically, politically, and emotionally situated in a learning space? How is this changed in the wake of online and hybrid education?
- What must we know about existing and invisible obstacles to learner agency in order to disrupt them?
- What is the role of interactivity, engagement, and critical contribution in the digital or digitally-enhanced classroom?
- How do we make our classrooms sites of intrinsic motivation, networked learning, and critical practice?
- How can the work of writers and educators like Paulo Freire, bell hooks, Henry Giroux, and John Dewey help us navigate our new educational terrain? And how are educators like Cathy Davidson and Howard Rheingold helping to further reimagine learning that happens in digital space?
- What is digital agency? What are its incumbent privileges and responsibilities?
- How can critical pedagogy help to examine, dismantle, or rebuild the structures, hierarchies, institutions, and technologies of education?
- And how can we gather together generously to bring Critical Digital Pedagogy more fully into the conversation about the changing landscape of education?

Pete Rorabaugh writes in "Occupy the Digital: Critical Pedagogy and New Media":

> Critical Pedagogy, no matter how we define it, has a central place in the discussion of how learning is changing in the 21st century because Critical Pedagogy is primarily concerned with an equitable distribution of power. If students live in a culture that digitizes and educates them through a screen, they require an education that empowers them in that sphere, teaches them that language, and offers new opportunities of human connectivity.

Critical Pedagogy is as much a political approach as it is an educative one, a social justice movement first, and an educational movement second.

So, Critical Digital Pedagogy must also be a method of resistance and humanization. It is not simply work done in the mind, on paper, or on screen. It is work that must be done on the ground. It is not ashamed of its rallying cry or its soapbox. Critical Digital Pedagogy eats aphorisms — like this one right here — for breakfast. But it is not afraid to incite, to post its manifestos, to light its torches.

WHAT IS A PEDAGOGUE?

SEAN MICHAEL MORRIS

It's not uncommon for people who teach to be unaware of pedagogy. That doesn't mean they don't practice pedagogy, or that they haven't engaged in pedagogical discussion. It means they are less conscious, or unconscious, of the pedagogy they employ in their classrooms than, say, the likely readers of this piece. I have taught many teachers who, before arriving in the seminar room for training, first looked up pedagogy in the dictionary.

This is, of course, perfectly fine. Pedagogy, like parenting, is a lot of what we've learned from our predecessors. We may raise our children as our parents raised us; likewise, we often teach as we were taught. If the majority of our instructors were lecturers, we're likely to lecture; if they centered class activities on group work, then we'll employ that instead. Most higher education instructors receive very little or no training in pedagogy, and so — thrust into the classroom because they have knowledge of their field — they teach with the tools available to them. Teaching is, a lot of the time, a matter of tradition, a matter of habit. And in a world where 60 to 75 percent of teachers are adjunct or dreadfully underpaid, habit is expedient.

Just as teachers are not all pedagogues, neither are pedagogues necessarily teachers. Notable pedagogues (Paulo Freire, bell hooks, John Dewey) have been teachers as much as writers, but this isn't true of all. For a pedagogue, the classroom is a laboratory, a place where experiments in learning take place. It's the pedagogue who looks for new ways to inspire active learning in a classroom; who invents the "flipped" classroom; who encounters an LMS and decides to break it instead of simply reside within it. The pedagogue looks at the walls of her classroom and instead of seeing mandatory boundaries, sees the invitation to take students outside.

And more: the pedagogue takes what she does in class, and she distributes it. She publishes, she blogs, she talks excitedly in conference seminar rooms (and conference elevators), she makes documentaries, she teaches teachers, she teaches the public.

I like to think of pedagogues as fashion designers. They can be a bit blithe to the quotidian concerns of classroom teaching. They move online discussions out of the forum and onto Twitter, and when a good teacher asks, "but how do you grade tweets?" the pedagogue replies: "Oh, I don't bother with grading!" The pedagogue is concerned more with big ideas, the themes of education, its ethics and morals and goals, and a lot less with grading mid-terms, quizzes, and preparing well-researched lectures.

This can be infuriating and confounding for teachers, especially when they need solutions to classroom issues that are very real, and very immediate. But asking a pedagogue for answers requires patience, and a willingness to take risks in the classroom. Pedagogy is at home in dialogue, not Q&A. When we have trouble with participation in an online discussion forum, the pedagogue may give us 10 useful tips, but may instead ask us to revise our syllabus, to look at the germ of our course planning for the problem.

It's not entirely true that pedagogues have no good ideas for classroom practice. They do. They've done little else in their classrooms besides solve problems. But the pedagogue's solutions are the solutions which, years after she implements them in her own classroom, become the habit and tradition of brand new teachers.

Pedagogy is essentially a critical thinking exercise directed at learning and teaching. Pedagogy asks us to never teach by rote: never assume the use of a podium, or an overhead projector, or desks situated in rows, or a chalkboard, or walls. Teaching should be a determined thing, an intentional thing; and every exercise we design, every component of the LMS we engage, every grade we assign should reflect our intentions. And more than that, our philosophies.

What is a Digital Pedagogue?

Entering a classroom, we think first about its walls. We think about where the desks sit. Where we will stand. Whether there are windows, where the doors are, how the chalkboard, whiteboard, or overhead projector are arranged. And then we make decisions about teaching based on these environmental considerations. Should we rearrange the chairs? Should we stand behind the podium, or should we sit on the desk? Making decisions about how teaching will occur — what it will look like, how it will be performed — is as much a response to the environment in which we teach as it is to the lesson we have planned.

What about when we teach online? Where are our walls and chairs and podium in digital space? For some, the coded boundaries of the LMS replace the solid borders of the classroom, and discussion fora become the arrangement of chairs. Video lectures have been used to replicate an instructor's presence on the screen, and quizzes with algorithmically automated teacherly responses offer feedback in lieu of written notes and gold stars. But it's important to think bigger about where the walls are, where our teaching territory lies.

And here's why: because when we teach digitally — whether online, or in hybrid environments (and all learning today is necessarily hybrid) — walls become arbitrary. All walls. And all seats and all podiums and all chalkboards, too. LMSs have more than snack-sized shortcomings, but the biggest dilemma they pose is that they create the illusion of digital learning without really ever encountering the Internet. Like all illusions, this is misleading, because digital learning (and by necessity, digital pedagogy) takes place all over the web.

Individual digital tools have been largely created in order to contain the Internet. They are like stalls at a public market. In one, you can buy fresh produce, in another jewelry, in another tie-dye shirts and aprons. Each is meant to give you a specific interaction with part of the whole. This is also true of traditional classrooms. You go to room 202 in the Humanities building to learn English, but you go to room 556 in the Science building to take your math class. The LMS, the market stall, the classroom all have this in common: they make particular and small that which is widespread.

But there are few true walls on the Internet, only the walls we choose. We may teach part of our class on-ground and part of it within an LMS, or we may put our syllabus online and conduct backchannel discussions on Twitter between classes. But as teachers we can never be certain that our students will choose the same walls we choose for them. While they are in our on-ground classroom, they are also on Twitter and Facebook. They've just "pinned" a photo of our slideshow to Pinterest. And by doing so, they've made the class extant, and their own participation ongoing. They've broken the walls of the classroom (or the LMS) on their own, and so broken down the boundaries of when and where learning takes place.

That students can break the walls between which we plan our teaching means that we must adjust our pedagogical approach. And that's the core of digital pedagogy: an acknowledgement that **the space of learning is more fluid and adaptable than we might have planned on.**

Before getting lost in the discussion of what tools to teach, or whether to teach tools in place of (or next to) teaching content, it's important to ask the question: are we teaching digitally? And if we are, there are a number of consequences.

1. Our digital pedagogy must inevitably acknowledge the ability of students to control and choose containers for their own learning.

2. We cannot compensate for all the ways that students will choose to process and curate their learning in digital spaces, and so it becomes vital to teach students not about particular tools, but about how to choose tools for their use.

3. In order for students to choose tools for their own use, they must have a sense of themselves as learners much more than a sense of us as teachers. Digital pedagogy is necessarily learner-centric.

4. We must empower students to use the web (because they will anyway) in ways that support their learning. This means integrating the use of smart phones, tablets, and laptops in on-ground classrooms. It also means inviting students to connect with each other outside of the ways we intend them to connect. Let learning go where they go.

Digital pedagogy is different from teaching online because it allows us to open up learning and teaching in ways that gravity-bound education doesn't permit. When we bring the Internet into our teaching, we open our students (and ourselves) to the potential of networked, connected learning.

DIGITAL PEDAGOGY: A GENEALOGY

JESSE STOMMEL

Digital pedagogy is not a dancing monkey. It won't do tricks on command. It won't come obediently when called. Nobody can show us how to do it or make it happen like magic on our computer screens. There isn't a 90-minute how-to webinar, and we can't outsource it.

We become experts in digital pedagogy in the same way we become American literature scholars, medievalists, or doctors of sociology. We become digital pedagogues by spending many years devoting our life to researching, practicing, writing about, presenting on, and teaching digital pedagogies. In other words, we live, work, and build networks within the field. But this isn't exactly right, because digital pedagogy is less a field and more an active present participle, a way of engaging the world, not a world to itself, a way of approaching the not-at-all-discrete acts of teaching and learning. To become an expert in digital pedagogy, then, we need research, experience, and *openness* to each new learning activity, technology, or collaboration. Digital pedagogy is a discipline, but only in the most porous, dynamic, and playful senses of the word.

You can't outsource digital pedagogy because it is inextricably bound up in the work of teaching and learning. Digital pedagogy is not a path through the woods. It's a compass (one that often takes several people working in concert to use). And in the next 10 years, digital pedagogy will become (and already is to an extent) coterminous with pedagogy. We do not, after all, talk about *chalkboard pedagogy*, even though the chalkboard is one of the most advanced and revolutionary educational tools. Digital pedagogy is also becoming, for me, coterminous with critical pedagogy, given the degree to which the digital can function both as a tool for and an obstacle to liberation. Digital pedagogy demands that we rethink power relations between students and teachers — demands we create more collaborative and less hierarchical institutions for learning — lest we use computers to replicate the vestigial structures of industrial-era education.

I have devoted nearly all my professional life to teaching, to the collaborative work I do with students. And, while I have sometimes focused on literary and media studies, my primary scholarly interest has always been pedagogy. Most of my pedagogies, including my digital ones, are rooted in thinkers like Emerson, Thoreau, Elbow, Dewey, hooks, and Freire. Pedagogy is not synonymous with teaching or talking about teaching, nor is it entirely abstracted from the acts of teaching and learning. It is the place where philosophy and practice meet (aka "'praxis'"). It's a surprisingly difficult line to toe, or wall to teeter upon: meta-cognitive reflection on, and investigation of learning, which is by its nature emergent.

Because it's responsive by nature, pedagogy can't be pinned down in a stable definition. Still, we recognize it when we see it, and it looks like a teacher or learner puzzled, hands-at-the-ready, mouth-agape, pausing just as they're about to speak or take action. It looks like careful planning without attachment to or fetishizing of outcomes. It looks like failure. And wonder.

The digital adds another not-at-all-discrete meta-level layer. The tools we use for learning, the ones that have become so ubiquitous, each influence what, where, and how we learn — and, even more, how we think about learning. Books. Pixels. Trackpads. Keyboards. E-books. Databases. Digital archives. Learning management systems. New platforms and interfaces are developed every week, popping up like daisies (or wildfires). None of these tools have what we value most about education coded into them in advance. The best digital tools inspire us, often to use them in ways the designer couldn't anticipate. The worst digital tools attempt to dictate our pedagogies, determining what we can do with them and for whom. The digital pedagogue teaches her tools, doesn't let them teach her.

John and Evelyn Dewey write in *Schools of To-Morrow*: "Unless the mass of workers are to be blind cogs and pinions in the apparatus they employ, they must have some understanding of the physical and social facts behind and ahead of the material and appliances with which they are dealing." This remark is not unlike the image Fritz Lang depicts at the outset of the 1927 film *Metropolis*: slaves to a machine becoming food for the machine. The danger in fetishizing machines is that we become subject to them. But turning away in the face of the digital will lead to much the same fate. Rather, we need to handle our technologies roughly — to think critically about our tools, how we use them, and who has access to them.

Digital pedagogy has been variously defined. Brian Croxall and Adeline Koh offered a very inclusive, broad-stroke definition at their MLA Digital Pedagogy Unconference, saying that "digital pedagogy is the use of electronic elements to enhance or to change the experience of education." And Katherine D. Harris offered up the components of her digital pedagogy — which she borrows in part from the "mainstays of Digital Humanities" — during a NITLE seminar on the subject: "collaboration, playfulness/tinkering, focus on process, and building (very broadly defined)."

Digital pedagogy is an orientation toward pedagogy that is not necessarily predicated on the use of digital tools. This is why I like Harris's focus on process and Croxall and Koh's use of the seemingly vague, but in fact quite lovely, phrase "electronic elements." The phrase dissects the notion of an educational technology, turning the discussion to a consideration of the smallest possible element that might influence teaching and learning: the electrical impulse. At this level, we're not talking about how we might use WordPress in a composition class, or how Smart Boards failed to revolutionize K-12 education, but about how the most basic architecture of our interactions with and through machines can inspire new (digital or analog) pedagogies. Thus, Kathi Inman Berens says that "the new learning is ancient."

In "Digital Humanities Made Me a Better Pedagogue, a Crowdsourced Article" in *Hybrid Pedagogy,* five of us argue that "the 'digital' in 'digital humanities' and 'digital pedagogy' refers less to tech and more to the communities tech engenders and facilitates." Similarly, Paul Fyfe asks, in "Digital Pedagogy Unplugged", "How do we break the thrall to tools and technologies which may limit the horizon of our pedagogical creativity?" Digital pedagogy is a pedagogy of hacking, which Fyfe defines as "adapt[ing], manipulat[ing], and mak[ing] productive use out of a given technology or technological context or platform." It also depends on collaboration. Cathy Davidson writes in "Collaborative Learning for the Digital Age": "Given the interactive nature of most of our lives in the digital age, we have the tools to harness our different forms of attention and take advantage of them." She goes on to argue for a distributed notion of expertise, because "the more expert we are, the more likely we are to be limited in what we conceive to be the problem, let alone the answer."

This discussion can't be strictly academic or administrative. Digital pedagogy necessarily involves both teachers and students — those at traditional institutions and lifelong learners. "We must develop a participative pedagogy," writes Howard Rheingold in "Participative Pedagogy for a Literacy of Literacies," "assisted by digital media and networked publics, that focuses on catalyzing, inspiring, nourishing, facilitating, and guiding literacies essential to individual and collective life in the 21st century." Students and learners should be central in mapping the terrain of digital pedagogy. Educational institutions should dedicate themselves to supporting this work. And, as Cathy Davidson recently remarked, all of us need to "sustain innovation by finding the cheapest, fastest, least bureaucratic way to make ourselves perpetual learners."

Digital pedagogy calls for "screwing around" (Ramsay) more than it does systematic study, and in fact screwing around is the more difficult scholarly work. Digital pedagogy is less about knowing and more a rampant process of unlearning, play, and rediscovery. We are not born digital pedagogues, nor do we have to be formally schooled in the ways of digital pedagogy. There's lots to read on the subject, but we can't just read our way into it; there is no essential canon. In fact, *expert* digital pedagogues learn best by forgetting — through continuous encounters with what is novel, tentative, unmastered, and unresolved.

BEYOND THE LMS

SEAN MICHAEL MORRIS

We are not ready to teach online. In a recent conversation with a friend, I found myself puzzled, and a bit troubled, when he expressed confusion about digital pedagogy. He said something to the extent of, "What's the difference between digital pedagogy and teaching online? Aren't all online teachers digital pedagogues?" Being a contemplative guy, I didn't just tip over his drink and walk away. Instead, I pondered the source of his question. Digital pedagogy is largely misunderstood in higher education. The advent of online learning and instructional design brought the classroom onto the web, and with it all manner of teaching: good and bad, coherent and incoherent, networked and disconnected. Whatever pedagogy any given teacher employed in his classroom became digitized. If I teach history by reading from my twenty-year-old notes, or if I lead workshops in creative writing, or if I teach literature through movies, I bring that online and — boom! — I'm a digital pedagogue. Right?

But that's not right. Not every teacher is a pedagogue. Pedagogy is a scholarship unto itself, a study of learning and the many ways it is fueled — in classrooms, in workshops, in studios, in writing centers — wherever learning is poised to occur. Pedagogy is also different from the study of education. Those with backgrounds in education understand the institution, and its relationship to students, in ways I expect I never will. Pedagogy has at its core timeliness, mindfulness, and improvisation. Pedagogy concerns itself with the instantaneous, momentary, vital exchange that takes place in order for learning to happen. That exchange may be between teacher and student, or between student and student; it can also occur between teacher and teacher, administrator and CEO, journalist and educator. The etymology of pedagogy reveals that leadership is at its core; and thus it is not limited to classroom practice in the same way that it is not limited to institutions of learning.

Pedagogy experiments relentlessly, honoring a learning that's lifelong. A pedagogy of writing, for example, recognizes that a teacher is not trying to pull essays like pulling teeth for fifteen weeks; instead, she is cultivating a desire to write that will last well beyond the end of the semester, well beyond graduation. And there are few limits to what can be attempted in the interests of meaningful, sustained learning. If it works to blindfold students and walk them around campus to add dimension to their sensory writing, or if it works to play hopscotch in order to stir memories in new writers, then the pedagogue will try it.

Not all teaching happens like this. Not all teachers are pedagogues, nor need they be. There is a place for all styles of classroom practice, I think, just as there is a place for learners of all capabilities and approaches. I am not here arguing for a particular teaching philosophy. What is important is seeing the difference — a difference that becomes much more acute when learning goes online.

THE RELIC OF THE LMS

The invention of the LMS (learning management system) was a mistake. And here I'm not going to make the same frustrated argument made numerous times before now that LMSs are limiting structures, that their interface and functionalities control how teachers teach online. The LMS was a mistake because it was premature. In a world that was just waking up to the Internet and the possibility of widely-networked culture, the LMS played to the lowest common denominator, creating a "classroom" that allowed learning — or something like learning — to happen behind tabs, in threaded discussions, and through automated quizzes. The LMS was not a creative decision, it was not pushing the capabilities of the Internet, it was settling for the least innovative classroom practice and repositioning that digitally. As a result classes taught within its structure generally land with a dull thud. No matter how creative and inspired the teacher or pedagogue behind the wheel, the LMS is no match for the wideness of the Internet. It was born a relic — at its launch utterly irrelevant to its environment and its user.

And worse, the LMS convinced us that teaching online was not only possible, it was easy — that digital pedagogy was a mere work of relocation. Take your lectures and your assignments, create a slideshow or a video or a piece of audio, load it all up, and there you have it: online learning. Many early instructional designers believed that if we employed interactive Flash exercises and scaffolded learning according to Bloom's taxonomy, we'd end up with robust learning that engaged students in a way duplicate to classroom interaction. (I was once one of these instructional designers. Mea culpa.) Sure, it took a little longer to set up your course, but once you did, it practically ran itself. Plus, you could reuse the content again and again! Design the course once, teach it *ad infinitum*. (Only a benefit when the instructor is not compensated well for course design, or not compensated at all.) The LMS largely erased mindfully aware teaching, and made excuses for unconscionable practice.

The real problem here is not that quality suffered, but that people mistook what they were doing within the LMS as pedagogical. It may be teaching — in the same way that reading from a handout is teaching — but simply slotting your pre-written materials into an online framework and calling it a class is not interesting or sound pedagogy.

The persistence of the onerous LMS, and the ways learners have already adopted the patterns and habits of the learning within it, indicates that we are not ready to teach online. Many talented instructors complain about the limitations of LMS-based teaching, and yet in the same breath discard all their best, most innovative pedagogies. Very few are using the approach of the digital to innovate *further* instead of innovate less. But just as the pedagogue will enter a room and rearrange the tables and chairs to suit his purpose, so too will the digital pedagogue happily hack the LMS, opening it to the wider web, or using it as a portal to a more expanded learning environment.

Pioneers on the Digital Plain

Digital pedagogy is important because it is willing to improvise, to respond to a new environment, to experiment. The digital pedagogue is not the same as an online teacher. The digital pedagogue looks at the options, refuses the limitations of the LMS, invites her students to participate in — indeed, create — networked learning. Her practice is mindful of the landscape.

Questions that the digital pedagogue asks regularly include:

- What tools are available for me and my students to play with?
- How can improvisation occur online to reinforce learning?
- Does digital learning end when the course ends, or is it sustained perpetually by the online learning environment (aka, the Internet)?
- Who are my students, and where can they be found? What are my students' URLs? What is mine?
- Do disciplines matter online? Do canons exist? What is the point of rote memorization when everything is available online all the time?
- Where is my authority now that all authority is a Google search away?
- And most importantly: What happens when learning is removed from the classroom and exposed to the entirety of the digital landscape?

For some, teaching begins with authority and expertise. For the digital pedagogue, teaching begins with inquiry. And that's why digital pedagogy is so important. It reminds us that the new landscape of learning is mysterious and worth exploring. The techniques of on-ground learning do not translate well. The LMS fails. Only an attitude of pioneering exploration will make heads or tails of the potential for online learning; and it is the digital pedagogue who will lead that charge.

LEARNING IS NOT A MECHANISM

JESSE STOMMEL

Digital pedagogy is not equivalent to teachers using digital tools. Rather, digital pedagogy demands that we think critically about our tools, demands that we reflect actively upon our own practice. So, digital pedagogy means not just drinking the Kool-Aid, but putting the Kool-Aid under a microscope. When I lead workshops for teachers interested in developing digital skills, I say right up front that I have little interest in teaching teachers or learners how to use the technologies they'll use in classrooms for the next three years. I am much more interested in working with teachers and learners to develop the literacies that will help them use and evaluate the educational tools they'll be using in ten or twenty years. Often, this means knowing when and how to put tools down, as much as it means knowing when and how to take them up.

Talk of teaching with technology is not altogether (or even close to nearly) new. Even well before John and Evelyn Dewey's 1915 book *Schools of To-Morrow*, the development and dissemination of educational technology has had political, as well as practical, ramifications.

The large-format blackboard was first used in the U.S. in 1801. The vacuum tube-based computer was introduced in 1946. In the 1960s, Seymour Papert began teaching the Logo programming language to children. The first Learning Management System, PLATO (Program Logic for Automatic Teaching Operations), was developed in 1960. At the invent of each, there was fear, resistance, and the thoughtless slobber of over-enthusiasm. After the introduction of the Radio Lecture in the 1930s, Lloyd Allen Cook warned, "This mechanizes education and leaves the local teacher only the tasks of preparing for the broadcast and keeping order in the classroom." This sentence is not all that different from the ones we've read about the Massive Open Online Course over the last 6 years, or about online learning over the last twenty five years. In the 19th Century, Emily Dickinson hinted at the mechanizing of education in her poem, "From all the Jails the Boys and Girls," where she equates schools with jails but ultimately determines, "That Prison doesn't keep."

Let's take a specific (and increasingly ubiquitous tool) by way of example. When I first taught online, I encountered the horror that is the gradebook inside most learning management systems, which reduces students (often color coding them) into mere rows in a spreadsheet. Over the last 15 years, I've watched this tool proliferate into all the institutions where I've worked. Even teachers that don't use the learning management system for its other decidedly more pleasurable uses have made its gradebook more and more central to the learning experience for students. On its surface, the LMS gradebook does not seem all that fundamentally different from an analog gradebook, which also reduces students to mere rows in a spreadsheet. But most learning management systems now offer (or threaten) to automate a process which is, in fact, deeply idiosyncratic. They make grading more efficient, as though efficiency is something we ought to celebrate in teaching and learning.

It seems easier to far too many teachers to imagine that students *do* work the way machines do — that they can be scored according to objective metrics and neatly compared to one another. Schools, and the systems we've invented to support them, condition us to believe that there are always others (objective experts or even algorithms) who can know better than us the value of our own work. I'm struck by the number of institutions that for all intents and purposes equate teaching with grading — that assume our job as teachers is to merely separate the wheat from the chaff. And I find myself truly confused when anyone suggests to me that there is a way for us to do this kind of work *objectively*. For me, teaching and learning have always been (and will always be) deeply subjective.

bell hooks writes in *Teaching to Transgress* about her experience in graduate school, "nonconformity on our part was viewed with suspicion, as empty gestures of defiance aimed at masking inferiority or substandard work." One of the problems with learning management system gradebooks, often mapped to rubrics and outcomes (which have run equally rampant of late), is that they assume students (and their experiences) are interchangeable. And they assume the same of teachers. The problem is that lesson plans and assignments can't be expected to work exactly the same with every set of students, with every teacher, or on every given day. Both teachers and learners must approach the classroom from a place of flexibility, willing to see the encounters, exchanges, interactions, and relationships that develop in a classroom as dynamic. Grades, and the (very bizarre) notion of their systematized objectivity, stand as an immediate affront to this kind of classroom.

I recently worked with a student that admitted to stopping doing the work for the current week, because she was distracted by — "lost within," to use her words — a subject from a previous week. My response was simple and encouraging, "sounds good, stay lost." There would have been no column sufficient for representing this exchange in a gradebook, and this kind of exchange has been the rule more than the exception in my work as a teacher. The text in question, Mark Z. Danielewski's *House of Leaves*, is about exactly what the student described to me, going on a quest and getting lost. This is, for me, what learning looks like — not finishing assignments, not following directions, not dotting "i"s and crossing "t"s. It's a process of discovery that has no outcome fixed in advance. This kind of learning is about sitting (sometimes uncomfortably) with our not knowing. Grading inside a learning management system too often obscures, does not reveal, this process.

I used these systems for years, struggling to find ways to subvert their worst intentions, until I ultimately determined to simply say, "I would prefer not to."

If there is a better sort of mechanism that we need for the work of digital pedagogy, it is a machine, an algorithm, a platform tuned not for delivering and assessing content, but for helping all of us listen better to students. And, by "listen," I decidedly do not mean "surveil." The former implies an invitation to open dialogue, whereas the latter implies a hierarchical relationship through which learners are made into mere data points. My call, then, is for more emphasis on the tools that help us fully and genuinely inhabit digital environments, tools like ears, eyes, or fingers. My call is to stop attempting to distinguish so incessantly between online and on-ground learning, between the virtual and the face-to-face, between digital pedagogy and chalkboard pedagogy. Good digital pedagogy is just good pedagogy.

bell hooks writes, in *Teaching to Transgress*, "The first paradigm that shaped my pedagogy was the idea that the classroom should be an exciting place, never boring." So, I want to end this piece with several questions: what kinds of tools can we find, build, or imagine that help make the work of learning "fun," as hooks advocates? Can we imagine assessment mechanisms even that encourage discovery, ones not designed for *assessing learning* but designed for *learning through assessment*? When do we decide that a tool isn't working, and how can we work together to set it down en masse?

TEACHING IN OUR RIGHT MINDS: CRITICAL DIGITAL PEDAGOGY AND THE RESPONSE TO THE NEW

SEAN MICHAEL MORRIS

As a child, I was a prolific liar. Or, storyteller. I improvised truth. In most cases, I did this in order to defy the orders of adults in my life; but in some situations, I did this to make the world seem like a shinier place. Happier. More full of wonder. School largely was a series of disillusionments. The relative lack of wonder I was educated into painted the world as a place in which I had little interest in participating. Adults didn't seem happy. Teachers didn't seem happy. Wonder and awe and curious mystery were the anathema to education and learning. So, I lied in order to make the world align better with my imagination.

I discovered dinosaurs very early in my life. Kindergarten? First grade? Certainly by the second grade, because that's when I wrote to Fisher Price to ask them to create dinosaur-themed toys. By the fifth grade, I was spending hours in the public library poring over every book I could find on the beasts. I memorized the length and height and weight of every one. I knew the Cretaceous from the Jurassic. I understood the evolution from Allosaurus to T-rex to Gorgosaurus. I rebelled when Brontosaurus was renamed Apatosaurus. I lived them and breathed them, I tried to imagine them walking the earth (an activity almost salivatingly tantalizing to the brain), I told my friends and family about them. And I never lied about dinosaurs. There was no need. They were wondrous enough already.

Sometimes, reality needs no elaboration.

Today, and for most of the last fifteen years, my work has been with and for teachers. Teachers of all kinds. Writing teachers, math teachers, teachers in K-12, teachers of teachers. What it *looks* like I do is help teachers come to grips with how digital culture and its tools have changed, shifted, made more or less sparkly the work of learning. But the truth is that the digital side of my job is just coincidence. It has to do with timing. Right now, the digital is relevant, present, and is that thing that seems to provide the most interesting possibilities and the most contentious challenges in the scholarship and practice of teaching and learning. But it would be a mistake to think that what I *do* is digital, because what I really do is human.

Take for example the friendship and collaboration that has grown between myself and Maha Bali, a professor in the Center for Teaching and Learning at the American University in Cairo. Maha was instrumental in organizing the first international Digital Pedagogy Lab institute, committing time and energy to bringing Jesse and me — two educators she'd never met in person — to her university. On the surface, Maha and I talk a lot about technology… and we talk *through* technology, utilizing Twitter, Slack, Google Hangouts, and e-mail to communicate. But what we are truly engaged in, she and I, is an ongoing conversation about relationships — between teaching and learning, between teachers and students, between ourselves and the interface. Across the distance, our professional collaboration is haptic, she in my periphery and I in hers, with an asymptotic reach through the screen as our praxis.

That space of nearly reaching but never quite reaching our destination — a space my colleague Amy Collier would call not-yetness ("Not-yetness and Learnification") — is tantalizing, tickling the brain in the same way it's tickled when we imagine dinosaurs really truly actually walking the earth. When I am talking to Maha, I am only just barely (not)present with her, and in that just barely lies a sliver of wonder: I can be in Egypt and in my home office at the same time.And because I can communicate with her at any moment, unexpectedly, I am *always* in Egypt and in my home office. Likewise, as a resident of the Pacific Northwest, but an employee at Middlebury College in Vermont, I am also always in Middlebury and always in Portland. When my coworkers sit in a presentation in the auditorium on campus, and I watch the live stream of the event, we can pass notes by text message, and brainstorm with one another in the moment as revelations arise.

The digital isn't magic. It isn't mysterious. It's regular human communication astride a new medium. There's no need to make it more than it is. No need to lie or elaborate. Because in the digital, there's wonder enough.

That wonder inspired the formation of Digital Pedagogy Lab (DPL), an educational offshoot of the journal *Hybrid Pedagogy*. Jesse and I founded DPL in order to provide both sustainable, flexible professional development for teachers and learners at all levels of education, and an environment of experimentation and fun (thus, the "Lab"). We didn't want to bog down digital pedagogy with best practices and jargon, instead seeking to crack open the raw possibility inherent in technology-inflected learning.

For some who instruct with the digital, or who are confronted by others instructing with the digital, this wonder can seem more like a sideshow than a relevant methodology. In part, this is because the use of digital technology to widen the parameters of human interaction and knowledge production is still in its most experimental stage. It's not kids reading about dinosaurs in books, it's passionate paleontologists picking at the dirt in the middle of Wyoming. Where they will or will not find a dinosaur egg or two, where they will or will not discover a new species.

Take the example of the work of digital educators like Dave Cormier, Bonnie Stewart, Jim Groom, Audrey Watters, myself, and Jesse Stommel.

Or the collaborative poetry exercise Jesse and I have run, in which 50 participants in a Google Doc collaborate over 30 minutes and only contribute a single word. Participants ultimately remixed the rules, contributing videos, images, and writing poetry within the rules themselves. When I showed a video of this exercise to a friend of mine — a traditional, on-ground poetry teacher at a public 4-year institution — he stared at me and then he asked, "Why?"

My answer: "To see what would happen."

This is precisely the kind of thing that looks on the outside like clumsy, un-academic behavior in the place of teaching. It's the kind of thing that many instructors new to the digital — or leery of its experimentation — shrug off as teaching that requires no real effort and no real accountability. Many assume that posting to Tumblr or Pinterest isn't or can't be educational, and they are confounded or upset by teachers who use Prezi. What these more traditional professors don't see is that something like this poetry exercise takes the same planning — and even more coordination — and even more critical reflection once it's done — to pull off. And while the lessons learned are not necessarily predictable, the exercise is not without merit.

In our collaborative article, "Beyond Rigor," Jesse, Pete Rorabaugh, and I argue that:

> Intellectually rigorous work lives, thrives, and teems proudly outside conventional notions of academic rigor. Although institutions of higher education only recognize rigor when it mimics mastery of content, when it creates a hierarchy of expertise, when it maps clearly to pre-determined outcomes, there are works of exception — multimodal, collaborative, and playful — that push the boundaries of disciplinary allegiances, and don't always wear their brains on their sleeves, so to speak.

And we say later: "Play is critical inquiry." What is happening today — what happens when digital technology, media, and tools enter the learning space — is that learning has become more encyclopedic. It is beginning to shrug off the binding of disciplinarity and has become, frankly, less disciplined. We can no longer look for the old structures of rigor echoed in this more rambunctious learning. Where in a traditional classroom, the instructor holds the keys to knowledge, and they can lock it away whenever and in whatever portions they deem fit, digital culture hangs its hat on the ideal of openness and access: anyone who wants it can have whatever knowledge simply by keying in a search, or pointing to a specific URL.

Students with digital access can now go to the library and pore over the books they are most interested in, with or without permission, with or without curriculum, and generally entirely without a rubric, learning outcomes, or scaffolding.

Dinosaurs were not a popular subject at my elementary school, and independent study for a fifth grader wasn't rewarded. My motivations were entirely those of my hungry imagination. For many of today's students, those dinosaurs of mine are everywhere. In every nook and cranny of their days. And in their back pockets.

And yet, not all students. And certainly not all teachers. Access and "open" aren't solutions in themselves. When PowerPoint and Canvas and Twitter are bigger mysteries than we can solve, all this superlative talk about the digital does no one any good. We must find a practicable and more inclusive route into wonder. The work of scholarship should be the work of imagination.

And when we are in our right minds, we are creative, constructive, hopeful people. And we can practice our way into wonder. Paulo Freire wrote in his final work, *A Pedagogy of Indignation,*

> If I am not in the world simply to adapt to it, but rather transform it, and if it is not possible to change the world without a certain dream or vision for it, I must make use of every possibility there is not only to speak about my utopia, but also to engage in practices consistent with it.

Neither is grungy pessimism nor unadulterated optimism going to pave the way forward into an educational landscape that will productively embrace the digital. What we require is a strategic hope, and creativity born from skepticism. It's useless to badger on about how digital technology must never change the iron-clad traditions of the institution; but it's just as useless to think that technology is somehow going to wake us from our thousand-year stupor and reinvent education. And this is what I mean when I say that it would be a mistake to think that what I *do* is digital. What I do is human. What Digital Pedagogy Lab does — what Jesse and Jim and Bonnie and Dave and Audrey all do — is as human as a child on the library floor, his nose deep in a book.

We learn. We commit to learning. For now, there are no texts, so we'll go digging in the dirt. In Cairo. In Prince Edward Island. Online. Finding bones, imagining behemoths. It's field work, fueled by that strategic hope and an unrequited inquiry.

IS IT OKAY TO BE A LUDDITE?

SEAN MICHAEL MORRIS AND JESSE STOMMEL

I feel a pinch as I approach the screen once more. A twinge, just the littlest bite of remorse. Sometimes, it's sizeable, the feeling I have that I want the digital to be more, the Internet to be tangible, the vacant gaping spaces between my colleagues and myself to be smaller, more a hands-breadth than the length of a whale. And sometimes it is this, a mosquito in the ear. Either way, I return to the screen wishing for relationships that are bigger than pixels, and words that are indelible.

I rail against technology at dinner parties. I curse it to my friends in Google Hangouts. And they call me a luddite.

The title of this post is inspired by an essay by Thomas Pynchon. He wrote presciently in 1984, "Since 1959, we have come to live among flows of data more vast than anything the world has seen." According to Pynchon, "Luddites flourished In Britain from about 1811 to 1816. They were bands of men, organized, masked, anonymous, whose object was to destroy machinery used mostly in the textile industry." The 21st Century has produced a whole new kind of altogether less revolutionary luddite. These are the folks who refuse to go on Facebook, who have tried Twitter but would never use it regularly. They keep pen and paper handy and nod with suspicion at the great green elephant of Evernote. For these people, the Internet has not brought on a new world of connectedness and community, it has reduced us to two dimensions, static portraits of faces meant to be lively with expression. The Internet hurts their eyes. And they secretly (and sometimes not so secretly) scorn it's denizens, reducing their work to blips.

Nicholas Carr writes in "Is Google Making Us Stupid?," "You should be skeptical of my skepticism. Perhaps those who dismiss critics of the Internet as Luddites or nostalgists will be proved correct, and from our hyperactive, data-stoked minds will spring a golden age of intellectual discovery and universal wisdom." Words that drip with irony. Says today's luddite, Google may not be making us stupid, but it is changing our minds (the ones in our heads and the ones we tap with vigilant thumbs) about what brilliance and idiocy are.

There are many who look at the Internet as the downfall of modern education. They decry online learning as necessarily sub-par, stating that the digital can never replace the face-to-face. These are teachers throwing sabots into the machine, hoping with words to stop the gross forward movement altogether, before all we do is reduced to microwaves.

Perhaps, there is some middle-ground, not skepticism or luddism, but what Sean calls digital agnosticism. So often in our discussions of online education and teaching with technology, we jump to a discussion of *how* or *when* to use technology without pausing to think about *whether* or *why*. While we wouldn't advocate for a new era of luddism in higher education, we do think it's important for us to at least ask ourselves these questions.

We use technology. It seduces us and students with its graphic interfaces, haptic touch-screens, and attention-diverting multimodality. But what are the drawbacks and political ramifications of educational technologies? Are there situations where tech shouldn't be used or where its use should be made as invisible as possible? How does tech reconfigure the learning environment, both literally and figuratively? When a classroom (virtual or otherwise) revolves around tech, what shape does it take? How is this shape different from the configurations of classrooms that don't revolve around tech?

Can we approach new digital technologies at once with wonder and also dismay — with a reflective curiosity that unabashedly pushes buttons but not without first brazenly dissecting them?

And what do we make of analog pedagogies? Is the chalkboard an anachronism, or does it remain (as we believe) one of the most radical and advanced learning technologies? How do we remind ourselves that when we go online, our feet (or some other parts of us) are usually still on-ground?

The student-made viral video "A Vision of Students Today" shows how the boundaries of the classroom have changed in recent years. It ends with a very moving ode to the chalkboard. It offers a critique of how we interact with technology in contemporary society, pointing out how important it is to remain critical — open-eyed both in awe and inspection — at our engagement with machines.

Technology may be *homo sapiens'* super power. It is everywhere all the time, whether digital, mechanical, or simply practical. We will do technology always, and so railing against it, or feeling a twinge at the loneliness of the pixel must be tempered. To fear a technological future is to deny a technological past and present. And there is nothing new about sounding the alarm. Luddism has roots in a powerful kind of human agency, but to assume that technology necessarily removes agency is to misunderstand its use. Even the luddites knew when and how to throw sabots.

WINONA RYDER AND THE INTERNET OF THINGS

JESSE STOMMEL

In the living room the voice-clock sang, Tick-tock, seven o'clock, time to get up, time to get up, seven o'clock!

~ Ray Bradbury, "There Will Come Soft Rains"

The more our tools are naturalized, invisible, or inscrutable, the less likely we are to interrogate them.

The 2015 film *The Experimenter* is based on the true story of Stanley Milgram, the Yale University psychologist who became famous for his 1961 social behavior experiments that tested the obedience of volunteers who thought they were administering electrical shocks to strangers. In the film, the character of his wife, Alexandra "Sasha" Milgram, is played by Winona Ryder, and she serves as the on-screen stand-in for the film audience. Our ethical response to what happens in the film is registered on her face. In several scenes, the camera focuses on the face of Winona Ryder watching the experiment unfold—her skin twitching, her body shifting uncomfortably, her eyes wide with both horror and also a certain awe at what humans are capable of.

In his experiment, Milgram asked a "teacher" (the subject of the experiment) to shock a "learner" (an actor) for getting wrong answers on a simple test. An "experimenter" (working with Milgram) would order the teacher to give increasingly powerful shocks, and more often than not, the teacher complied. The study is not without baggage, but the results remain compelling nonetheless. At one point in the film, Winona Ryder as Sasha Milgram asks to experience the shock herself, the same very small shock that the teachers were also given during the setup of the experiment. The scene is played out with a certain menace as the various accoutrements are put into action. Visually, she is overwhelmed by the devices that surround her: the electrodes, the teacher's microphone, a series of digits that light up to show the learner's answers, a pen, a clipboard, the gray of the experimenter's lab coat, a recording device, and the large box of switches through which the teacher delivers the shocks.

Milgram himself describes this particular device as "an impressive shock generator. Its main feature is a horizontal line of thirty switches, ranging from 15 volts to 450 volts, in 15-volt increments. There are also verbal designations which range from SLIGHT SHOCK to DANGER-SEVERE SHOCK." I sense glee in the language Milgram uses ("impressive"), something theatrical in the excess ("thirty switches"), and a fastidiousness in his attention to detail in reporting all this.

The mechanisms and the machine, but also the clipboard, the lab coat, etc. play clear roles in maintaining and even eliciting compliance. And the subtler and more intricate or inscrutable the mechanism, the more compliance it appears to generate — because the human brain fails to bend adequately around it. The camera works a similar magic on the film viewers as it ominously traces over these objects. Like our on-screen surrogate, Winona Ryder, we too sit still — complicit, both horrified and awed by what we see and our inability to stop it.

The less we understand our tools, the more we are beholden to them. The more we imagine our tools as transparent or invisible, the less able we are to take ownership of them.

At the interview for my current job at the University of Mary

Washington, the inimitable Martha Burtis asked me to reflect on the statement: "It's teaching, not tools." What assumptions does this oft-bandied-about phrase make? What does it overlook? Like Martha, I find myself increasingly concerned by the idea that our tools are without ideologies — that tools are neutral. Of course, they aren't. Tools are made by people, and most (or even all) educational technologies have pedagogies hard-coded into them in advance. This is why it is so essential that we consider them carefully and critically—that we empty all our LEGOs onto the table and sift through them before we start building. Some tools are decidedly less innocuous than others. And some tools can never be hacked to good use.

In 2014, the EDUCAUSE Learning Initiative (ELI) report "7 Things You Should Know About the Internet of Things" noted: "The Internet of Things (IoT) describes a state in which vast numbers of objects are interconnected over the Internet and can collect data and transmit and receive information." I find something ominous about the capital-I and capital-T of the acronym IoT, a kind of officiousness in the way these devices are described as proliferating across our social and physical landscapes.

The ELI report continues, "the IoT has its roots in industrial production, where machine-to-machine communication enabled the manufacture of complex items, but it is now expanding in the commercial realm, where small monitoring devices allow such things as ovens, cars, garage doors, and the human heartbeat to be checked from a computing device." At the point when our relationship to a device (or a connected series of devices) has become this intimate, this pervasive, the relationship cannot be called free of values, ethics, or ideology.

I'll be candid. I am quite often an unabashed fan of the Internet of Things. I like that my devices talk to one another, and I enjoy tracking my movement and my heart rate. I even find myself almost unable to resist my curiosity about something like the ridiculous bluetooth-enabled cup that can track how much water I drink. I like controlling my car from my phone and feeling the tickle of an incoming text message on my wrist. But my own personal curiosity and fascination are outweighed by my concern at the degree to which similar devices are being used in education to monitor and police learning.

I am worried by sentences like this one from the ELI report, "E-texts could record how much time is spent in textbook study. All such data could be accessed by the LMS or various other applications for use in analytics for faculty and students." I am worried by how words like "record," "accessed," and "analytics" turn students and faculty into data points. I am worried that students' own laptop cameras might be used to monitor them while they take tests. I am worried that those cameras will report data about eye movement back to an algorithm that changes the difficulty of questions. I am worried because these things take us further away from what education is actually for. I am worried because these things make education increasingly about *obedience,* not learning.

Remote proctoring tools can't ensure that students will not cheat. The LMS can't ensure that students will learn. Both will, however, ensure that students feel more thoroughly policed. Both will ensure that students (and teachers) are more compliant. In his 1974 book *Obedience to Authority: An Experimental View,* Milgram described "the tendency of the individual to become so absorbed in the narrow technical aspects of the task that he loses sight of its broader consequences." Even if I find the experiment itself icky, Milgram offers useful reflections on the bizarre techno theater that made his experiment go.

When Internet-enabled devices have thoroughly saturated our educational institutions, they run the risk of being able to police students' behavior without any direct input or mediation from teachers. By merely being in the room, the devices will monitor students' behavior in the same way that the cameras and switches and lab coats did in Milgram's experiments. How will learning be changed when everything is tracked? How has learning already been changed by the tracking we already do? When our LMS reports how many minutes students have spent accessing a course, what do we do with that information? What will we do with the information when we also know the heart rate of students as they're accessing (or not accessing) a course?

Winona Ryder was caught on camera and arrested for shoplifting in Saks Fifth Avenue in 2001. How do we respond when a security guard peers through the slats of a dressing room to witness a very rich person, "scissors in hand, clipping sensor tags from store items?" The jury convicted her. She was vilified even as "Free Winona" t-shirts started flying off shelves. An early web meme was born.

I maintain a great deal of excitement about the potential of the Internet of Things. At the same time, I find myself pausing to consider what Milgram called "counteranthropomorphism" — the tendency we have to remove the humanity of people we can't see. These may be people on the other side of a wall, as in Milgram's experiment, or people mediated by technology in a virtual classroom.

Winona has very few lines of dialogue in *The Experimenter*, and yet her performance is a pivotal one because she offers a guide, a moral compass, for the off-screen audience. She is complicit in her passivity and yet rebellious in her willingness to register raw and genuine emotion, something no other character can muster. And as the film unfolds, the shock and awe on her face gives way to compassion. As she looks upon the scene of the experiment, she sees human beings and not the experiment.

We must approach the Internet of Things from a place that doesn't reduce ourselves, or reduce students, to mere algorithms. We must approach the Internet of Things as a space of learning, not as a way to monitor and regulate. Our best tools in this are ones that encourage compassion more than obedience. The Internet is made of people, not things.

ADVENTURES IN UNVEILING: CRITICAL PEDAGOGY AND IMAGINATION

SEAN MICHAEL MORRIS

There never were going to be any dinosaur bones. Not on that cloudy day, nor on any other. But we went out anyway. With sandwiches and chips, an apple or two. Out to the open space around Boulder, Colorado. Me, my mom, and hope for a brontosaurus.

I'd been an elementary school amateur paleontologist for years already. Studying everything I could about dinosaurs, about the science of finding them and digging them up. I knew enough about geology to be dangerous. I could recite the periods of the eons when dinosaurs ruled the earth by heart: not just the Triassic, Jurassic, and Cretaceous, but the early, late, and middle, and the beasts that roamed, and how long they stomped across the plains.

Colorado had been underwater in those prehistoric days. So, I told my mom, if we find anything, it will be amphibious or water-dwelling. A sauropod, maybe. Or a plesiosaur.

She'd kept me home from school so we could go dino hunting. We parked the car along a country road, crossed over a fence, and found our way to a high creek bed where, I was certain, I could make out the strata of sediment that marked the ages gone past.

Not the one or two hundred years they actually marked, but the billions I thought they could.

It didn't matter that there weren't going to be any dinosaur bones. My mother knew that. Because learning doesn't require accuracy.

#

Several years later, at Boulder High School, I had an American Studies Honors teacher who sometimes threw chalk at students. On good days, she threw erasers. I was a senior, happily in love for the first time, enjoying my burgeoning sense of adulthood, and I thought this teacher—we'll call her Ms. G.—both riotously laughable and uniquely intelligent. I respected her precise criticality. I recognized the difference between her capacity and my own on the first day of class, when she assigned an article from *The Atlantic Monthly*. An article that, while not above my reading level, certainly was beyond my ken.

On the second day of class, when she asked again and again, "What was this article *really* about?" and answers like "homelessness" and "poverty" weren't enough, I realized I had a long way to go. (That was also the same semester I was introduced to the five-paragraph essay, a form so elegant in its monotony, and yet so revelatory in its logic, I couldn't believe I hadn't been taught it earlier.) The thing that really got me about Ms. G. was her insistence that we push ourselves beyond our assumptions about our adolescent intellectual capability. She wanted us to be *smart*. As smart as she was. As critical, as temperamental about insight. She didn't want us throwing erasers in class, of course, but she would've loved it if we were throwing them in our imaginations.

What Ms. G. never suspected, I suspect, is that she was growing in me an academic courage unwanted in a high school senior. And for my final project that term, I undertook a research paper about the Civil War, focusing my attention on Robert E. Lee. Egged on by her encouragement, I read his diaries, I read second hand accounts about him, and I drew maps of his military strategies. In the process, I came upon what I thought was a tremendous discovery, a thesis so unshakable and so awe-inspiring that Ms. G. would be proud enough to hand me an eraser or piece of chalk herself.

I claimed that Lee lost the Civil War on purpose, in order to preserve what was left of the South.

I was thrown out of class. I was told I should not try to be a scholar, and I was moved to a different, remedial section of American Studies. I spent the rest of the year in a room where boys and girls kissed in the back row while the teacher tried to lecture from the text.

#

Why is imagination important to the project of critical pedagogy? By which, I'm also asking why is imagination important to the project of social justice? Critical pedagogy doesn't reside solely in classrooms; in fact, it cannot, because its project is the work of vision and change within all sectors of society. Held captive in the classroom, critical pedagogy will never reach those for whom school is not a central location for learning. If learning is done in the home, or at work, or in the survival of poverty, violence, or depression, school can feel arbitrary, unnecessary, a hindrance, or a site of a false hope of escaping hardship. Critical pedagogy's project is to sharpen and concentrate learning where it happens, privileging no location over another as that place where critical consciousness (conscientização) can rise up.

Imagination is important to the project of critical pedagogy precisely because of the responsive nature of its practice. We must be able to think on our toes if education (of all kinds) is meant to be liberative. Liberation depends upon a thought—a thought that *things as they are can be different than they are*. That there is a reality beyond that which Paulo Freire, in *Pedagogy of Indignation*, calls "objective reality, one purely realized and around which nothing could be discussed."

It is imagination that enables us to believe that things can be changed.

Teaching with this in mind is as necessary as it is concerning. To sport imagination in the classroom is to call into question the axes upon which the institution of education turns—credentialing, seat time, standardization, testing, grades, academic integrity. The bearing of imagination looks fragile. It can look like whimsy, unprofessionalism, uncertainty. It is not the power suit or patched elbows that academia expects. It betrays a vulnerability, an important vulnerability, to which not all teachers are prepared to confess, especially in front of a classroom of students. And yet, if Maxine Greene is correct and "it is a primary purpose of education to deny people the opportunity for feeling bored" (*Releasing the Imagination*), then filling our teaching lungs with imagination is unavoidable.

The idea of bringing imagination to bear on subjects as critical as math and science may give us pause. But the imagination is as accurate as the intellect. It has its own rigor. The results simply aren't the same. The intellect, and its hound of empirical practice, produces results that can be cataloged and categorized. Written in a paper. Abstracted. Tested. Posted for tenure. The intellect goes hunting and brings home a duck for dinner.

The imagination, led by an entirely wilder mutt, produces results that are intangible, and that are usually questions rather than answers. "The role of the imagination," Greene tells us, "is not to resolve, not to point the way, not to improve. It is to awaken, to disclose the ordinary unseen, unheard, and unexpected." The imagination goes hunting and brings back a whangdoodle.

But the imagination also brings back hope. (This is where it is rigorous.) Just as the imagination enables us to believe things can be changed, so it is hope that drives us to change them. "Without a minimum of hope," Freire writes, "we cannot so much as start the struggle." Change is predicated on hope; hope is predicated on imagination. Criticality is not enough. "A more critical understanding of the situation of oppression does not yet liberate the oppressed." Freire again. "But the revelation is a step in the right direction." What follows upon that revelation is imagination.

Simply put: critical understanding + imagination + hope is the only recipe for meaningful change. If we don't make imagination available in our classrooms, neither do we make hope available.

And is there education without hope? What would be its purpose? What is the purpose of hopelessness? These are not rhetorical questions, either. There are answers to them. Answers from which has risen educational technology—in large part an attempt to homogenize learning, to produce people who are archives of information but never change agents, who are *qualified*. Qualified for *what* matters less than that qualification has been achieved. The process of education, without imagination or hope, resembles a chore board, upon which boxes are checked, from which we derive our sense of direction for the day, week, or our tenure, and which gives us a that sense of accomplishment, however fleeting, that we have done what needs to be done.

Just doing what needs to be done, though, is a far cry from believing that things can be different, and then struggling to make them so. It is a far cry from denying people the opportunity for feeling bored.

Without imagination, education shrivels to training, which is an occupation without hope, and one which doesn't even long for hope. Training seeks to maintain the status quo, and assumes that the systems already in place are not only satisfactory, but beyond question. Systems that are, as Freire laments, " as obvious as that Saturdays precede Sundays."

Education that *doesn't* withhold or resist imagination inquires, assumes questionability—and does so benevolently, with the hope that inquiry leads to deeper understanding, to improvement, to equity, and to mending the flaws of systemic bias, discrimination, and disparity.

#

I would never have proved that Robert E. Lee surreptitiously surrendered the Civil War in order to save Southern lives, because he didn't. To seek to uphold the humanity of a man who supported a bloody war in order to defend slavery is beyond problematic. My concern, however, is not my thesis, but rather the teaching I received in response. Freire writes:

"Never does an event, a fact, a deed, a gesture of rage or love, a poem, a painting, a song, a book, have only one reason behind it. In fact, a deed, a gesture of rage or love, a poem, a painting, a song, a book are always wrapped in thick wrappers. They have been touched by manifold *whys*."

Where my teacher failed me, where teachers fail, where educational technology fails, where the LMS and the gradebook and standardized assessment all fail, is in not recognizing the manifold *whys* behind all learning. Behind every wrong answer, every right answer, every creative answer, every question, every fear of asking questions. The *whys* of learning cannot be assessed or quantified, they cannot be listed somewhere on a spreadsheet, nor recorded in the findings of an evidence-based educational research project.

School dismisses the imagination, the strange unlikely path of manifold *whys*. This is its grandest, profoundest failing. You see, I had all my facts mixed up, and my insights into Lee's brain incorrect, my assumptions about military strategy reaching for amateur; but the process of my insights, the serendipity that led me to the facts, the cognitive, imaginative leaps that I made, even the presumption that I could understand the complexities of military strategy as a high school senior—these last were the real stuff of my learning. It was my imagination at play in that paper, in that research; it was my gleeful sense of discovery. And that, *that* is what Ms. G. should have responded to.

Difficult, yes. Impossible? The impossible is what the imagination is for. "The difficult task for the teacher is to devise situations in which the young will move from the habitual and ordinary" (the five-paragraph essay, the litany of all that has already been said about the Civil War) "and consciously undertake a search." Yes, Maxine Greene, yes.

I hold up my 16-year-old self's research project as an example—with its troubling, gross thesis—precisely because it is troubling and gross. The imagination doesn't always lead us to correct answers; instead, imagination can lead us astray precisely so we can learn. But that is the process of a progressive education. An "adventure in unveiling," Freire calls it in *Pedagogy of Hope*. Education shouldn't be a matter of simple solutions, memorization, passing objective reality from one older mind to dozens of younger minds. Education is an operation of imagination, discovery, and unveiling. When the imagination leads us astray, when it takes us down paths our teachers would not advise we walk, it "poses the issues of decision, of option, of ethics," even, says Freire, "of education and its limits."

Teachers tend to, are taught to—either through received teaching or an education in teaching—read the world *to* their students, rather than giving them room to read it themselves. And more, through the mechanism of their syllabi, their lesson plans, their assignments and assessments, teachers expect students to navigate by the charts provided them in the form of lectures, textbooks, handouts. The misunderstanding here is not one of the night sky and stars, or the charting of navigable routes, but a misunderstanding of the sea. For it is the student's mind, not the teacher's, that's meant to be navigated. This is pivotal to an understanding of critical pedagogy: it is the student's mind, not the teacher's, that's meant to be navigated. And for that, the student's mind must be unveiled—their *whys* must be heard and listened to.

A teacher who says "these have been my *whys*; these have been the questions that formed the academy; these have been the questions of the field, and its answers, and my answers" is teaching history, not the present. That teacher does not teach possibility, but rather conformity. "If teaching can be thought of as an address to others' consciousness," Greene writes, "it may be a summons on the part of one incomplete person to other incomplete persons to reach for wholeness." It is an illusion of the profession that the teacher holds the answers, that the institution does, or the field does. If this were the case, academia would be unnecessary, for its primary mission is to explore. And exploration, not the geography of the known, is the heart of education.

#

There might have been dinosaur bones. There were definitely sandwiches. And climbing fences we should not have. And child-like explanations of the sediment under our fingers. Excitement and apples and hope.

There didn't need to be dinosaur bones. In taking me out to the creek bed to fish for fossils, my mother not only stoked my imagination, she also meant to "combat life's anaesthetics," as Greene encourages of all teachers, and to move me to reach out toward a horizon that only my imagination and hope could see.

LEARNING ONLINE

Educational campuses have libraries, coffee shops, cafeterias, quads, lawns, amphitheaters, stadiums, hallways, student lounges, trees, park benches, and fountains. Ample space for rallies, study-groups, conversation, debate, student clubs, and special events. Few institutions pay much attention to re-creating these spaces online.

ONLINE LEARNING: A MANIFESTO

JESSE STOMMEL

Online learning is not the whipping boy of higher education. As a classroom teacher first and foremost, I have no interest in proselytizing for online learning, but to roundly condemn it is absurd. Online learning is too big and variable a target. It would be like roundly condemning the internet or all objects made from paper.

Much of the rhetoric currently being used against MOOCs is the same rhetoric that has been used against online learning since the 90s (and against distance education since the mid-1800s). There are important questions to be asked, such as *how do MOOCs change the business models of higher education,* or *how do we maintain online the intimate and tailored experiences some of us create in the classroom,* but these are not new questions. What I find exciting about the rise of the MOOC is that it brings with it a new level of investment in discussions of online learning. This isn't to say that MOOCs are necessarily good or bad (they are, in fact, a lot of different things, depending on the MOOC), but to get lost entirely in the stories being told about MOOCs is to *miss the forest for the trees,* so to speak.

Since I started teaching in 1999, I've frequently encountered an anti-pedagogical bent amongst fellow teachers and faculty, a resistance to thinking critically about our teaching practices and philosophies, especially regarding online learning. What we need is to ignore the hype and misrepresentations (on both sides of the debate) and gather together more people willing to carefully reflect on how, where, and why we learn online. There is no productive place in this conversation for exclusivity or anti-intellectualism. Those of us talking about digital pedagogy and digital humanities need to be engaging thoughtfully in discussions about online learning and open education. Those of us in higher ed need to be engaging thoughtfully with K-12 teachers and administrators. And it's especially important that we open our discussions of the future of education to students, who should both participate in and help to build their own learning spaces. Pedagogy needs to be at the center of all these discussions.

I say elsewhere in this collection that "MOOCs are a red herring," because there is a bigger beast in the offing. I would not proselytize for online learning or MOOCs, but I *would* for open education, participant pedagogy, critical voraciousness, and play. The internet didn't invent collaboration or solve all the problems of institutional access, but it does allow for new forms of collaboration and does bring educational opportunities to new audiences. (In my own online classes, for example, I've taught housebound students, new mothers in rural areas hundreds of miles from a university, and soldiers stationed abroad.)

I have no interest in debating the *whether* of online learning. That bird has most assuredly flown. What I'd like to do here is outline **a pedagogy of online learning** — not best practices, but points of departure to encourage a diversity of pedagogies.

1. Online learning happens at many different scales. Not all online learning, though, is scalable. The MOOC is one possible approach, and it is neither a panacea nor a pariah. It might function well for certain learners or for certain courses, but it should be viewed as one of many available approaches. Online learning can happen alone or in groups of 2, 20, 500, or 100,000. The scale of the activity, event, or course changes the experience (but does not *define* the experience).
2. I've argued that "all learning is necessarily hybrid." The best online learning should engage us in an immediate

and physical way. Learning shouldn't happen entirely at a desk. The best online courses — the best courses of all types — ask students to do work in the world (outside their houses and/or outside the online course portal).

3. The *openness* of the internet is its most radical and pedagogically viable feature. This isn't to say that every class should be entirely open, but we should not assume in advance (or use systems that assume) we need a learning space to be closed (or password-protected). Some learning happens best in rooms with walls, but some learning happens best in fields or in libraries or in town squares.
4. A class should not be made open purely as a publicity ploy (though publicity can be a happy consequence). We need to ask ourselves how openness serves the students (both the official for-credit students and the unofficial not-for-credit students). The mission of an educational institution is both to serve its students and also to serve a much broader public. Putting these two audiences into direct conversation is (in many cases) an effective pedagogical strategy.
5. Rigor fails to be rigorous when it's made compulsory. It can't be guaranteed in advance by design. Academic rigor shouldn't be built into a course like an impenetrable fortress for students to inhabit. Rigor has to be fostered through genuine engagement.
6. Designing an online course involves building both the course and its interface. Online course development requires more preparation, more advance planning, and more technological support. At many institutions there's a problematic divide between instructional designers and teachers — between those building online courses and those teaching them. Expert teachers need to build their own online courses or we need to create closer collaborative relationships between teachers and instructional designers.
7. Online learning is not the domain of for-profit

institutions. While online learning has been most-visibly used by for-profits, this leaves no permanent black spot upon its hide. Innovative, pedagogically-sound, and ethical work is being done online. That is the work we need to be talking about and advancing with gusto.

8. Don't wield outcomes like a weapon. Online learning activities should not be overly designed or too-strictly standardized. In "Explaining Rhizomatic Learning to My Five Year Old," Dave Cormier writes, "We shouldn't decide beforehand what we're going to learn." Improvisation, play, and experimentation are essential to learning.
9. FERPA is not an excuse for bad pedagogy. FERPA is designed to protect students and does not outlaw public work. Some simple guidelines: If you're asking students to do public work online, let them know their work will be public, offer the option of anonymity, never post grades publicly, and don't forget about intellectual property (which is separate from FERPA).
10. There is no one-size-fits-all approach to online education. Learning is not neatly divisible into discrete chunks (like courses). We make courses, because they suit a business model and because they're practical (i.e. gathering a community in the same place at the same time). The chunks, though, 10 weeks, 15 weeks, semesters, quarters, are arbitrary. The course is not always the best container for learning.
11. Community and dialogue shouldn't be an accident or by-product of a course. They should be the course. You can't just stick people into a room and expect them to talk. The same is true for online space. We must create platforms that both actively facilitate and passively encourage interaction. Then, we work to model constructive interaction. The best online courses have a personality, create genuine relationships, and ask hard intellectual questions.

12. Content-expertise does not equal good teaching. The internet already has lots of experts in all manner of things. A good pedagogue, rather, relies on a variable mixture of content-expertise and careful thinking about teaching practices. The teacher is not merely a facilitator, but uses her own learning of a subject (its histories, theories, and methodologies) to design, structure, and scaffold a learning experience. Once a course begins, the growing expertise of the students, and not the teacher, should be the primary focus.
13. Online learning needs less quantitative and more qualitative assessment. Students are not columns in a spreadsheet. Most learning management systems make assessment far too neat and tidy. Certainly, some things can be objectively assessed, but that's not the stuff of learning that we should be focusing on so intently. Numerical data should be a guide only, a way into the deeper conversation about what was learned, a reference point for more productive and qualitative assessment. The most important form of assessment, though, is self-assessment by the students of their own learning.

The first mistake of many online classes and the majority of MOOCs (so far) is that they try to replicate something we do in face-to-face classes, mapping the (sometimes pedagogically-sound, sometimes bizarre) traditions of on-ground institutions onto digital space. Trying to make an online class function exactly like an on-ground class is a missed opportunity. There's a lot that happens in F2F classrooms that just can't be replicated in an online environment, and that's okay. Better to ask ourselves what *can* be achieved online and what sorts of classes (or learning experiences) we can construct to leverage the potentials of the specific interface or community.

HOW TO BUILD AN ETHICAL ONLINE COURSE

JESSE STOMMEL

The best online and hybrid courses are made from scraps strewn about and gathered together from across the web. We build a course by examining the bits, considering how they're connected, and creating pathways for learners to make their own connections.

The design process is what distinguishes online teaching most from traditional on-ground teaching. When we teach an on-ground class, the room in which we teach has been built for us in advance. Usually, it's in a school, on a campus, has chairs, desks, tables, windows, walls, a door. Sometimes there's a computer, a projector, a screen. Hopefully, the desks and chairs are moveable and there are chalkboards on multiple walls. When we enter these rooms, we still make (or, rather, *should* make) intentional design decisions. How will the chairs be arranged? What direction will we face? Will the blinds be open or closed? Where will the teacher's desk be? Will the room have a *front*? Will we rearrange from day to day or maintain a consistent configuration?

All of these decisions require careful contemplation and experimentation. Letting the default configuration of a classroom dictate how we'll teach is to allow the bureaucratic (and in this case architectural) trappings of schooling subsume our pedagogies. I've taught in many classrooms where the desks were arranged by default into rows, each student forced to stare into the back of another student's head. This is not a prime configuration to encourage active engagement, critical thinking, collaboration, interaction, making, doing, or discussing, all of which are (in varying degrees) essential for learning. I would say, though, that *any arrangement* is problematic if it's fixed permanently in advance. The learning space should be constructed intentionally from one activity to the next and preferably by or in consultation with students.

When we teach online, we have to build both the course and the classroom. A good learning management system is a tool that can help with this process; however, we should never let its design decisions — its architecture — dictate our pedagogies. We should also not blindly follow our institution's choice of learning management system. Certain tools work well for building certain kinds of learning experiences, but there's no universal solution. Teachers should be instrumental in making decisions about the technologies used in their classrooms (virtual or otherwise). And a single course should leverage several solutions and configurations, given the specific needs of the day, activity, or student.

Hybrid classes demand an even more complex architecture, requiring consideration of the physical space(s) we'll work within, the virtual space(s), as well as the various ways we'll move between the spaces. When we build a hybrid class, we must consider how we'll create pathways between the learning that happens in a room and the learning that happens on the web. A hybrid strategy can be as simple as a single but powerful hyperlink embedded in an e-mail or as complex as replacing the syllabus for a course with a multi-author WordPress installation.

In "Online Learning: a Manifesto," I offer a series of tenets, which I describe as "points of departure to encourage a diversity of pedagogies." Here, I want to drill down a little deeper into the nuts and bolts of online and hybrid course design, exploring more specific strategies for implementing several of the tenets from my earlier piece:

> The best online learning should engage us in an immediate and physical way.

For an online or hybrid course, I create activities that ask students to venture out into their communities. As often as possible in my courses, I use tools that play well with mobile devices, like Layar or WordPress, to allow us to do our work in the world and not just behind a desk. The best tools make themselves as invisible as possible, serving not as a distraction but as a way of extending the landscape beyond its bounds. So, I might ask students to blog about Thoreau's *Walden* while on a hike, including pictures from their adventure. And if students tweet their post with geotagging activated, they contribute to a humongous archive of location-tagged tweets. By sharing and interacting with this kind of work online we bring each other into a shared sense of physical space. Rather than merely redistributing learning, a hybrid pedagogy asks us to reflect on and make connections between learning that happens in classrooms, online, at a desk, aboard a bus, on a mountaintop, by ourselves, and in conversation.

> The openness of the internet is its most radical and pedagogically viable feature.

I've taught hybrid classes since 2001 and fully online classes since 2007. **Almost every class I've taught has been an open course, but few have been massive.** Designing for openness means giving careful thought to both what registered students can do inside a course and what passersby can do. I began by putting all of my syllabi online, but I've increasingly asked students to do public work and to have online discussions in open fora. For me, openness means allowing access to all or a significant portion of a course without registration. Some of the best learning opportunities are ones we fall haphazardly into. A certain amount of immediacy is lost when we are forced to trade personal data for access — to *pay* for our entrance into a course with personal information (which is what makes most MOOCs decidedly not *free*).

I've built course sites from scratch, but I've also found WordPress and Canvas to be extremely robust tools for designing open courses. Both allow entirely open components but can require registration or password-access at various points to enable different levels of engagement. Unlike most other learning management systems, any page in Canvas or WordPress generates a unique hyperlink, creating multiple points of entry to a course. There are a number of LMS plugins for WordPress, although most put far too much emphasis on grading and assessment for my taste. Don't put the cart before the horse, so to speak, by choosing an LMS because it offers a convenient gradebook.

> Academic rigor shouldn't be built into a course like an impenetrable fortress for students to inhabit. Rigor has to be fostered through genuine engagement.

When I design an online course, I start by thinking about the nature of the learning community I hope to foster. Most learning management systems offer tools for engagement, but they are usually closed asynchronous forums, which can be valuable, but only for a very specific kind of interaction. One of the drawbacks of these systems is that students usually don't retain access to their work once the course is over. Using tools like Twitter or Disqus for online discussion gives students more direct control over their own data, allowing them to delete, archive, and (in some cases) edit their contributions at will.

I'm of the mind that we can't make our courses "academically rigorous" *by design*, especially at the level of content or assessment. Rather, **rigor arises through the development of a critically voracious learning community**. This can't be compulsory, but has to be encouraged through intrinsic rather than extrinsic motivation. In other words, making participation worth points does not help build community. (Handing out a grade to every person talking at a party would not encourage them to talk to us. In fact, probably just the opposite.) Rather, build or leverage a space that encourages open contribution and trust learners to navigate the space. The single best tip I have on this front is to avoid the *ping-pong ball effect,* in which the teacher responds to every (or nearly every) comment made by students with immediate correction or affirmation. This very quickly reinforces a hierarchy in which students are constantly looking to the teacher for approval. **Ignore any "best practices" or "quality assurance" measures that encourage the teacher's voice to dominate online discussion.** Model thoughtful engagement and responsiveness with several well-placed comments/questions and leave space for the learners to follow suit.

> Don't wield outcomes like a weapon. Online learning activities should not be overly designed or too-strictly standardized.

Courses should be designed by individuals or small groups of collaborators not by committees. We should also not use systems that etch curricula into stone. This means supporting (financially and culturally) course development and frequent course redevelopment. It also means eschewing altogether stock courses. Where possible, students should guide the curriculum and create course content. This means using or enabling tools that give students at least some measure of control over design. With a small group of students, this might mean building the course site together in a wiki or multi-author WordPress installation. With a larger group of students, where administering permissions for each student might become cumbersome, embedding Google docs or allowing comments on course pages can foster and facilitate student collaboration.

> There is no one-size-fits-all approach to online education. Learning is not neatly divisible into discrete chunks (like courses).

Online and hybrid course design should be motivated not by cost savings but by the pedagogical benefits of learning that happens and persists beyond the classroom. Online and hybrid models should not replace classroom instruction. We should design courses that actively reconsider when and where learning happens. One of the benefits of online learning, for me, is that I can have a local group of students collaborating with people elsewhere in the world, disturbing the notion that learning happens best in a single course, at a single institution, or within a single country. Social media allows us to bring together teachers and students working in similar courses around the world to create collaborative "textbooks" using curation tools like Pinterest, ScoopIt, Reddit, or Delicious. There are ways to make learning massive and accessible that don't involve stuffing 100,000 people into a closed-room MOOC.

> Content-expertise does not equal good teaching. The internet already has lots of experts in all manner of things. A good pedagogue, rather, relies on a variable mixture of content-expertise and careful thinking about teaching practices.

We won't figure out online and hybrid learning — in higher education, at least — until we truly value faculty development and pedagogical training. The minimal top-down efforts I've seen toward this end have been largely ineffective. We need to start at the grassroots level to weave pedagogical work into our research and publishing. If teaching is indeed 40-90% of our jobs (depending on the type of institution), then the sessions at our disciplinary conferences should be 40-90% about teaching (or at least make explicit connections between our research and teaching). **Pedagogy is not the domain solely of Schools of Education and should be a respected specialty or sub-field in every discipline.** And departments developing online and hybrid courses need to start by hiring full-time or tenure-track faculty who specialize in online learning and/or digital pedagogy.

Most importantly, educators at every level must begin by listening to and trusting students. This means building space in every course for students to reflect upon the course's pedagogy — an ongoing meta-level discussion of learning with student voices at its center. Teachers stand to learn more from students about online learning than we could ever teach. Many students come to an online or hybrid class knowing very well how to learn online. It's often *our failure* to know as well how to learn online that leads to many of the design mistakes in this generation of online courses. Recognizing this demands a culture-shift — demands that we acknowledge the diverse expertise of students as tantamount to our own.

THE FAILURE OF AN ONLINE PROGRAM

SEAN MICHAEL MORRIS

It's evening. An Irish pub in Louisville, Colorado. Fish and chips. Beer. A game of soccer on the TV. I'm sitting down with one of my faculty to revisit the department's Developmental English course (ENG 090). My goal: bring the course fully online, eliminate the text book, and make it a deeper learning and community building experience for all who enroll. The trick is, almost no one enrolls in ENG 090 because they want to. They enroll because they failed a test. How do you take a student from "You failed. Take this class." to "Writing is fun!" And how do you do that online?

My meeting started with that question, and the course itself grew out of more questions. We spent our time asking how a thing could be done — "How can we eliminate a text book?" "How can we make assignments that are meaningful, student-centered, and relevant?" "How can we make this course equally accessible to native English speakers and second language learners?" — and very rarely, if ever, saying that something could not be done. We opened our minds to the ways that we could open the LMS. We decided on quizzes that were iterative, formative and not summative. We chose to create a voice for the course that was friendly and work that united students in collaboration rather than making them compete against the machine or us.

That evening, and in the semesters that followed, the ENG 090 course evolved to become more open, more engaging, and over time inspired higher and higher retention.

I was Program Chair of the English Department at an institution that existed next to the community college system in Colorado. We provided online courses for all 13 system colleges. Because our audience — teachers, students, on-ground administrators — was diverse in both their expectations and abilities, always at the fore of any course design was ease of use. How flexible and facile could our courses be? How low-maintenance, too, and thus adoptable? In addition, I faced my personal expectation that every course we offered be as pedagogically sound — and not just sound, but also as innovative as possible. Working within the dim corridors of the Blackboard and WebCT LMSs, it was often challenging to provide enough illumination to help learning happen.

I had long believed that online learning didn't understand itself. That it was as a two-year-old child who discovers he can walk but doesn't really understand the nuances of the ambulatory act, nor really even what walking's for. For years — and especially after the widespread adoption of the LMS — there had been a kind of "because we can" attitude among instructional designers and online educators. No one was asking whether we should or, more importantly, what exactly online learning was for.

My institution at the time, like many then and many now, thrived in a climate of non-inquiry. We created courses that met state-mandated standards, that enjoyed consistently higher and higher enrollments (in my short tenure, my department went from offering 25 sections to 50 sections each term), and we aspired to be a model for online learning programs everywhere. On paper, we looked great. But failure was inevitable.

In Fall of 2012, the Developmental English course that was birthed that evening at the pub, and which has also enjoyed tremendous growth in enrollment and attendance over the last five years since I left my post, was redesigned. It was redesigned by the administration, Frankensteined together from bits and pieces of variations on the course, armed with incredibly rigid rubrics for discussion posting, assignments, and other student contributions, engorged with hard-to-take and hard-to-grade weekly quizzes, and derailed by inconsistencies between assignments, discussions, and lectures. Before this redesign, ENG 090 justified an offering of ten to fifteen sections in a single term. And the semester following, only four sections filled.

It seems natural to assume that students spread the word and chose to take the course at other institutions. What at one time was a meaningful, interesting developmental class had become a nightmare, a punishment for failing the English comprehension test.

So what went wrong? Clearly, instructional design choices are partly to blame. But why were those choices made?

A climate of non-inquiry can create a robust online learning program. But it corrupts that program from the bottom, up. A climate of non-inquiry, where we all hold our meetings with our blinders firmly strapped about our cheeks, corrodes the best-intentioned online programs because it allows us as administrators and teachers to never be learners. And the truth is, there is a great deal of learning still to be done. An insistence on doing things as we've always done them, on trying to match piece to piece, part to part, learning object to learning object, only limits us. Non-inquiry blinds us to the environment in which we're actually teaching.

Online learning not only will fail; in its current iterations it already has. We should not try to fix what's wrong with online learning now; instead, we should pretend it never happened, start from scratch, and begin playfully outside the borders of how we've always taught and how we relate to the machines that can help us teach. The only way we can surface from this quagmire of poor teaching, uninformed design, and lackluster (or lack of) pedagogy is to admit that we've wandered a long way down the wrong path. We need to sit down, have some fish and chips, maybe a beer, and start asking questions again. Freely, openly, curiously, and without fear.

A USER'S GUIDE TO FORKING EDUCATION

JESSE STOMMEL

At exactly this moment, online education is poised (and threatening) to replicate the conditions, courses, structures, and hierarchical relations of brick-and-mortar industrial-era education. Cathy N. Davidson argued exactly this at her presentation, "Access Demands a Paradigm Shift," at the 2013 Modern Language Association conference. The mistake being made, I think, is a simple and even understandable one, but damning and destructive nonetheless. Those of us responsible for education (both its formation and care) are hugging too tightly to what we've helped build, its pillars, policies, economies, and institutions. None of these, though, map promisingly into digital space. If we continue to tread our current path, we'll be left with a Frankenstein's monster of what we now know of education. This is the imminent destruction of our educational system of which so many speak: taking an institution inspired by the efficiency of post-industrial machines and redrawing it inside the machines of the digital age. Education rendered into a dull 2-dimensional carbon copy, scanned, faxed, encoded and then made human-readable, an utter lack of intellectual bravery.

The learning management system is a perfect example. Most of these systems recreate the bureaucracies of education without capturing the joy and rigor. At their worst, learning management systems turn students into row in a spreadsheet, and their work into columns, taking all that's ineffable about learning and making it grossly manifest. Learning management systems aren't all bad, but the idea is bad, the impulse is bad, at its core. They make homogenous what is fundamentally heterogeneous, standardizing what shouldn't be standardized. Fetishizing the learning management system is to confuse educational administration with learning. Perhaps, the administration of education does need managing, but learning needs to be given a frame and then set loose. Very few online learning tools encourage the sorts of risk-taking that make for the best pedagogies. Quality should not be assured; it should be discovered.

The discussion forum, currently the holy grail of "engagement" inside most online courses, is particularly problematic. Exchanges within forums are usually too strictly controlled and reduce honest interaction to busy-work scored by a rubric. These interactions rarely resemble the many and varied kinds of discussions possible in a classroom. And many teachers require things of online discussions that they would never demand in an on-ground classroom: one post of at least 250 words, properly cited, and exactly 2 responses to fellow students. Imagine trying to create a lively classroom discussion with these kinds of constraints.

Draconian learning management systems, hierarchical discussion forum tools, and automated grading systems replace the playful work of teachers and students with overly simplified algorithms that interface with far too few of the dynamic variables that make learning so visceral and lively. There will be no going back from this fundamental error in judgment. Within even just a few years, structures will be too decidedly built, customs and norms too firmly entrenched. I worry that we may be too far gone already. But, we need to hesitate at this very important threshold, for even just a moment, and decide carefully how to proceed.

Rather than simply transplanting the Lego castle of education from one platform to another, we need to start dismantling it piece by piece, all the while examining the pieces and how they fit together. Only then can we reassemble the pieces thoughtfully inside the digital environment. Nothing can be taken for granted. Everything must be broken in order to be creatively and ethically rebuilt. Everything. The course. The degree. Accreditation. Assessment. Rubrics. Standardized testing. Tenure. Intellectual property. FERPA. Peer review. The power dynamics of teachers and students.

This doesn't mean we should necessarily eliminate tenure or guidelines for intellectual property altogether, but we should leave no stone unturned, no Lego piece uncontemplated. And things like FERPA and assessment must be refashioned to make them even remotely relevant to the work we do online. I'm not proposing to break and rebuild education as it happens at brick-and-mortar institutions (at least not in this article). Different work must be done there to keep those institutions viable. What I'm proposing is forking education, in order to begin to build something revolutionary in digital space. This work has already been lovingly done in pockets, but now it needs to happen at a much grander scale. The MOOC will have its day, but we need to help guide its course, recognize that it's just one of many kinds of online learning, and insurgents need to be ready to rise up in its wake.

So what do we break and how do we rebuild:

The course. The semester. The quarter. The credit-hour. We need to devise learning activities that take organic (and less arbitrary) shapes in space and time. We need to recognize that the best learning happens not inside courses but between them. So, for example, I am working to create collaborations between courses at several institutions and assignments that bridge a course offered one term and a different course offered the next. I ask students to reflect on the connections. Most importantly, we need to create more contexts and communities for learning that don't live inside courses at all.

The lecture. Teachers need to talk less and listen more. We need to put the work of students at the front of our courses. For example, replace the video lecture that begins many online "lessons" with a video made by a student. Let the voices of authority proliferate rather than congeal. If we want our students to learn from each other (as we should) then they need to be looking at themselves, not us. The job of the teacher is to allow for and foster community, not to be at the center of it. This is not to say that we should never lecture or share our expertise with students, but we need to significantly level the playing field.

Assessment. Cathy N. Davidson writes, "We're so obsessed with assessment we're missing the fact that, in the real world, excitement and joy and challenge are real motivators of learning and, indeed, success" ("The Year of the MOOC"). We should build hype around learning, generate genuine interest, and pander to intrinsic rather than extrinsic motivations. I so often hear variations of "my students won't do this assignment if it's not worth points." We need to give students reasons less banal than points to do the work of learning. For example, I have my students do projects that have real-world audiences — projects that have an immediate impact on them and their world. I tell them that there is no "busy work" in my classes — that they should make noble efforts but ultimately re-imagine any activity that doesn't feel useful.

Rubrics. The problem with rubrics is that they are usually structured so that students produce something determined in advance by an instructor (or, in more progressive classes, by the students themselves). By determining a model for assessment in advance we presume to know (even roughly) what students will produce and what their learning will look like while it's happening and after it's done. What we need are un-rubrics that invite experimentation, loose frameworks that allow improvisation to flourish. Or we should create rubrics in hindsight as a way to debrief after a learning activity is finished. Sometimes, clear objectives or outcomes are important at the outset of an assignment or course, but we need to leave room for those outcomes to be more roughly handled.

Intellectual property. These two words are, for me, fundamentally at odds. We need to encourage sharing, remixing, and productive and creative forms of plagiarism. For example, how about an activity where the words of one student are asked to live coherently inside the words of another? Or an assignment that asks a student to intentionally mimic the voice, word-choice, and style of another writer? This is how children learn language, and we don't police their plagiarisms. Creative Commons Search is a lovely resource in this respect, offering lots of words begging for playful appropriation (with attribution).

The authority of the teacher. Active learning puts students at the center of the learning space. Participant Pedagogy asks students to help create the space. For participant pedagogy to flourish, participants have to take full ownership of their own learning. Participant pedagogy is not only about students being pedagogues but about teachers coming to class as full participants.

The syllabus. A good syllabus is not a contract, because by the end of a class, the syllabus should be broken. Participant pedagogy requires not that we work to add stuff to our syllabi but that we work to take stuff away. For example, I often create two versions of my syllabi, the institutionally sanctioned version and then a website that links to the "official syllabus" but also becomes a living document that changes as the term proceeds. I also make sure that the site has ample places for the students to insert themselves through a massively co-authored blog, hackable rules for assignments, and a schedule that we revise together.

Tenure and pay structures for online teachers. We need systems that reward the best teachers, foster their professional development, and support the work they do with students. We encourage good teaching by hiring (and adequately compensating) the teachers thinking critically about their own practices and working closely with peers and students to develop new pedagogies. All teachers (and especially online and hybrid teachers) need to be trained in and fairly compensated for course design, which is often the most difficult and time-consuming component. We also need contracts or job security for online teachers that allow for adequate lead-time to design courses (at least 6 months and sometimes longer).

The divides between K-12, community colleges, universities, libraries, and non-institutional learning spaces. We need everyone in the room as we do the work of rebuilding education in digital space. For example, most universities have actively resisted online learning for the last 15+ years. Now, those very same institutions are diving head-first into partnerships with Coursera and the like. In higher education, we need to turn to the experts, many of whom are teaching at community colleges, don't have Ph.D.s, and don't have active research agendas beyond their teaching. We need to champion the non-traditional academics that have been doing this work and bring those with experience fully to the table.

Competition. Backbiting. Intellectual elitism. Anti-intellectualism. Online learning should be more friendly, more collaborative, more open, and more accepting. We need to create pedagogies of care online and allow what we discover in these new spaces to influence what we do at brick-and-mortar institutions.

The intellectual bravery we need right now is to believe that we can imaginatively rebuild something valuable in digital space, something that has what we value most about education: the protections, the safety, the excitement, the moments of ecstatic learning, the epiphanies, the collaborations, the debates, the discoveries, *and* the moments of quiet reflection.

THE DISCUSSION FORUM IS DEAD; LONG LIVE THE DISCUSSION FORUM

SEAN MICHAEL MORRIS AND JESSE STOMMEL

There are better forums for discussion than online discussion forums. The discussion forum is a ubiquitous component of every learning management system and online learning platform from Blackboard to Moodle to Coursera. Forums have become, in many ways, synonymous with discussion in the online class, as though one relatively standardized interface can stand in for the many and varied modes of interaction we might have in a physical classroom.

The rhetoric of a physical classroom — its pedagogical topography — can certainly dictate how we teach within it: where the seats are, which direction they face, whether they're bolted down, what kind of writing surfaces are on the walls, how many walls *have* writing surfaces, whether there are windows, doors that lock, etc. The same is true of the virtual classroom: is it password protected, what kind of landing page do we arrive on when we enter the course, how many pages allow interaction, can students easily upload and share content. Each of these predetermined variables allows (and sometimes demands) a certain pedagogy. The physical classroom, though, can usually be rearranged (to some extent) on the fly. Most online learning platforms make customization slow or difficult enough to deter responsiveness or impulsivity. The pedagogies of most online classes, then, are fixed in advance.

However, as teachers concerned with critical pedagogy, it is our task to always reconsider that which may seem fixed, unmoveable. Henry Giroux writes in "Rethinking Education as the Practice of Freedom: Paulo Freire and the Promise of Critical Pedagogy," "Critical pedagogy forges both an expanded notion of literacy and agency through a language of skepticism, possibility and a culture of openness, debate and engagement." Our aim here, then, is to engage discussion forums in a discussion, to develop new ideas about how they may be used, how they should not be used, who they're for, and what alternatives are available.

We argue in "Why Online Programs Fail, and 5 Things We Can Do About It," that building community is at the heart of learning, whether on-ground, online, or hybrid. Some tools allow for more flexibility in this than others. Any digital tool can be used well or misused, depending on its application. With rare exception, software applications are neutral parties to their use. Even the ugliest of educational technology can be hacked to good ends, and most of it has been created with the best intentions. Every tool, though, demands imagination and critical investigation.

Discussion forums are the sort of ed tech you hope creative teachers will hack mercilessly, creating in their place a means through which students and teachers can interact in substantive, relevant ways. The forum itself does not automatically promote meaningful conversation — or conversation at all, unless conversation can be reduced to monotone interjections by its participants — but that does not mean good things can't happen there. In truth, discussion forums have the same potential all digital pedagogy tools have. In the right hands, wonders occur.

However, even as we hope teachers will recast and remix the tools they're asked to use, this is not generally the case with discussion forums. Instead of providing fertile ground for brilliant and lively conversation, discussion forums are allowed to go to seed. They become over-cultivated factory farms, in which nothing unexpected or original is permitted to flourish. Students post because they have to, not because they enjoy doing so. And teachers respond (if they respond at all) because they too have become complacent to the bizarre rules that govern the forum.

With the right teacher and engaged students, discussion in the classroom includes carefully cultivated spontaneity, more akin to an organic garden. Online discussion forums require the same careful attention and engagement, the same understanding of when to train and prune and when to allow things to take their own course, flourish in their own way, on their own time. And in order for that to happen, the technology must make room for that spontaneity.

Having worked several years within learning management systems that employ discussion forums as their only measure of class participation, we've both seen how draconian regulations for the quantity and quality of posts have overtaken any creativity, inspiration, or engagement that would, in the best on-ground classroom, motivate participation. And most learning management systems prompt teachers to grade each discussion (and sometimes assign points to *individual* interactions), which would never seem reasonable in our on-ground pedagogy. The most terrifying thing about all of this is that, more and more, learning management systems offer pre-set rubrics and auto-grading to assess these sterilized interactions. The discussion forum becomes a shackle, an assessed, graded component of a student's performance. It defeats its own purpose.

It might seem laughable, but these are the kinds of instructions offered frequently to students to "encourage" participation in discussion forums:

You must post three times each week. Your first post should be an original thought with at least one secondary source. Your second and third posts should respond to two other students. Be sure to write your first post (of 500 words) by Wednesday, and at least one of your responses (of 250 words) by Friday. You will lose 5% off your participation score for this discussion for every 24-hour period that you are late.

The resulting posts do not constitute participation; they constitute attendance. What's being measured is a student's willingness and ability to check into the course twice each week. And while the required length of a post can force students to do more "talking" than they might otherwise do, this does not necessarily qualify as real engagement.

Thomas P. Kasulis writes in "Questioning":

> A discussion is not only the process of collectively examining a set of issues; it is also the persons involved in that task . . . To prepare for a class discussion without taking into consideration the personalities, strengths, and needs of the people in the course is to depersonalize teaching. It is to teach the course and not the students.

In the room with our students, we can know if they're engaged and participating, even as each of them participates in his or her own unique fashion. In an online discussion forum, it's difficult to observe such nuance, and impossible to quantitatively evaluate it. Still, teachers working inside the pedantic confines of an LMS and its discussion forum usually acquiesce to its obsolescence. Rather than hacking the system to fit our pedagogy, we can easily become the teachers the LMS wants us to be, which quickly feels less like teaching and a lot more like data entry.

What's interesting about the increasingly digital nature of our students is that they can be found actively participating almost everywhere else on the web (Twitter, Facebook, Pinterest, Youtube, Tumblr) outside the LMS. We've heard online teachers talk about how difficult it is to get their students to join in, usually citing their lack of preparation for online work; but the truth is most students, no matter how diverse, are already online, using the tools familiar and relevant to them, tools connecting them to communities that compel them to engage. It is not, in other words, the tool that confuses the student, but the student that confuses the tool. Discussion forums, as they're often used, do not encourage, or in some cases do not allow, students to meet, greet, challenge, question, and collaborate in the dynamic ways they do elsewhere on the web.

The illusion offered by discussion forums is that they build community. And while certain kinds of communities can be built through regular posts and responses to those posts, these are communities of commentary, and not the kinds of communities that further online and hybrid learning. In a classroom, we work diligently to unify our students, to foster a supportive environment, and to encourage cooperation and collaboration. At their worst, discussion forums are less like classrooms and more like bus stops — each participant stopping by, saying a few words, and then going on their way. Whereas discussion forums are isolated, digital communities are dispersed, uncontained, and this allows them to be as rampant as we hope our online classes will be.

Rampant online discussion requires flexible technology and requires that we choose our tools carefully. As Giroux suggests, "Education is not neutral. It is always directive in its attempt to teach students to inhabit a particular mode of agency; enable them to understand the larger world and one's role in it in a specific way..." The best forums for online discussion actively open the world to the student, without dashing her upon its rocks, rather than box her in (technologically, pedagogically).

Here are a few tools that can be used in concert with or in place of the discussion forum in an LMS, and which can allow for delightful, persistent, meaningful conversation:

Disqus: The Disqus platform allows forum-like threaded discussions to be embedded in a blog post or any other web page. Think an open-access forum distributed across the web in habitats where discussion arises organically. Disqus uses a single sign-on that allows teachers and learners to create profiles that include an archive of comments from anywhere they use Disqus. Individual comments can be easily linked to and shared.

Twitter: Twitter can be used both synchronously (in hashtag chats) and asynchronously to engage learners, instructors, and others outside the classroom. It can be used creatively to analyze literature, build community, and even do collaborative work. Twitter encourages sharing of links and dynamic exchanges of ideas. While some might argue that the character limit doesn't allow for deep inquiry, we disagree. Twitter can be a tool for a *collective* inquiry, creating depth through the metonymic relationship between tweets and between tweets and what they link to.

Note: Since we are compiling the pieces in this collection, sometimes more than 5 years after they were written, not all the tools we point to have proven equally effective (or ethical) over time. For example, we have increasingly moved away from Twitter as a pedagogical tool, because of concerns for privacy and safety, particularly for marginalized persons. What's most important is turning a critical and thoughtful eye toward any tool, what it affords, and whom it might exclude.

Vanilla Forums: Vanilla forums is an open source forum tool that strips away much of the more elaborate functionality of traditional discussion forums and keeps the focus on the interactions as opposed to the interface. The system relies on robust search for navigation rather than an excessive flurry of nested folders or drop-down menus. Vanilla Forums can be embedded inside other sites and plays nice with social media. We have recently begun experimenting with the tools Discourse and Slack, as well.

Facebook: The closed nature of the Facebook network makes it less ideal for class-related conversation. It's not really a good idea (and a privacy issue) to require students to friend everyone else in a class. A Facebook Page or Group, though, can be used relatively effectively to link to posts created elsewhere and to assemble discussions about them in a single place.

Google Hangouts: Google Hangouts, and similar tools, offers opportunities for synchronous engagement. The drawback of Hangouts being limited to 25 simultaneous video feeds can be addressed by having groups of learners (with or without a teacher) act as a roundtable with a backchannel on Twitter or in the chat box inside the Hangout.

Other options for building virtual learning communities include Google Groups, Buddypress (if you're using Wordpress as an alternative to the LMS), the not quite extinct e-mail list, and even World of Warcraft.

What almost all of these tools have in common is their openness on the web, in stark contrast to the password-protected forums inside an LMS. The best LMSs leverage these existing networks and are increasingly making the capacity for openness part of their design. When learning environments are opened (or left open) to a wider community of voices, the benefits resound throughout a student's learning process.

Participants' personal learning networks can, in an open forum, be that much more diverse and expansive. Students are no longer only speaking with other students in the same class, but now can speak with other students in their discipline, students at other universities, professionals in their field, other instructors, and people outside of academia who nonetheless share an interest in the subject matter and who may have radically different perspectives. Students become part of the wider conversation distributed across the Internet. Their thoughts and works reside adjacent to the top names in their field, and can be collected, curated, and archived along with all other nodes of the discourse.

The vast majority of students are already living their lives in the open, and so an open platform for discussion amplifies the presence of learning in their day-to-day lives. And helps them develop critical skills and literacies for working in these spaces.

READING THE LMS AGAINST THE BACKDROP OF CRITICAL PEDAGOGY

SEAN MICHAEL MORRIS

The pupil is thereby 'schooled' to confuse teaching with learning, grade advancement with education, a diploma with competence, and fluency with the ability to say something new.

~ Ivan Illich, *Deschooling Society*

1

What if we were to theorize that the learning management system (LMS) is designed, not for learning or teaching, but for the gathering of data? And what if we were to further theorize that the gathering of data, as messaged and marketed through the LMS, has become conflated with teaching and learning?

Part of the work that I do as an instructional designer and critical pedagogy agonist is to ask questions of the tools used in digitally mediated education. Because critical pedagogy encourages us to consider carefully the assumptions handed to us, a critical instructional designer begins first not by learning the tools before them—most digital tools work essentially the same way, with few exceptions, and are designed to be easily adopted—but by stepping back and looking at those tools from a distance. The critical instructional designer ask questions like:

- Why was this tool created? What is its primary objective? What are its other objectives?

- What assumptions about education and learning lie behind the design of this tool? Where do those assumptions come from?
- How does this tool offer what Freire might call a determinant, or something that seems to resist our agency to change or resist?
- How do the objectives and assumptions of this tool measure up against my own? How effectively does it resist my capacity to resist it, to change or hack it?

There are other considerations as well. How does this tool represent a politics of oppression—the surrender of privacy, data, authorship, authority, agency, as well as issues of representation, equity, access? Who owns the tool and what are their goals? How is the production of this tool funded? What influence does the maker of this tool have on culture more broadly writ? What labor is rewarded and what labor is erased? What is the relationship between this tool and the administration of the institution? Who must use this tool and who is trained to use this tool, and is that labor compensated? These are all important questions to ask, and the answers may play a role in the adoption of any given tool in a classroom or learning environment.

But in many cases, and especially with the LMS, adoption comes regardless of consent. In only a minority of situations are faculty and students part of the discussion around the purchase of an LMS for an institution. In those situations, we must abide by the use of the LMS; however, that doesn't mean we must acquiesce to its politics or its pedagogy. In order to intervene, then, we must step back and rather than learn the tool, analyze the tool.

When we do that with the LMS, we find that its primary operation is the acquisition of data, and the conflation of that data with student performance, engagement, and teaching success. As Beer, Clark, and Jones cheerfully report in their article, "Indicators of Engagement,"

> A fortunate effect of the almost ubiquitous adoption of LMS for online course delivery in universities, is their ability to track and store vast amounts of data on student and designer behaviour (Heathcoate & Dawson, 2005) . Typically, LMS record all actions made by users once they are logged into the system and this data is subsequently stored in an associated database. The process of analysing institutional data captured by an LMS for decision making and reporting purposes is called academic analytics (Campbell, Oblinger, & DeBlois, 2007) and it has been shown that analysis of captured LMS data is directly relevant to student engagement, evaluating learning activities and can usefully answer other important questions (Shane Dawson & McWilliam, 2008).

And earlier in that same report, the authors write:

> It could be said that the online learning environment facilitates the interactions required for learning and therefore have an influence on student engagement. It could also be said that measuring student participation within a learning environment and contrasting this measure with student results can provide an approximation of student engagement.

In other words, usage becomes engagement and engagement gets equated with successful learning and expert teaching. But we cannot let ourselves believe that usage is anything besides usage—and even that assumption is subject to a certain questioning.

But when we assume that data points to behavior, and that points to the means to control behavior, we become authorized to create methods, approaches, and technologies that fulfill that promise. I offer as Exhibit A a promotional video for Hero K12, a student monitoring system that gathers data from student behavior in on-ground learning environments (aka, the augmented reality LMS). The video shows an adorable cartoon (aimed at administrators) to explain how its approach to student behavior modification. As the caption on the video reads:

> The concept of student behavior tracking may not be immediately easy to understand. If you have 2 minutes, this short video will fol-

> low the story of two students and how Hero solves some interesting behavior problems for schools. Hero helps schools encourage and recognize students who demonstrate positive behavior, and enforce consequences for the behaviors schools want to curb.

The video, which compares the stories of Jack — a star student who shows up on time to class and is rewarded with a "fast-pass" ticket to the lunch line, is invited to a special school celebration, and whose parents are called about his excellent behavior — and Jill, who shows up late to school and thus misses out on the lunch pass, the celebration, and praise from her school and parents.

I've shared this video out on Twitter (with a nod to Audrey Watters, who originally shared it previously), and the overall response was one of horror. My network was concerned about this level of monitoring, about the reduction of students to data, about the fact that Jill's home or family situation, her access to transportation, nor any other factor outside of her name and grade level are considered by the Hero K12 human management system. For myself, I am most concerned about the inability of students to fully understand and to resist or change the system. While I have no doubts students are capable of breaking the system, or making it work for them, Hero K12 represents a determinant, one which students must adapt to, one which requires a surrender of their agency. They become their data, and while they may find ways to feed certain data into the system, they have no power to resist their own reduction to numbers, patterns, and statistics.

(As a side note, the Hero K12 video was removed shortly after Audrey Watters openly critiqued it on Twitter.)

The LMS threatens the same reduction of human complexity to simple data. I say "simple" because even when data is nuanced and complex, it fails to be an accurate representation of a human being. This is not to say data cannot indicate certain behaviors, nor that it is useless, only that it has limitations. But it is not those limitations that are advertised, not those limitations that we're trained to observe; instead, we are encouraged to see data as descriptive, not just indicative. And when that happens, a surfeit of data erects a barrier between students, teachers, and administrators. But most importantly, and least spoken about, data as a determinant erects a barrier between a student and themselves.

Most LMS data isn't different from website data. Pageviews, time on page, number of posts in a discussion, the number of announcements a teacher sends out in a semester, the number of modules, quizzes, assignments, and files in a course, etc. And like with website data, pageviews and time on page are equated with engagement. The "hits" on a given course indicate the quality of the teaching taking place, and can be aligned with the number of assignments, quizzes, files, and more in that course to point the way to best practices.

Except they don't and can't. Any more than Jill showing up late for school can be equated with the kind of learner she is, or whether she will learn anything from detention mandated upon her by her data. And yet it is the use of data that makes the LMS so potentially destructive, especially as that data is used to punish or correct behavior.

B. F. Skinner, an innovator of the behavioral psychology that most positivist approaches to education is founded on, wrote that "behavior is shaped and maintained by its consequences". He believed that, by controlling the environment in which learning happened, learning could be made more efficient, more effective, and that outcomes could be guaranteed. Put simply (too simply, I admit), a belief in Skinner's approach has led to evidence-based teaching, which uses data to determine the effectiveness of certain pedagogical practices based on whether students achieved the desired outcomes.

This is precisely the same as testing the reactions of a rat in a maze. In Skinner's own words: "Comparable results have been obtained with pigeons, rats, dogs, monkeys, human children, and psychotic subjects." Shall we repeat part of that? Rats, monkeys, human children, and psychotic subjects. Collecting data has always been part of the "science" of education, control has always been the end to that effort, and learners have necessarily been equated with rats and pigeons all along.

2

There is an essential difference between the 'science' of education, positivism, evidence-based teaching, and behaviorism (which I see as coterminous within the LMS) and the ideas of education forwarded by critical pedagogy. The two are, in effect, almost impossible to engage in a dialogue because their aims for and perspectives on learning are fundamentally different. Whereas the LMS (and all that the technology implies) provides a data-driven means of controlling student behavior—modifying it through methods of reward and punishment—critical pedagogy's primary aim is the liberation of students from systems that oppress them. To achieve this, critical pedagogy engages in operations of analysis and inquiry focused on structures like the LMS—but also grading, assessment, and more—that are normally assumed quantities in the equation of education.

But more than that, critical pedagogy is pedagogical precisely because its efforts are not solely trained on school. Rather, school becomes the site where students' critical apparatuses can be explored and applied. The classroom becomes a lab for critical pedagogy, where, in discussion with a teacher, learners come to recognize the shape and content of the means of oppression—both at the school and in society at large. Henry Giroux writes in *On Critical Pedagogy*,

> I expand the meaning and theory of pedagogy as part of an ongoing individual and collective struggle over knowledge, desire, values, social relations, and, most important, modes of political agency ... For me, pedagogy is part of an always unfinished project intent on developing a meaningful life for all students. Such a project becomes relevant to the degree that it provides the pedagogical conditions for students to appropriate the knowledge and skills necessary to address the limits of justice in democratic societies.

In other words, becoming critical in a classroom is preparation for remaining critical when students enter the mainstream of work, consumerism, politics, and, increasingly important, the digital society of social media, entertainment, news media, and more.

The LMS was not designed to, as Giroux puts it, "address the limits of justice in democratic societies." In some of my talks with leadership at Instructure in the early days of their Canvas LMS, they seemed very much in agreement with me about ideas like student agency, identity, empowerment, student-centered classrooms, and the like. They hoped that their LMS made room for teachers to adopt all kinds of pedagogies, including critical pedagogy. These were exciting discussions, and the first I'd heard of an educational technology company that was truly interested in education and not just technology.

However, in those discussions we were skipping upon the surface of the water. In order for an LMS to function, it must assume itself integral to the learning process, must operate as a determinant in education. The makers of Canvas couldn't look at their product as optional, couldn't market it as a by-product of a philosophy that reduces students to "rats and pigeons," nor could they build a container for learning that invited students to question the notion that learning can be contained.

At all levels, the LMS is a capitalist structure that participates in the idea that education is about production. The LMS must, as Illich says in the epigraph above, "confuse teaching with learning, grade advancement with education." If it fails in that project, it fails to be saleable. And in the end, the LMS is for sale. As with anything that's for sale, the user (in this case, the institution, then the teacher, then the student) must be convinced that the product is essential.

Critical pedagogy never assumes any product is essential. It assumes that human agency is essential, identity formation is essential, justice is essential, and the human will and capacity to resist and create change are essential. Paulo Freire writes, in *Pedagogy of Indignation*:

> To the extent that we accept that the economy, or technology, or science, it doesn't matter what, exerts inescapable power over us, there is nothing left for us to do other than renounce our ability to think, to conjecture, to compare, to choose, to decide, to envision, to dream.

By choosing to inspect a product—in our case, the LMS, but this can apply to any educational technology or teaching practice touted by ed tech makers (e.g., the Google certified educator whose practice is supplanted by product placement)—we enter into a critical relationship with our tools and practices, stripping them of their mystique and unassailability, and can come to conclusions about them that are not foregone, not written by an advertiser.

All of that said, the ubiquity of the LMS must be dealt with. We cannot simply wish it away, nor wish it to be different. It's not the approach of critical pedagogy to ignore the tools and systems that oppress, nor to engage in wishful thinking. Rather, critical pedagogy focuses on the way things are in order to construct an understanding of the way things can or should be. Giroux writes "education has a responsibility not only to search for the truth regardless of where it may lead but also to educate students to make authority politically and morally accountable" (Loc. 261). We cannot see our way clear to justice if we don't see clearly the systems that obscure justice.

Yet, one of the objections I encounter often when talking about critiquing and confronting the LMS and other educational technology is that it is mandated for use by an institution. Especially for adjunct teachers—an academic population that's persistently increasing and whose continued employment is precarious—butting heads with the LMS and the administration that supports it is too risky. Similarly, teachers whose authority in the classroom is less immediately visible because they are not straight, white, cisgender men are understandably cautious to engage the work of critical pedagogy when simply asserting presence can be a challenge.

So, how do we face off with the LMS in ways both critical and which might yet allow us to cooperate with our institutions and reasonably succeed as instructors? Is it necessary to stop using the LMS? Or are there ways to invite students into an inspection and critique of this tool even while they are asked to use it?

For example, in many online courses the designer or teacher will ask students to complete a "syllabus quiz," an over-architected assessment of a student's willingness and ability to uncover the requirements of a class. What if instead, students were invited to talk about their assumptions about the LMS—about discussions, about how assignments are submitted, about grading—and to say openly both what they like and find problematic about the platform? What if students were asked to research the LMS itself, the company that created it, the politics behind it, its pedagogical assumptions? Or, what if a teacher confided in students the ways in which their teaching philosophy aligned or did not align with the pedagogies baked into the LMS?

When I enter a physical classroom, the first thing I look for is the arrangement of chairs. I want moveable chairs, seats that can be formed into a circle, that don't necessarily situate learners in rows in front of a podium. Podiums have their use at times, but I want options. Perhaps inviting students (and teacher) into an inspection of the LMS right at the start of the term is a way of "rearranging" the chairs by calling out the architecture of the digital room we find ourselves in.

A step beyond this initial inspection might find us offering students the opportunity to participate in digital education in new ways. Do they want to "meet" somewhere besides the LMS? Twitter? Slack? Facebook? What are the affordances and problems with those platforms? What happens to grading when we leave the LMS (and what role does grading play in learning)? Is there a desire for more synchronous interaction, and how can that be facilitated; similarly, what are the affordances of asynchronous interaction?

While this sort of exploration and inquiry may seem to interfere with the curriculum of a course (the learning objectives, required materials, mastery), I argue that they could be the first, most important steps when teaching online or in a digitally mediated environment. This is critical thinking—divorced of assessment, divorced of learning objectives—that aligns with the goals of a critical pedagogy. Giroux provides that

> Critical pedagogy asserts that students can engage their own learning from a position of agency and in so doing can actively participate in narrating their identities through a culture of questioning that opens up a space of translation between the private and the public while changing the forms of self-and social recognition.

In fact, in a classroom where success will be measured by the mastery of specific material, a critical inspection of the learning environment may be students' only opportunity to "actively participate in narrating their identities."

It's possible that the single most important action we can take as digital educators and critical instructional designers is to ensure that learners have laid before them the capability to both know how the LMS exerts control over their learning, and to intervene upon that control to change it.

Put simply, I do not believe that the LMS is a useful or productive tool for learning. Its structure and infrastructure are too deeply biased by a "scientific" approach to teaching. It is built upon research and best practices, and its aim is the collection of data, the control of student behavior, and the production of narratives of power. Freire offers:

> Our testimony ... if we dream of a less aggressive, less unjust, less violent, more human society, must be that of saying 'no' to any impossibility determined by the 'facts' and that of defending a

> human being's capacity for evaluating, comparing, choosing, deciding, and finally intervening in the world."

I would like to imagine a less aggressive, more human digital learning, even if that seems impossible.

WHY ONLINE PROGRAMS FAIL, AND 5 THINGS WE CAN DO ABOUT IT

SEAN MICHAEL MORRIS AND JESSE STOMMEL

Online learning in its current iterations will fail.

The failure of online education programs is not logistical, nor political, nor economic: it's cultural, rooted in our perspectives and biases about how learning happens and how the internet works (these things too often seen in opposition). For learning to change drastically — a trajectory suggested but not realized by MOOCs — teaching must change drastically. And in order for that to happen, we must conceive of the activity of teaching, as an occupation and preoccupation, in entirely new and unexpected ways. We must unseat ourselves, unnerve ourselves. Online learning is uncomfortable, and so educators must become uncomfortable in their positions as teachers and pedagogues. And the administration of online programs must follow suit.

Early failures in online education have led us to a place where many believe we know exactly what we're doing; but what we've done, more than anything, is close down space for possibility, evolution, and experimentation. We've created happy little caskets inside which learning fits too neatly and tidily (like forums, learning management systems, and web conferencing platforms). We've timed learning down to the second, developed draconian quality assurance measures, built analytics to track every bit of minutiae, and we've championed the stalest, most banal forms of interaction — interaction buried beneath rubrics and quantitative assessment — interaction that looks the same every time in every course with every new set of students.

Online learning programs fail because they've been told, and they believe, they must operate within the same paradigm of learning and teaching that on-ground programs obey. This is a falsehood, a misconception, and at times a deception. More and different types of learning and teaching are available in the digital environment. We must convince ourselves that we don't yet understand digital education so we may open the doors more broadly to play and creativity. At the expense of regimentation and bureaucracy.

WE ARE ALL THE UNIVERSITY OF PHOENIX

Most online programs believe they're not — couldn't possibly be, would never even border upon being — the University of Phoenix. We have serious problems with the business model of University of Phoenix, particularly their marketing practices, insidious reliance on contingent labor, and strict standardization of courses and curricula. However, it's folly for any school to imagine they could avoid becoming University of Phoenix just by having the intention not to.

There are very smart folk working for University of Phoenix, some good teachers, and a lot of really great students. University of Phoenix has been in the business of online learning since 1976. They have a lot of intellectual and economic capital. It's just being aimed in some very bad directions. The New York Times reports that "students and some of its own former administrators say the relentless pressure for higher profits, at a university that gets more federal student financial aid than any other, has eroded academic quality." Most new online programs are started with less expertise, less intellectual and economic capital, and usually steer themselves in the exact same directions without realizing it. If we don't change course, then every online program is a runaway train on its way toward becoming the University of Phoenix.

It's seductive: the notion that we could draw more students and contribute to our institution's bottom line by simply moving our existing curriculum, classes, and faculty online lock, stock, and barrel. But imagine the most lively on-ground classroom with all its various sights, sounds, and smells, then compare that to the horribly restrictive interface of any learning management system. We are not arguing that nothing happy or good can happen within the LMS. Nor are we saying we can't create lively opportunities for learning online. But the online environment is fundamentally different and requires fundamentally different input to attain similar output. Online learning requires a meticulous attention to the container and the permeability of that container. We have to carefully build our classroom and educational space online before we start populating it, lest text, hierarchical menus, and pop-up windows be confused with interactivity and community.

We shouldn't set off on a cruise, and build the ship as we go. Educational campuses have libraries, coffee shops, cafeterias, quads, lawns, amphitheaters, stadiums, hallways, student lounges, trees, park benches, and fountains. Ample space for rallies, study-groups, conversation, debate, student clubs, and special events. Few institutions pay much attention to re-creating these spaces online. The work done outside and between classes (which is the glue that holds education together) is attended to nominally if at all. Imagine this scenario: a business student shares a table at the campus coffee shop with an English major. A conversation kicks off with the inevitable, "What's your major?" When and where does this conversation happen in online programs? How can we facilitate the interdisciplinary dialogues that bring a campus to life? What spaces can we build online that aren't quantified, tracked, scored, graded, assessed, and accredited? How can we use open source tools and social media to build the hallways between our online classes? Many individual educators have begun to do this work, but we need a larger discussion about the future of online education that privileges these spaces as central and indispensable to learning.

What we are doing right now is merely expanding our online course offerings so students can get degrees online. Enrollment in online courses at post-secondary institutions grew from 9.6% in 2002 to 29.3% of total enrollment in 2009, or 5 and a half million students taking online courses ("The Student Cyborg"). By 2014, this number is expected to increase to 18,650,000. As of February 2013, 1.7 million students had registered for at least one Coursera course (Gutierrez 2013). What we have is a series of online classes with no real infrastructure to support the work students do on college campuses outside and between those classes. Online programs have the bureaucratic trappings of formal education without the rich ecosystems. Meanwhile, learning communities thrive online extra-institutionally, supported by the 1500+ blog entries, 98,000 tweets, and 695,000 Facebook status updates posted every 60 seconds (Gizmodo 2011).

FIVE WAYS TO BUILD ETHICAL ONLINE PROGRAMS

Truly successful online programs pay attention to what's already happening in digital culture. They inspect and then makes use of blogs, social media, and the permeability and collaborative organization that takes place there. Up to now, online learning has taken little notice of the web upon which it's suspended.

We've both watched the failures of online learning firsthand. Between the two of us, we've taught dozens of online classes at every level of higher education and have led the development of online programs. Yet, neither of us had fully realized our ethics online until we went rogue and developed our own online course extra-institutionally. MOOC MOOC, our meta-MOOC about MOOCs, changed our perspectives and we realized something profoundly good could happen online.

Online learning has been a strange elephant in the room of far too many conversations we've been in over the last decade, but the need to examine online learning has, with the advent of MOOCs, become all the more pressing. Ripe with potential, a great deal may be revealed, repurposed, and renewed to create innovative learning experiences online. Lots of heavy-lifting needs to happen at the level of development to build the necessary infrastructure. However, the most important work to be done is a series of paradigm shifts. We must:

1. Stop conflating on-ground and online learning models, which require different pedagogies, administration, economies, curricula, and communities.
The key failure of online learning has been its attempt to duplicate, replicate, or simply dump into an LMS the content and strategies of on-ground learning. We need to recognize that online learning uses a different platform, builds community in different ways, demands different pedagogies, has a different economy, functions at different scales, and requires different curricular choices than does on-ground education. Even where the same goal is desired, very different methods must be used to reach that goal.

Mark Sample reminds us in his essay, "Intrusive Scaffolding, Obstructed Learning (and MOOCs)," that "Unless online teaching — and classroom teaching as well — begins to first, unscaffold learning problems and second, rediscover embodied pedagogy, we will obstruct learning rather than foster it. We will push students away from authentic learning experiences rather than draw them toward such experiences." Because so many have been afraid that learning would not happen in online courses, we've focused on the machinations of technology to (en)force that learning. But in doing so, we've missed an opportunity to create unique learning experiences.

The machinations, which Sample refers to as "scaffolding", have led to further obscenities, including the "learning object" and the canned and endlessly duplicated course. The former is an attempt to reduce learning to atomic building blocks — discussion topics, quizzes, flash-based interactive modules — swapped out like trading cards no matter the course or students. The latter is the all too common practice of teaching from a single "master" course, reused semester after semester by various faculty without substantive changes to the content.

Online learning has been so involved with the facility of the technology that it has overlooked the complication of good pedagogy.

2. Rely more on pedagogues and less on tech.
The invention of online learning and digital pedagogies should be driven by educators, not industry. The AAUP proclaimed in their "Statement on Online and Distance Education": "Faculty expertise and experience are indispensable for selecting appropriate technologies for distance education." That was written in 1999, and yet the norm is still for technological decisions to be made at the administrative level, for online classes to be taught almost exclusively by contingent faculty, and for online curricula to be designed by faculty with little-to-no expertise in digital pedagogy. We need to work to help technological decision-makers at institutions of education understand that technology is a pedagogical decision — that the choices made around technology don't drive pedagogy but are driven by careful decisions and thinking about teaching and learning.

Supporting innovative digital pedagogies means investing in robust inter- and intra-institutional collaborations, and it means hiring and creating a culture for the development of digital pedagogues. Institutions shouldn't outsource online learning to Coursera, Pearson, or the like, as a substitute for developing internal expertise in and discussion about online learning. What we need is to gather together experts in digital pedagogy willing to turn their attention toward solving the problem of online learning, toward innovating new methodologies, and toward rebuilding what we value most about education in digital space. And, if we are going to successfully automate any bit of the work of teaching and learning, we must make our machine relationships altogether more intimate. Our algorithms are not sufficiently complex to capture the dynamic, sometimes poetic, nature of learning.

3. Stop worrying whether online learning will usurp traditional education.

More than one college instructor has worried over predation by online learning. Many teachers are concerned online courses, especially massive ones, will automate their jobs, making them and their very human teaching methods obsolete. Additionally, teachers fear that MOOCs, led by celebrity instructors, will further reduce attendance in their on-ground and even hybrid classrooms, and they worry they're being made to compete with digital pedagogies they have no training and/or interest in.

However, online classes have not historically poached students from on-ground classes. In fact, the online student is generally a different type of student altogether than she who takes a class on campus. According to the report from Joseph Cavanaugh, "Are Online Courses Cannibalizing Students from Existing Courses": "Online students are more likely to be female and older and are less likely to live on campus. They live significantly further from campus and are more likely to be part-time students who often take only online courses." These are students we're not likely to see in classrooms anyway. And online learning opportunities bring them into our virtual classrooms. This expands the reach of higher education, and offers more learners more opportunities. For this reason, we need to stop worrying about whether online learning will cannibalize on-ground learning, and work harder to offer something unique for audiences that might not otherwise have access to education.

4. Let go of fears and take more risks.

Online learning initiatives require courage. This is not a mere aphorism, or platitude. Courageous digital pedagogy, course design, and online program administration doesn't worry itself into corners, avoiding confrontation with tough questions about political economies, contingency, FERPA, plagiarism, and intellectual property. It tackles these subjects bravely, willing to assume solutions instead of handicaps. We need to develop hybrid models with robust online communities and more experimental approaches to LMS-based classes. Massive courses should be massively taught (and not by fleets of contingent or volunteer laborers). And we need to rethink what we mean by "institutionally supported" technologies and platforms to include a much broader and rapidly changing landscape of digital tools. We cannot afford to get hung-up on arguments relevant (or barely relevant) to the on-ground classroom simply because those arguments are familiar.

To support innovative pedagogies, we must participate in and help spur more robust faculty development around online learning. This does not look like a training seminar in the current technologies used to deliver online courses. Rather than training, we need to include faculty in, as Cathy Davidson says in *Now You See It*, "inquiry-based problem solving wherein solutions are not known in advance." We need to create a culture around online learning that incites new ideas, elicits fiery discussion, and excites teachers about the possibilities inherent in digital pedagogy. We should not assume we know how online learning works, but rather set out for new territory in these discussions.

5. Hold massive "town meetings" to develop broader strategies around online learning, because so far this conversation isn't big or inclusive enough.

Most online programs are designed for administrators and accreditors and not for students. We need to bring students more fully into this discussion, building a robust network of participant pedagogues reshaping what, when, and how we learn online. We need to create more open and transparent discussions about rights and principles and not deeper and more oppressive quality assurance measures. We must work to create institution-wide conversations about the present and future of online learning, and must also bridge conversations across institutions and disciplines.

There is no one in education untouched by online learning. We need everyone in the room, thinking and taking action across the artificial divides between K-12, higher ed., computers and writing, digital humanities, STEM, non-profit, for-profit, open education, and edtech. Reimagining education for the digital age begins with a single honest exchange, a line of code, a recognition, a declaration, a demand, an occupation.

THE CATACLYSM OF ONLINE LEARNING

As Cathy Davidson rightly notes, "The fourth great age — cataclysmic, paradigm-changing age — in human history is now, with the internet ... Anyone can think a thought, publish a thought, and it's out there to the world." Traditional institutions of higher education were founded on a proliferation of books, on the idea that knowledge was available through libraries and colleges if we could find the road to access. Today, the road to access doesn't necessarily detour through the university.

But universities, and more importantly educators, still have a role to play in the production and circulation of information, in the cultivation of a digital citizenry. To fulfill that role — indeed, in order to see it with any clarity at all — we must begin to think differently about online learning. It's not what we've thought it was, and it has never been what we hoped it would be. Education as a whole needs some reassembling; but digital education — borne thus far from a mimicry of on-ground learning — needs immediate reexamination. Online learning is yet in its impressionable infancy, and can be molded, grown, and led into a meaningful maturity.

THE MARCH OF THE MOOCS: MONSTROUS OPEN ONLINE COURSES

JESSE STOMMEL

MOOCs are a red herring. The MOOC didn't appear last week, out of a void, vacuum-packed. The MOOC has been around for years, biding its time. Still, the recent furor about MOOCs, which some have called "hysteria," opens important questions about higher education, digital pedagogy, and online learning. The MOOCs themselves aren't what's really at stake. In spite of the confused murmurs in the media, MOOCs won't *actually* chomp everything in their path. And they aren't an easy solution to higher education's financial crisis. In fact, a MOOC isn't a *thing* at all, just a methodological approach, with no inherent value except insofar as it's used.

MOOCs are like books, good when they're good and bad when they're bad. There is evil they can help do and evil they can help undo. Emerson writes in "The American Scholar," "Books are the best of things, well used; abused, among the worst" (56). Cathy Davidson writes similarly about MOOCs: "There are bad versions of MOOCs, and bad versions of traditional education." This is echoed again by Tanya Sasser: "Some variables remain the same, no matter what the medium of instruction. Boring is boring." Like the worst college classes of *every* variety, the worst MOOCs supply content without helping to facilitate learning.

Content and learning are two separate things, often at odds with one another. "The delivery of course content is not the same as education," Siva Vaidhyanathan writes in "What's the Matter

With MOOCs?". He continues, "Education is an imprecise process, a dance, and a collaborative experience." Most content is finite and contained; whereas, learning is chaotic and indeterminate. It's relatively easy to create technological infrastructures to deliver content, harder to build relationships and learning communities to help mediate, inflect, and disrupt that content. MOOCs, though, don't only have to be about static content. MOOCs are trainable.

Too many people are drinking the MOOC Kool-aid (or dumping it out hastily) when what we need to do is look closely at the Kool-aid to see what we can learn from it. At this point, MOOCs are all untapped potential, mostly misunderstood and only potentially gangrenous. Audrey Watters writes, in "The Language of MOOCs," "It's clear to me that there's a failure of acronyms here."

"**Massive**": What happens if we take the "Massive" out of "Massive Open Online Course"? In "We've been MOOCed", Jim Groom writes, "The scale of MOOCs is all they have been reduced to, the massive has taken over, the rest is always already secondary." There are financially sound reasons for making college classes bigger, but there are rarely pedagogical ones. Learning inevitably happens in every (on-ground and online) classroom, no matter the size, place, or shape. Learning is nascent and inexorable; however, it must also be cultivated and shared. The process we take through a course should be collaborative and dialogic. Massiveness does not always (or usually) lend itself to engaged participation of this sort. Without the "massive" part, there is still something revolutionary about MOOCs, perhaps something with even more potential — something lurking and embryonic.

"**Open**": The first "O" in "MOOC" has been dangerously misread. The pedagogical value in openness is that it helps create dialogue by increasing access and bringing at once disparate learning spaces into conversation. Open, though, does not mean free. Everything is monetized, whether overtly, indirectly, or insidiously. To say that a MOOC is *free* is like saying that reading a book I found on the street is free. The book was manufactured from raw material. A publisher marketed it. Someone bought the book. And I spent time (that I could have been working) reading the book. I paid for the book. And we'll pay (and already do pay) for MOOCs. The question is whether we'll also dedicate the necessary energy and commitment to making them work.

"Online": The second "O" in "MOOC" is a misnomer. Learning doesn't happen online, at least not for humans. It happens in our brains, in our bodies, and in the world. The internet is a window not a world. The course for a MOOC is not, in fact, online. That would be like saying that a syllabus for a course *is* the course. It's what jump-starts the course, and what organizes it, but it isn't the course. The learning of the course happens in the moments that overstep the bounds of the syllabus and curriculum — the moments that happen in several places simultaneously. David Brooks writes, in "The Campus Tsunami," "A brain is not a computer. We are not blank hard drives waiting to be filled with data. People learn from people they love and remember the things that arouse emotion." A successful MOOC is a hybrid MOOC that confronts us online but engages us in the world — thoughtfully, physically, and emotionally.

"Course": Education of this sort can't be contained tidily inside of a close-walled "course." Those boundaries too must be breached. Sean argues in "Courses, Composition, Hybridity" that learning is "creative and spontaneous, umbilical and imminent. A course is an act of composition, of the drawing together of thoughts through the use of tools to create — birth, deliver, discover, startle — not an artifact of learning, like a paper or final exam, but a use." Learning is playful and random, which is *not* to say that it's indiscriminate. If it were, we would have no need *at all* for syllabi, curriculum, or courses. Learning, rather, happens in the attentive unfolding of the rules — in their clever disruption and wild instantiation. We still need courses, at least as conceptual containers, but we can learn from the best MOOCs (like connectivist ones) and make our courses more and more boundless.

Emerson writes, in "The American Scholar," "The state of society is one in which the members have suffered amputation from the trunk, and strut about so many walking monsters, — a good finger, a neck, a stomach, an elbow, but never a man." These are the horrors Emerson imagines: severed heads, floating stomachs, fingers clicking away while bodies stiffen and minds wander. But there is also something exuberant promised in these horrors, a monster of another sort in the offing:

> The scholar of the first age received into him the world around; brooded thereon; gave it the new arrangement of his own mind, and uttered it again. It came into him, life; it went out from him, truth. It came to him, short-lived actions; it went out from him, immortal thoughts. It came to him, business; it went from him, poetry. It was dead fact; now, it is quick thought. It can stand, and it can go. It now endures, it now flies, it now inspires.

Learning, for Emerson, is emergent and copulative *not* parthenogenetic. Education does lively work in the world, like a contagion, always spreading, always reaching. MOOCs have this potential, but only when we read them right. Even more importantly, the proliferation of MOOCs has broader implications for higher education, so turning away in the face of their incessant march would be *both* perilous *and* a missed opportunity.

ON PRESENCE, VIDEO LECTURES, AND CRITICAL PEDAGOGY

SEAN MICHAEL MORRIS

I have been criticized for standing up in front of a class. Criticized, cajoled, heckled—usually in a friendly way—because my pedagogy asks that teaching and learning decenter the instructor in the classroom. Yet, I stand, and where I stand the front of the classroom follows. Whether I am behind a podium, whether I am standing amid tables where groups are gathered, whether I am in the back of an auditorium and speaking. I stand, and I am the front of the classroom.

In part—probably to a greater degree than I am aware—this is because I'm a white male. A white male who passes for straight (but isn't), and who passes for neurotypical (but isn't). A white male whom one supposes has a Ph.D., but never pursued one. A white male who passes for an academic, but who not only eschews that title, he also was never indoctrinated into academic life. But none of those intersections of my social location matter when I have a mic, a podium, or a classroom.

To another degree, the front of the classroom follows me because I am the teacher. Of anyone in the room, I know more in its entirety the circumference of the community there. I know the end of the semester or quarter, it's final thesis, at least in theory; and in many cases, I have sailed these waters before. But more than that: the community needs me. If education is an act of freedom, of liberation, as bell hooks posits, then it is also risky. I am in the room to minimize that risk, to keep the boat from capsizing while students rock it as hard as they can.

That may smack of control, but it's compassion. I don't want anyone to fall overboard; and if they do, I would like to be sure they know how to swim.

My presence is important especially when I acknowledge it, especially when I allow that I am a white, cisgender, straight-passing male, and especially when I acknowledge that my presence would be different, and equally as vital to the community of the classroom, if I were not white, cisgender, straight-passing, and male. My presence is important when I am transparent to my intersectionality so that the power differential in the room—between teacher and student—can be shone a light on and, if not diffused entirely, at least understood.

Presence, in other words, is not simply showing up to call on raised hands, answer questions, or deliver Powerpoint lectures. Presence is human, all-too human, because education is human, and learning is a problem that humans must solve. And a teacher's presence must welcome students' presence so that the community can begin to answer the questions education demands we address.

Community in a classroom, though, is complicated. Students' presence is more nuanced, more implicated, than our own. It is not enough to include students' intersectionality, their social location and stories in the narrative of the classroom. It is not enough because to ask them to share their stories without sharing our own, to refer to the literature of "diversity," to talk about the "marginal," is to center the teacher in more dangerous ways than taking the podium. The instructor's own social location must be included in the narrative of the classroom so that there is a chance to decenter it. If we do not speak up about our own power—if we don't do more than simply concede the podium or the center of the room—we have done too little to undo that power. Then, our presence is an elephant in the room; our social location the litmus for all social locations. A silent authority silences without ever saying a word.

In "Making the Invisible Visible," Kisha Tracy and Katherine Covino write,

> As instructors, we have the responsibility to challenge this simplification and the blind acceptance of categories — or boxes — that either inherently limit human potential or are intended to prevent full participation and representation. In particular, whatever our disciplines, it is imperative we design pedagogical methods that will help our students make the invisible — those threatened with erasure, those who lack representation, those who defy the definitions imposed upon them, those struggling against the political machine — visible and expose the power structures that work to maintain the invisibility of marginalized individuals.

As someone who is neurodivergent and gay, the problem I see with this approach is that I am not invisible to myself; no one has erased me—because I am alive and I write and I speak. I struggle against the political machine, but I also know so does my neighbor, and you, and whomever my teacher may be.

The fullness with which we talk about the injustices done to "marginalized" people, I fear, not only fails to acknowledge all the ways they/we have spoken, do speak, want to speak, but also centers the hetero, white, cisgender, male assumptions of education. In other words, if an instructor decides what marginal is and what marginal does, then those in their classroom already must follow social rules they cannot defend themselves against.

Difference cannot become canon. Because canon means passing muster, and we cannot ask difference to pass muster. Rather than put marginalized folk under a microscope in order to understand their struggle or develop compassion for difference, might we not instead wreck the classroom with story?

In digital environments, this story-making, difference-sharing, power-exposing activity becomes much harder. Not only does the learning management system or a course web site stand in for the instructor (I was recently asked why simply assembling the curriculum—textbooks, reading schedule, quizzes, assignments and the like—wasn't suitable to demonstrate instructor presence in an LMS), but the platform itself silences difference. To quote myself, "Despite any stubborn claims to the contrary, instructional design assigns learners to a single seat, a single set of characteristics." Students are sorted alphabetically; they appear as small profile pictures (if not anonymous avatars) in discussion; they are rows in a spreadsheet. Instruction isn't modulated, but doled out when students press a button.

As Inside Higher Ed (and others) reported, the question of instructor presence online is no laughing matter. Western Governors University, a horror of digital learning that bases its teaching on competency-based courses, was recently called upon to return over $700 million in federal financial aid. The Department of Education, which recommended the action, cited "concerns about an inadequate faculty role" in online courses. When instructors don't show up, students don't learn.

Unfortunately, the response of most instructional designers and online teachers is to turn to tools. As Jean Dimeo reports there are "a variety of video-audio production tools [that] can help instructors better connect with online learners." Dimeo's article outlines four of these tools recommended by presenters at the 2017 Quality Matters Connect conference in Fort Worth, Texas. And while I too have been recently wowed by the smooth operation of a video production tool (Instructure's Arc), I am far from believing that the tools will preserve the very complicated, nuanced need for presence in an online environment.

That we turn to tools for digital learning indicates we don't understand, or have abdicated our understanding, of pedagogy. In fact, most tools perpetuate problems of censure, erasure, racism, heteronormativity, and other harmful assumptions of "same-ness." They are designed for lowest common denominator teaching and learning and do not feature genius in their methods.

As well, I'm unconvinced by Arc, Screencast-O-Matic, Snip, Sway, Panopto, and the rest precisely because these tools do nothing in and of themselves to make transparency, human connection, the problem of learning that can only be solved by the community of a class, more express. Tools and rubrics and best practices will not solve these concerns. Western Governors University cannot rise from the ashes by the power of a video lecture. Yet this is precisely the wool they attempt to pull over our eyes.

What is missing from digital learning is the recollection that I am human and you are human. That we are vulnerable and needy. That we are brave and terrified. That we watch the news at night and tremble and that, for better or worse, we believe education holds some of the answers to our fears. Students can stare at our faces on a screen all they want, or for as long as we require it, but will that suffice as presence?

THE COURSE HATH NO BOTTOM: THE 20,000-PERSON SEMINAR

JESSE STOMMEL

Sean and I wrote in "Pedagogies of Scale," "Meaningful relationships are as important in a class of three as they are in a class of 10,000." In the rest of that article, we wonder at questions of scale: how to scale up, when to scale down, and what it might mean to scale *sideways*. My question here: is it possible to scale up and down simultaneously — to create more and more intimate learning experiences for larger and larger groups of learners?

As I'm co-teaching Shakespeare in Community, a Massive Open Online Course from University of Wisconsin-Madison. The goal of the course is to bring thousands of learners into conversation. While I've taught MOOCs since 2012 on several platforms, this is the first time I've developed a Coursera MOOC. Coursera is a platform well-oiled for content-delivery. In fact, when I sat down with Daphne Koller, the founder and president of Coursera, she used the word "content" several dozen times. I asked about "conversation", "dialogue", and "community". Her responses showed that these are, for Coursera, an afterthought. And after playing around inside the guts of the tool, it remains clear to me that these are, indeed, an afterthought. All the proof I need is that it's about ten times easier to upload a video, and track the watching of that video, than it is to administer the discussion forum. But Coursera does content-delivery incredibly well. My content feels stroked and adored by the platform. It feels genuinely loved. As learning management systems go, I am happy to go on record saying that Coursera is one of the best.

However, I remain certain that learning is not something that ought to be managed. The better we become at managing learning, the more damage we do to learning. This is the cruel irony of the learning management system. The better designed it is for doing its core function, the worse off the learning that happens inside of it. As a technology, the learning management system is genuinely Orwellian. I like best the learning management system when it is still a baby, before it has fully grown up, before it has earned its stripes. But every learning management system is almost immediately on its way toward extinction. They die quick deaths at the point they forget that learning is an encounter, not a spreadsheet. The gradebook, and the demands it places on every single other feature, ultimately kills the learning management system. (Thus, I wouldn't blame the technological systems so much as I'd blame the institutional and political climates that drive them.)

If we are to use these systems, we need to carve out more space in them for nuance — fashioning simpler platforms that serve as launching pads to places outside their own orbit (both physical and virtual). And every course inside a learning management system should ask students to reflect on the "rhetoric of the room" — the ways the shape of the room affects the learning we do inside of it. We either critically interrogate our tools or are subject to them. There is no middle ground between these two.

THE MOOC'S THE THING

At this point, every MOOC fails if it isn't, at least implicitly, about how we learn in a MOOC.

There has been much pontificating about MOOCs. Much discussion of the *ifs* and *whys*and *whethers*. There has been decidedly less practical discussion of how we might make better MOOCs. There has been little discussion about what the MOOC can teach us about learning. And I don't mean what we can learn from machines, from big data, from so-called "objective" or "quantifiable" research. I don't mean what we can learn from IRB-authorized participant surveys or some other "study" that proves what is proven already through plain observation. Instead, we need more deeply subjective work on MOOCs. Many of us don't have time for the years that can pass in legitimizing the double-blind-peer-reviewed claims of an academic article. The folks for whom this work can do the most good are designing and taking courses right now, *this week*, not in two years. What can we learn from (and *with*) them?

The bulk of the MOOCs I've taken or eavesdropped upon have not been particularly well-designed. And I find this equally true of the connectivist MOOCs I've encountered and the ones from Silicon Valley MOOC-providers like Coursera and Udacity. The problem is not that the MOOC is experimental but that it is often not experimental enough. The MOOC landscape has been cut up into neat and tidy categories, and too many MOOCs conform to pre-established scripts. Most Coursera MOOCs, for example, look identical to traditional online courses circa 2005 or earlier, and efforts to scale up those courses has meant more content and less attention to interaction. Coursera is a triumph of marketing a decade-old approach to online learning, not a triumph of learning design.

I say this, and yet I am just now teaching a MOOC using Coursera and have been more often than not delighted by the elegance of the platform — especially the stark lack of feature bloat I've seen infect almost every other learning management system I've worked within.

Connectivist MOOCs (cMOOCs), which encourage a conversation that is distributed across the web, have also fallen into the trap of conforming themselves too often to a script. The cMOOCs I join now, with a couple exceptions, do not feel as though they've evolved from early cMOOCs, as much as they feel beholden to them. Most cMOOCs are disasters of learning design. Beautiful disasters. Joyous disasters. Productive disasters. But disasters nonetheless. As if a course literally exploded onto the internet, leaving a smear of barely intelligible bits across the web.

I say this, and yet I have designed a half-dozen cMOOCs. I love them all like children, but I find myself wanting to kill all of my darlings. And not just in the name of experimentation. But because killing our darlings is at the root of pedagogy. Never do the same thing twice, because the same thing twice is already rotten. We learn from every one of our successes and mistakes, and we encounter each learner and each learning environment anew. Sean and I write in "If Freire Made a MOOC: Open Education as Resistance," "the *best* best practice is to imperil best practices."

All of which is to say that even if I've become a genuine fan of the MOOC medium, I continue to wish the medium would ask more questions of itself. And not the kinds of questions that can be answered by an objective study. The control group is a violence we can not afford. Surveys do not with patient ears attend. And snark or dismissiveness is not the answer either. Instead, we need to sit right down in the MOOC. But be always so light on our feet as to remain unentrenched.

The folks most poised to think with the MOOC are the ones building and rebuilding them. The folks most poised to think with the MOOC are the ones taking them. Everyone else is a cipher to this great accompt, working only upon imaginary forces.

And this is why I continue to teach online — not because I love teaching online, but because I'm determined to get to the bottom of online learning. Determined to see that it hath no bottom. There are many things about which I remain uncertain. What I know thus far is that content can not be poured neatly from one container to another — from the face-to-face class into the online one. What I know is that none of these technologies will save education or us — except, perhaps, from the urge to look to tech (and not to ourselves) for saviors.

CONTENT IS DEAD AND GONE

At the point that our content feels *stroked and adored,* we know that actual learning has stopped. Learning is at direct odds with content. In fact, learning does battle with content. If content wins, learning loses. We do, instead, in the best learning environments, grapple with content — we kill it on the road when we meet it there.

And so, I approached Shakespeare in Community, my latest foray into MOOC-development, with the goal of creating content that was, at every turn, self-undermining. My aim was, from the start, for everything I created for the MOOC to facilitate and be secondary to the dialogue among the learners. And I created more content (at least twice as much) than I've ever created for a course, but this MOOC wears its content with a difference.

Some choices I've made in my work on this MOOC and how they are motivated by its pedagogy:

- Before the Shakespeare MOOC, my own face (aside from a mere avatar) has *never* appeared in a single online course I've made. *Best practices* for online learning insist the teacher should be *present* and that one of the best ways to show this presence is through lecture videos featuring the teacher at the head of every unit within the course. My consistent response to this imperative has been to put videos featuring students (and not myself) at the head of the MOOCs I've taught.
- With this MOOC, I determined that I'd approach the production of lecture videos like I would a documentary film shoot. My goal was to find the collaborative energy of Al Filreis's Modern Poetry MOOC — but asynchronously. Ultimately, I filmed over 40 hours of interviews with just under 70 experts, from child

actors at the Young Shakespeare Players and the Children's Theater of Madison to adult actors from the American Players Theatre, students from George Washington University and the UW Odyssey Project, faculty from GWU and UW-Madison, administrators from the Folger Shakespeare Library, and more.

- From this footage, I edited about two hours of video (all of which is also available outside the course). While I shot *much more* footage than is likely shot for most Coursera MOOCs, I included in the course *much less* video than is included in most Coursera MOOCs. This was a *design* decision. I wanted to leave as many gaps as possible in the conversation for learners to fill with their own voices. Long monologues do not encourage dialogue. My hypothesis, though, is that 15-minute video documentaries, each with many voices, *do*.
- The first moments of the course, the first remarks in the videos, the first text on the page reflect uncertainty. There is no authority in this course, except insofar as everyone is an authority. I did not select and highlight footage that foregrounds what is known. Rather, many of the videos begin with a stumble, a glitch, a false start, a moment that shows even experts at their most vulnerable. And, ultimately, every video champions discovery more than knowing or certainty.
- Facts are shared, details are offered, and content is delivered. But never at the expense of questions or openings to discussion. I aimed not to withhold content, or obscure it, but to make it secondary. Content comes as a relief to many learners who are primed by Coursera for a pedagogy that equates content-delivery with learning. Admittedly, the videos I've made pull the rug out from under some learners, because I am not also offering the *trappings* of traditional education, like quizzes, grades, one static path through the material,

etc. My approach is not to alienate these learners, but to give them just enough stability to find their footing as they venture into the course. There are no imperatives, though, so efforts to merely follow instructions are frustrated.

- I decided to bring myself more fully into this MOOC than any of my previous online courses. I position myself in the videos as a conductor, what Howard Rheingold calls a "chief learner," showing up quite a bit in the first video, orienting learners to the course, but less and less as the videos proceed. However, I do appear, even if only briefly, in most of the videos. (My co-instructors also appear consistently but infrequently.) My goal is to establish presence the way I would in a classroom — by making eye contact with every student — even if the bulk of the learning happens with me not at the front of the room or on the sidelines, but in the midst of (and as a member of) the rest of the learners.
- I wanted to teach this course with as large a group of co-instructors as possible. I believe massive courses should be massively taught. In this case, I'm working with three other primary instructors: R L Widmann, Sarah Marty, and Catherine DeRose. And, while I directed and produced the videos myself, I worked closely with Mark Neufeld, the graphic designer for the course, in thinking about the MOOC's pedagogy. The course also features guest instructors for one or more weeks, including Sean Michael Morris, Joshua Calhoun, Eric Alexander, and James DeVita. Finally, every one of the nearly 70 interviewees becomes a defacto instructor, as do all the learners in the peer-driven learning environment.

In my introduction to the course, I write,

> Shakespeare begins *Hamlet* with the words, 'Who's there?' The ques-

> tion is deceptively simple, but it is one that opens a whole host of potential rabbit holes for us to tumble down. What I know is that how we begin something new is important. The first thing we say. The first question we ask. The first part of ourselves we show.

I am, from these first words in the MOOC, showing my pedagogical hand, talking about Shakespeare and also about the nature of the course itself. Then,

> The second line, 'Stand, and unfold yourself,' is a command in response to the first question [...] Taken together, the two lines offer uncertainty, curiosity, and also distrust. They wonder at humanness but worry at its edge.

R L Widmann (my long-time collaborator and mentor who inspired this MOOC) writes in her introduction to the course,

> My Shakespeare, the one I love best, offers me an opportunity to explore the world in which I live and those worlds to which I will never be able to travel in real time.

And in our first posts to the discussion forum, we each reveal something of ourselves, something personal and honest, not scripted. But our posts are lost there almost immediately, among the hundreds of other posts, none clamoring for attention more than the others. The notion that one or two or even four experts could deliver knowledge of Shakespeare to the world is, honestly, incredibly strange to me. The work in this course is an encounter with the text, and there are lots of guides and lots of people to engage in discussion about what we find. The course functions much like a face-to-face class does when I break students into small groups. I can't possibly be in all of the groups at once, and it is better for the learning environment that I'm not. Instead, the voices in the room break from murmur to cacophony, and we leave having deeply heard several of our peers and having heard beyond them the hum of a much larger room.

THOSE THAT ARE MOOCS ALREADY — ALL BUT ONE — SHALL LIVE

Shakespeare in Community launched a little over a week ago and currently has over 18,500 students enrolled from 157 countries. But numbers are not what the course is after. Most of the seminars I've taught have been groups of 15 – 35 people. My task for myself in this much larger course is to find a space where I can be both "lost" (in productive ways) and "found" in the sense that I see people and let them see me. My goal is to help create an experience in which the learners can do the same. Functionally, it doesn't feel all that different from a class of 15 – 35 people (although a MOOC could *never* replace that). This course scales the experience, not up but across, through the network of participants — which changes the nature of the experience in all manner of ways.

In a thread from our public Facebook group, a student remarked that the course, to her, felt "scattered." It also feels scattered to me. In the way that Central Park in New York City is scattered. I can't be everywhere at once, and I'm easily overwhelmed by the scale, but if I find a calm corner to hang out, I start to meet people and see stuff I wouldn't have otherwise seen. And the course is glad to have me, even if I end up just passing through.

The key for me is to recognize that almost 20,000 students means lots of different kinds of stuff will be happening that appeals in different ways to different students. Not all of these things will appeal even to me. And there will be corners of the course that I never see (could never even hope to see, because of the sheer volume). But there are people here, ones I would have otherwise never met. They talk to me about Shakespeare and also about their own learning. And there is something marvelous about every syllable they write, tapped out in the incessant vibration of my various devices that beckon to me throughout the day and night. Because of them, and the hum of their voices, I go to sleep bleary-eyed and wake up bleary-eyed.

O brave new world, that has such people in't!

CRITICAL INSTRUCTIONAL DESIGN

SEAN MICHAEL MORRIS

When I co-founded Digital Pedagogy Lab in 2012, I wanted to address the widespread lack of critical thinking about learning online. I write in "The Failure of an Online Program" that "An insistence on doing things as we've always done them, on trying to match piece to piece, part to part, learning object to learning object, only limits us. Non-inquiry blinds us to the environment in which we're actually teaching."

Design of online courses also suffers from a perceived need for efficiency. More students means more courses which means more teachers. And these are largely adjunct and contingent teachers, most of whom have only the time to receive the most preliminary kinds of training before (but most usually after) starting teaching online. And, that training usually consists of how-to lessons scaffolding to best practices.

But digital pedagogy should not be reduced to a set of best practices, tools, or interfaces. So, when Jesse and I started Digital Pedagogy Lab, we centered its philosophy on critical pedagogy, or on a critical digital pedagogy, as seen in the work of Paulo Freire, bell hooks, Henry Giroux, and others.

A critical digital pedagogy, we argued, was one that would ask questions about technology, about the assumptions we make about technology—its includedness in education, its politics, its economics and labor, and its repercussions for privacy and surveillance—and not simply about the use of technology. We wanted participants in Digital Pedagogy Lab to push beyond the "how" to use a tool, and into the "why" and "whether."

The seat of critical digital pedagogy is one of inquiry and observation. It is mindful of all the variety of dimensions the digital has in our and our students' lives. The "why" and "whether," then, are not just about lesson planning, choosing video over text, or learning on campus versus learning online. The why and whether must begin with questions about what happens when learning goes digital, when it goes online.

Jesse reminds us, in "Why Online Programs Fail, and 5 Things We Can Do about It," that:

> Educational campuses have libraries, coffee shops, cafeterias, quads, lawns, amphitheaters, stadiums, hallways, student lounges, trees, park benches, and fountains. Ample space for rallies, study-groups, conversation, debate, student clubs, and special events. Few institutions pay much attention to re-creating these spaces online. The work done outside and between classes (which we would argue is the glue that holds education together) is attended to nominally if at all.

Since on-ground college life and learning is deeply integrated into not just the student's life but also the life of the surrounding community, critical digital pedagogy would ask: how is or does the LMS or VLE integrate into the student's life online—whether that life takes place on social media, or in text messages and e-mails, or on other platforms where that student works, shares, and learns online? Is the LMS a walled garden? Or does it participate in meaningful ways in the wide range of digital experiences that students and teachers both have online? How are the conversations that become the marrow of learning on-ground accommodated in online space? How is diversity embraced or represented? Where does not just interdisciplinarity lie, but intersectionality? Where do chance encounters occur?

And, of course, if we venture outside of the LMS and into, say, social media, we need to wonder: what kinds of participation are we asking our students to enact online? What communities will they belong to? What are the compromises they will make, what benefits will they reap, how will their privacy be sacrificed and how can it be protected? Where there may be specific drawbacks to a LMS that doesn't look or act like the internet despite its belonging on the web, there may be some benefits to the ways it can isolate students. For example, does the LMS provide a space for identity formation in the way university life might? Does it provide a testing ground for citizenship? Does a platform bent on content and learning management offer opportunities to safely bridge the public and the private?

Henry Giroux writes, in "On Critical Pedagogy", that:

> Critical pedagogy asserts that students can engage their own learning from a position of agency and in so doing can actively participate in narrating their identities through a culture of questioning that opens up a space of translation between the private and the public while changing the forms of self-and social recognition.

This is increasingly important in a world where authoritarianism seems to be on the rise. Does the LMS, or do any of our strategies for online learning, provide a space where students participate in narrating their identities, or in beginning to understand the interdependent nature of their own identity with the identities of others in their communities? And if so, where and how?

Because critical pedagogy asserts that learning is a matter of engaging in a process of becoming conscious—and not just becoming knowledgeable of a certain set of facts, ideas, precedent—a critical pedagogy that fronts the digital must inquire how each new tool, environment, or network makes possible that becoming conscious. It is, in other words, asking much more foundational questions of learning online than simply "how do I post to the discussion board" or "where do I post grades." And it expects more of its teachers than analysis of learning analytics.

Consider, for example, that certain kinds of surveillance and control are possible in an on-ground classroom. And to a certain extent, students have come up in a system where they understand the ground rules of authority in even the most liberative learning environments. In digital environments, though, are we certain that students understand what is being surveilled and by whom? Do they know what analytics are being kept, who is checking those analytics, and what the repercussions of their actions or inactions online might be?

The VLE might not be as permeable, as vulnerable, as Facebook or Twitter, but it is decidedly different in its capacities for control and observation than a room where we all gather together to learn. In fact, it is less private even than students, learning alone in their bedrooms and living rooms at home, think it might be.

What students learn online is never just the content we load into the LMS.

Which is why, at its most practical, critical digital pedagogy looks askance at the tools we use, the tools we are asked to use, the tools that are sold to us, which then prompts us—as learners and teachers online—to ask after the promises that digital technology offers. Promises of efficiency, time savings, greater engagement, higher test scores, increased retention, and even deeper relationships with our students through the mediation of algorithms and digital clickers.

When we think through the whole context of learning online, it becomes apparent that it is never enough to *do* teaching with technology, to suffice with content and learning objectives and assessments. We must always step back and inquire:

- Are students online cared for? Have we found ways within the LMS or other platform to, as bell hooks writes, "respect and care for the souls of our students"?
- Have we engaged students in some way not measurable

by clicks, hits, and discussion posts, or, are we letting the the technology teach in place of us?

- Is learning online rich with the problem-solving Freire recommends as an alternative to "banking education", or does it amount to a checklist for satisfactory performance and completion? Have we laid the foundation for student agency?

What is needed, what has always been needed. is an effective digital pedagogy that lets us span the interface, cross the digital, and find one another where we are.

A critical digital pedagogy is one where learning and teaching online provides the material from which students can forge themselves into ethical subjects in the context of their lives as hybrid learners and complicated human beings.

Tim Amidon writes in "(dis)Owning Tech: Ensuring Value and Agency at the Moment of Interface,"

> Educational technologies, as interfaces, offer students and educators opportunities to discover and enact agency through strategic rhetorical action. Yet, realizing this agency is complex work because "participat[ing] fully and meaningfully in [the] technological activities" that comprise so many aspects of our social, civic, and professional lives requires an increasingly sophisticated array of multiliteracies.

Critical digital pedagogy has as one of the primary ends to its inquiry the development of these multiliteracies. Look beyond the tool to how we use the tool. Look beyond how we use the tool to how the tool uses us. Look beyond how the tool uses us to how we can resist, hack, change, or simply "prefer not to."

This doesn't just apply to the LMS, or Twitter, Turnitin, a cool new app, or an online proctoring service. Education is itself one of those tools. We could ask: how might students use and shape their educations? How do their educations use and shape them?

And how might they resist, hack, change, or simply prefer not to? We don't get to stop asking questions about the why and whether of our teaching simply because the digital provides algorithms that approximate answers.

Learning online still needs—really really requires—human teachers. Because what it comes down to is, we are the most important technology involved in digital and online learning.

A Call for Critical Instructional Design

Since the beginning of 2016, I've been working out an idea which I call *critical instructional design*. And I'm not the only one. Teachers and researchers in composition studies, sociology, and other fields have been at this endeavor for years. For my own part, my ideas are a response to the truly banal solutions I've witnessed a traditional instructional design provides for the complications of online learning—solutions which tend to reduce the complexity of learning to straightforward methodologies that provide replicable results.

Critical instructional design is an early, emerging attempt to get at some concrete methodologies for creating agentive spaces in online and hybrid learning environments.

It's not an iteration of traditional instructional design. It doesn't find its roots in behaviorism or the ideologies of B. F. Skinner. Rather than researching an instructional design based on positivist, research-driven, evidence-based methods, critical instructional design turns to critical pedagogy—to Paulo Freire, bell hooks, John Holt, Seymour Papert, Maxine Greene, and others for both inspiration and complication.

The critical instructional design approach prioritizes collaboration, participation, social justice, learner agency, emergence, narrative, and relationships of nurture between students, and between teachers and students. It acknowledges that all learning today is necessarily hybrid, and looks for opportunities to integrate learners' digital lives into their digitally-enhanced or fully online learning experiences.

Importantly, in keeping with its social justice roots, critical instructional design seeks to create learning and educational opportunities for students of all backgrounds, leveraging techniques especially to give platforms for those voices most usually suppressed or oppressed, including the voices of women, people of color, LGBTQ folk, people with disabilities, and more. It works against the standardization of so many educational technologies, and aims for the fullest inclusion possible.

I believe we must conceive of an instructional design that approaches the very human task of learning, the impulse to learn, and the increasingly urgent need for learning to result in the wisdom of agency.

Stanley Aronowitz writes, in *Against Schooling: For an Education That Matters,*

> Few of even the so-called educators ask the question: What matters beyond the reading, writing, and numeracy that are presumably taught in the elementary and secondary grades? The old questioning of what a kid needs to become an informed "citizen" capable of participating in making the large and small public decisions that affect the larger world as well as everyday life receives honorable mention but not serious consideration. These unasked questions are symptoms of a new regime of educational expectations that privileges job readiness above any other educational values. (xii)

Where critical pedagogy, and critical digital pedagogy, offer questions about "what a kid needs to become an informed citizen," critical instructional design attempts to provide a platform where those questions are given a forum that pairs them with curriculum. In other words, an approach to online teaching and learning that creates a space where student agency and critical consciousness can be fostered in a way that grows knowledge and expertise in a given subject.

Of course, the first question that comes to mind when I say that is: "How?" What are the methods employed by a critical instructional design? What are its best practices? How is it replicable?

The worst best practice is to adhere to, or go searching for, best practices. I have been in countless rooms with teachers, technologists, instructional designers, and administrators calling for recommendations or a list of tools they should use, strategies that work, practices that cannot fail to produce results in the classroom. But digital tools, strategies, and best practices are a red herring in digital learning. Learning always starts with people. Instead of asking "What tool will we need?," ask "What behaviors will need to be in place?"

For critical instructional design to work, we have to find a way to re-approach what we know about teaching and learning, about learning theory, about the digital. In Zen terms, we have to find "beginner's mind." This may sound strange, but the truth is that critical instructional design isn't an iteration of the instructional design that came before. It's new, while at the same time being old; it is familiar while at the same time disorienting.

In other words, for critical instructional design to begin, those undertaking the design of learning must themselves become more critically conscious of the work at hand. The most critical stance we can take as educators is to assume we know nothing and become profoundly observational.

If we want critical instructional design to work, we can't approach the virtual learning environment, or the student, or the writing of our syllabus, or the idea of assessment while our brain is loaded up with old stories about those things, and our habits for fronting them. Instead, we have to essentially clear our cache, assuming nothing, and think through each step of design as it arises.

The reason we have to do this is that traditional instructional design *seems* to work; educational psychology and behaviorism *seem* to work. The way we've been doing things has resulted in analytics that tell us something is going well (of course, the algorithms behind those analytics only measure, only can measure, statistics that help sell the platform). Too often, because we have something that works, we assume little else will.

Paulo Freire offers, in his book *Pedagogy of Indignation*, that

> To the extent that we accept that the economy, or technology, or science, it doesn't matter what, exerts inescapable power over us, there is nothing left for us to do other than renounce our ability to think, to conjecture, to compare, to choose, to decide, to envision, to dream. (33)

Instead of saying "I've always done it this way," we need to say "How should I do this now?"

That is literally the first and, as far as I can imagine, the only best practice associated with critical instructional design. Where critical pedagogy centers on social justice and liberation, and critical digital pedagogy fronts with the complications of learning in digital environments, critical instructional design looks directly at application and asks, open-eyed and slack-jawed, "What is the best first step, the right action for the circumstance, right now?"

And what happens when we begin to let go of our old ideas of instructional design and learning theory is that we feel the return of invention and imagination to the acts of learning and teaching. Freedom occurs, only to remind us that we've always been free.

Giroux writes in *On Critical Pedagogy*, "For me, pedagogy is part of an always unfinished project intent on developing a meaningful life for all students." This is vitally important to the project of learning online. I have long believed that online learning doesn't understand itself. That it is as a two-year-old child who discovers they can walk but doesn't really understand the nuances of the ambulatory act, nor really even what walking's for. As such, teaching online, designing online learning, is in fact an act of learning online... both learning in an online environment and learning what "online" even means.

At the same time as I encourage the idea of "beginner's mind", though, we cannot literally go back square one. Education has become too shrouded in technology for us to return to the mere classroom, mere pen and paper, chalk and chalkboard. But we can retreat to that point in our minds, to make it back to a figurative, theoretical square one, and consider what choices we *would* make from there. And then begin making them for the first time. What technology would we include? What technology would we veer away from? What practices are we most afraid of losing, and so what practices must we carefully and with passion fight for?

WRITING AND READING

A course today is an act of composition, of the drawing together of thoughts through the use of tools to create — birth, deliver, discover, startle — not an artifact of learning, like a paper or final exam, but a use.

COURSES, COMPOSITION, HYBRIDITY

SEAN MICHAEL MORRIS

The course is an old idea. In the old days of teaching, a course was a path, a set of obstacles, or a journey through ideas toward some end. The path was marked by learning objectives, and further broken down by units and lesson plans, exercises and quizzes. Scaffolding, people called it: the building of knowledge upon incremental ideas. A student graduated from this course either by enduring its duration — as a course of antibiotics — or by safely navigating its waters — as when one canoes the course of a river. Learning was a thing accomplished. It resided at the end of the journey, glimmering on the horizon at the beginning of the semester, and drawing ever closer as the student followed the path laid out by the instructor. Following along objective to objective, project to project, exam to exam until, standards satisfied, the student reached out and grasped her final grade.

But the course is an old idea. Learning has changed.

Or, more correctly, learning has revealed itself for what it really has been all along: creative and spontaneous, umbilical and imminent. A course today is an act of composition, of the drawing together of thoughts through the use of tools to create — birth, deliver, discover, startle — not an artifact of learning, like a paper or final exam, but a use. To create a use for those tools, a use for those ideas, a use, indeed, for the course itself. To complete a course today means a student finds himself at the beginning, but well equipped. The course as composition is not fundamentally instrumental, producing an article or living up to an outcome; but rather the course as composition is an action which has intrinsic value.

The first hybridity occurs (hybridity, too, is an action, and not a state) between the mind and the tool it controls. Consider the mind as one site of movement — biochemical movement, neuron to neuron, or metaphysical movement, inspiration to dream to spontaneous revelation to curiosity. Into the mind rushes memory, observation, calculation, confusion and resolution, error and correction. All of these things remain in the mind, impotent and useless without tools to bring them to light.

Hybridity occurs when the thinker picks up the hammer, the beam, the pen, the paper — all things decidedly not the mind itself. Hybridity occurs when mind and matter cooperate to create. There is in fact no creativity without hybridity — there is only thought or action. But the movement of hybridity causes thought and action, which make process into use.

The internet, and all the digital worlds, are impotent and useless without the synthesis of hybridity. Without the sense-making and use-making capabilities of the creative mind, web sites are flotsam, the trillions of lines of code are silent and meaningless. It is the human who composes who gives use, meaning, and order to the jumble.

THE TWITTER ESSAY

JESSE STOMMEL

Consider the tangible violence technology has wrought upon grammar. We rely on automated grammar and spell-check tools in word-processing software (so much that they've become a crutch). E-mail shorthand fails to live up to the grammatical standards of typed or handwritten letters. And many believe our language is being perverted by the shortcuts (and concision nearly to the point of indifference) we've become accustomed to writing and reading in text messages and tweets.

For many teachers and writing pedagogues, this is a travesty, a torturous fact of modern life that we all must contend with and defend against in our classrooms. However, I would argue that we are at a moment in the history of the English language where the capacity for something wondrous is upon us. This isn't to say that there haven't been other wondrous moments in the evolution of human language, but there has not (and may never be again) a moment just like this one, a moment where the very fabric of how we speak and how we express ourselves through language has become so tenuous that every new textual utterance threatens to either devolve into gibberish or reinvent the very way we speak and write.

The evolution of written language is speeding up at an exponential rate, and this necessitates that we, as writing teachers, reconsider the way we work with language in our classrooms. We can no longer be the staid grammarians that taught so many of us to write, nor can we simply dismiss or overlook the teaching of grammar entirely. Rather, we must think consciously (and practically) about how our students' conceptions of (and contexts for) writing are changing, and we must approach the teaching of grammar in new and innovative ways.

While I agree that technology has wrought a certain violence upon grammar, I would argue that writing instructors can exact an even more punishing and permanent sort of violence. Students aren't terrified to send text messages or post status updates to Twitter or Facebook, but they are often terrified to write academic papers.

David Crystal writes, in *txtng: the gr8 db8*, "The popular belief is that texting has evolved as a twenty-first-century phenomenon — as a highly distinctive graphic style, full of abbreviations and deviant uses of language, used by a young generation that doesn't care about standards. There is a widely voiced concern that the practice is fostering a decline in literacy. And some even think it is harming language as a whole." His use of the word "deviant" here is telling, suggesting that, in the eyes of detractors, text-messaging as a medium threatens not just grammatical errors, but moral infractions. It isn't just that technology, and text-messaging in particular, threatens to undermine language, but in so doing, it threatens to undermine the very culture upon which literacy is so precariously perched.

Crystal goes on to refute this belief a few pages later, writing, "All the popular beliefs about texting are wrong, or at least debatable. Its graphic distinctiveness is not a totally new phenomenon. Nor is its use restricted to the young generation. There is increasing evidence that it helps rather than hinders literacy." He points out that the average texter is aware when they are breaking the rules. He or she is aware of the ways that text-message-speak distorts Standard English — aware, in fact, to the point of revelry.

One of the primary goals of abbreviations in text- or Twitter-speak is to condense an utterance to fit the 160 character limit of a text message or the 140 character limit of a Twitter post (or Tweet). However, there is also a certain charm, a playfulness, involved. There is pleasure in the act of composing with these constraints, an intentional and curious engagement with how sentences, words, and letters make meaning. Composing a text message or tweet is most certainly a literate (and sometimes even literary) act. And, interestingly, the average text message or tweet distorts grammar much less than the naysayers would have us believe.

In fact, more often, text messages and tweets rely on very conventional sentence structures and word order to create clear contexts for the various abridgments. However, like a poem, this form has the ability to condense what might otherwise be inexpressible into a very small and self-consciously constrained linguistic space. And, also like a poem, a clever text message or tweet unravels, offering layers of meaning and interpretability for the reader. For example, neologisms are quite common in the world of texting. In a recent exchange I had via text, "hiyah" came to mean both a greeting (as in "hi ya") and the sound effect accompanying a karate-chop, a calculated portmanteau, a "hello" that feels like an assault. Granted, this sort of inventiveness is not always rampant in the wild, but the medium certainly offers and encourages this potential.

I've recently experimented in my composition classes with an assignment I call The Twitter Essay, in which students condense an argument with evidentiary support into 140 characters, which they unleash upon a hashtag (or trending topic) in the Twitterverse. Tweets often attempt to convey as much information in as few words as possible. A tweet could be seen, then, not as a paragon of the many potential horrors of student writing, but as a model of writerly concision. In composing their Twitter-essay, I have students proceed through all the steps I would have them take in writing a traditional academic essay, including brainstorming, composing, workshopping, and revising. I also have them consider and research their audience, the Twitter members engaged in discussion around a particular hashtag. Finally, I have them work dynamically with the Tweets of their peers, responding to them on Twitter and close-analyzing them in class. I ask the students to consider their word-choice, use of abbreviation, punctuation, etc. To model the activity for them and to give them a sense for the shape of a Twitter Essay, I compose my instructions for the assignment in exactly 140 characters and post them to Twitter.

For example, in my upper-division writing course, "Queer Rhetorics," I instructed the students to,

> Write an essay about #queer in 140 characters that does real work in the world, not wasting one character. Make something happen with words.

The most interesting response I got to this particular prompt was from a student that had never used Twitter previously:

> #queer #kwear #qu'eer #ckwewr #QuEeR #qr
> #kuere #CWEER #qawear #kwier #cawe're
> #ckuere #cwear #qwere #chweir #q-u-e-e-r

Without even fully understanding the function of hashtags, the student managed to disrupt (or queer) the primary organizational structure of discussions on Twitter. The essay was about #queer in both its content and its form, while also savvily disrupting how we tag ideas within a discourse.

I assigned a similar activity to a group of composition students in a class on "The Posthuman," another topic that lends itself well to experiments with modality and the disruption of language and discourse. I asked these students, again in exactly 140 characters,

> What is the posthuman? Write a Twitter essay on #posthuman in 140 characters that explores or complicates the term. Don't waste a character.

More interesting than the responses I got for that particular question were the ways my students took to using Twitter after doing the activity. Twitter became a space for investigating and troubling language. Outside of any required class activity, one student tweeted,

> #Rhetoric is a means by which humans imbue each other with their ideas. Through the use of ideas, authority, emotions, and logic.

My students also decided to send @replies (or messages tagged for a particular Twitter user) to one of the authors we were studying in class, Steven Shaviro, asking questions about and responding to his work in an attempt to bring him into the conversation we were having in class. This particular author, though himself an avid Tweeter, didn't respond; however, for me, the success of the activity was measured by the hum in the room as the students realized they could use Twitter to communicate directly (and in real-time) with the author of the essay we were discussing that day.

Here is the text I used for the Twitter Essay assignment in my "Monstrous Bodies" course in Fall 2011:

INSTRUCTIONS: THE TWITTER ESSAY

1. Write what I call a "Twitter Essay." In the next few weeks, we will return to some of the overarching questions of the course, so let's use this activity as a way for us to begin formulating the revised thinking we have about monstrosity, the human, horror, etc. Here are the instructions:

> What is a monster? Answer in a Twitter essay of exactly 140 characters using #twitteressay. Play, innovate, incite. Don't waste a character.

(The instructions above are *exactly* 140 characters, so this gives you a sense for how much space you have to work with.) Post your essay on Twitter. The only rule is that you must include the hashtag "#twitteressay" somewhere in your Tweet. You can add additional hashtags or links, but you can only write one

Tweet and it must be *exactly* 140 characters. Feel free to address any aspect of monstrosity. (No need to use our course hashtag, #monstersclass, unless it makes specific sense for you to include it.) You can offer a revised definition of the word "monster" or narrow in on a more specific topic. Spend time carefully composing, making sure every character of your tweet is necessary and meaningful. As you work, think also about the components of a traditional essay: a hook, an argument, supporting evidence, etc. While you can take creative license in how you interpret the word "essay," you should at least be able to make an argument (if pressed) for how your Tweet functions as an essay.

2. Now, peer review. Search #twitteressay on Twitter to see all of the Twitter Essay tweets. Respond to (and, perhaps, retweet) at least two of the ones you find. In your response, analyze the choices the author made and/or offer additional thoughts. Include the author's handle and our course hashtag "#monstersclass" somewhere in your tweet. So, for example, if I were peer reviewing my own instructions:

> @Jessifer's use of "incite" in the #TwitterEssay is unusual juxtaposed with "play." Incite often has negative connotations. #MonstersClass

(Note that the peer review tweet does not have to be *exactly* 140 characters.)

Gary Small writes, in *iBrain: Surviving the Technological Alteration of the Modern Mind*, "The current explosion of digital technology not only is changing the way we live and communicate but is rapidly and profoundly altering our brains . . . Because of the current technological revolution, our brains are evolving right now — at a speed like never before." David Crystal concludes his book on texting in a similar way, "Some people dislike texting. Some are bemused by it. Some love it. I am fascinated by it, for it is the latest manifestation of the human ability to be linguistically creative and to adapt language to suit the demands of diverse settings. In texting we are seeing, in a small way, language in evolution" (175).

Small and Crystal locate the evolution they each describe in different places. For Small, it is our brains themselves that are evolving, whereas for Crystal, it is language doing the evolving, as though words are somehow distinct from the people uttering them. Both highlight the way that learning and language are defiantly dynamic processes. The perversion of language in a text-message or tweet has both use value and intrinsic value. There is both the end result of concision and the fun to be had in attaining it. There is both the undoing of language for the purpose of making meaning and the undoing of language for its own sake, calling attention to the fundamental oddity of its rules and structure.

DIGITAL WRITING UPRISING

SEAN MICHAEL MORRIS

The intellectual is still only an incompletely transformed writer.

~ Roland Barthes, *Writing Degree Zero*

There could be many epigraphs hailing a discussion of digital writing, many pithy observations about its nature, becoming, qualities, mysteries, dilemmas. From Oscar Wilde: "A writer is someone who has taught his mind to misbehave." Virginia Woolf: "We are nauseated by the sight of trivial personalities decomposing in the eternity of print." Gertrude Stein: "They thought they were welcome and it did not make any difference." All these from writers who were writing long before digital writing was good breakfast conversation. Yes, epigraphs are easy.

First sentences, on the other hand, are hard. Here are a few:

- Digital writing is a rebellion.
- Today there is no value to our writing except as it is made useful.
- Essays quake and tremble at the digital.

The problem with first sentences is that they are either alluring and declarative, or simply declarative. They set the stage for the discussion to follow. "Coursera is silly." "Teaching is a moral act." "But, you may say, we asked you to speak about women and fiction — what, has that got to do with a room of one's own?" And, of course, "Call me Ishmael." Good first sentences prompt us to perk up our ears. We read a good first sentence, the lights go down, the music starts, and we look around for our popcorn and candy. First sentences allow us to predict what the language that follows will do. Peeking at the roadmap, we know our destination, at least implicitly. And that's a problem.

Because digital writing provides no road map. At least not yet. Where it goes, what it does, how it lives when we're not watching is something we cannot foretell. First sentences, then, fall flat. I may write one (I've written several here), but what becomes of the story I set out to tell once I state, question, or exclaim my presumed final thought is something I can't predetermine.

As a self-proclaimed Internet non-user (a proclamation that elicits hoots and howls from my friends), the allure of digital writing for me does not lie in its medium; instead, I'm tantalized by the proposition that digital writing is action. Not that the writing inspires action, or comes out of action, or responds to action. But that the words themselves are active. They move, slither, creep, sprint, and outpace us. Digital words have lives of their own. We may write them, birth them ourselves, but without any compunction or notice, they enact themselves in ways we can't predict. And this is because digital writing is communal writing.

In his article, "Organic Writing and Digital Media: Seeds and Organs", Pete Rorabaugh says that the "Growth [of ideas or compositions] is determined by the encouragement and critique of the community." Note that it is not "affected" nor "influenced" by the community. No, the growth of ideas is *determined* by the community. What gets said is inevitably communal. We create the choir as we preach, and the choir creates us. Pete is talking about the compositional process of a piece of writing, within and without the classroom; but if we take digital writing out of the academic, intellectual environment, we discover an organic quality by which natural hybridization takes place — seeds that beget seeds. Living text so dynamic that it defies our first-sentence hopes for organized paragraphs, supporting proofs, and tidy conclusions.

And so when I say digital writing is always communal, I do not mean it is always so by consent. As our writing practices become more and more digital, we discover that immense collaboration is possible, and we create meaningful networks using social media tools that help us steer that collaboration, monitor it, make it purposeful. But it's communities we don't subscribe to, those we're unaware of, who will be the ones to come upon the wreckage of our work, turning our treatises into trifles, our essays into dross.

Essays quake and tremble at the digital. They weep in awe and fascination. And they throw themselves into the abyss. As authors, we go unsuspecting about the Internet, never realizing that our words have lives of their own, that they gallivant about in the wired ether the way that Whos do — living, dying, decomposing, resurrecting. We try to impose sequence and structure on a medium more familiar with non sequitur, and what we get back is revolt. Digital writing is a rebellion. An uprising against our sense and sensibility. Différance. The digital texts we create have a sentience beyond sentences. What we think we're doing is not what we're doing. We're flapping our wings in Tokyo.

Academic writing, intellectual writing — this writing right here — cannot know how it will be excerpted, repurposed, discovered, reimagined, plagiarized, undone. Undone by human author or by computer. Discovered through random Google search, corrupted by code, made poetic by an accident of electronic interference. Therefore our reflections upon digital writing are always already ironic. Nevertheless, Kenneth Goldsmith offers in his book, *Uncreative Writing*, that words "very well might not only be written to be read, but rather to be shared, moved, and manipulated, sometimes by humans, more often by machines, providing us with an extraordinary opportunity to reconsider what writing is and to define new roles for the writer" (15). Through digital writing we form a new relationship to our words: text becomes functional.

There is no value to our writing except as it is made useful. If what we say is only made valuable by what readers say with what we say — how what we say is reconstructed, not just interpreted, how it is rebuilt, re-fabricated, repurposed — then we must write accordingly. This is third-order thinking: we are no longer involved in the wave of language, but neither are we responding to language now, and instead we are allowing meaning to come from meaninglessness. "While a writer today is challenged by having to 'go up' against a proliferation of words and compete for attention," Goldsmith says, "she can use this proliferation in unexpected ways to create works that are as expressive and meaningful as works constructed in more traditional ways." Our writing is in a state where every text begins at meaninglessness, until it finds harbor and use elsewhere, becoming meaningful only by association.

Digital writing is both compiled and original. The thoughts of the writers of words today lie between the words and the way they've been assembled. But the real novelty of digital writing comes when words are repurposed, when they are reflown, for that is when we begin to detect multiple intentions and, like archaeologists, discover meaning lying below meaning. Our texts the many layers of Troy.

And so we come upon a need to say what we want to say, and not to be contracted 'round our ideas within the death of our form. We are no longer responders to History, no longer makers of Literature. We are the writers of partially-realized ideas *and* their rewriters.

THE PEDAGOGIES OF READING AND NOT READING

JESSE STOMMEL

There is more than one way not to read, the most radical of which is not to open a book at all.

~ Pierre Bayard, *How to Talk About Books You Haven't Read*

Not reading is serious scholarly business. It is a crucial part of the work of critics, students, teachers, and reviewers. Pierre Bayard writes that not reading constitutes "our primary way of relating to books. We must not forget that even a prodigious reader never has access to more than an infinitesimal fraction of the books that exist." Stephen Ramsay writes similarly in "The Hermeneutics of Screwing Around; or What You Do with a Million Books," "The world is vast. Art is long. What else can we do but survey the field, introduce a topic, plant a seed."

Prepared is best, but unprepared is always better than overprepared. This is what I believe about preparing for class, about analysis, about reading. What's important is that we make careful decisions about how best to prepare for the act of learning. It is equally important, though, to leave gaps in that preparation for what is unexpected and uncertain. The best books, fiction or non-fiction, as I write in "Toward an Interactive Criticism: House of Leaves as Haptic Interface," "hit me sidelong when I least expect it. They bubble to the surface at inopportune moments." Reading feels sometimes like eating. But more often like the murmur of hunger just before eating.

When I read, I'm not sure what room I'm in. Increasingly, I read online and forget I'm in any room at all. I'm often reading more than one thing at a time, shuffling between browser windows. The room around me — with its dog to be fed and dear people to be listened to — becomes somewhere else entirely. An endless hallway where things pass by me and half-heard questions get added to the queue in my brain. And the stacks of books I've not yet read, the ones that beckon from so many rooms, are as important to me and my learning as the stacks of finished ones. Each of them is a decision I've made, and I've spent much of my academic life deciding not to read. I've been an English major from B.A. to M.A. to Ph.D., and I've read surprisingly few books copiously from cover to cover. Reading for me has always been more akin to a series of willful cursory glances. And my not reading has been intensely active. It has included talking, researching, writing, making, teaching, wondering, holding, glancing, flipping, filming, watching, etc.

As a teacher, I try to encourage students to be honest about how much they read, what that reading looks like, when they stop reading, when they start again, etc. Most importantly, I ask *why*. It's often as interesting to know why we put a book down, as it is to know why we pick one up — to examine our looking away and to examine our compulsion to avoid thinking about or theorizing that looking away. I don't actively discourage students from reading, but I also do not police their reading. If they're having trouble, I talk to them about reading strategies (which often involve skimming or thoughtful skipping). I never assume students aren't reading because of laziness. I always assume their reasons are as complex as my own. And I never work to fill the gaps of their not reading with shame. Like teaching and learning, reading cannot be compulsory.

Reading is an encounter. When they're about to read a more challenging text like *House of Leaves*, *Moby Dick*, or *Mrs. Dalloway*, I tell students that finishing should not be the goal. I would argue this is how *these particular* books are meant to be read, but also how *any* book is meant to be read, as an act of volition. I've taught Mark Z. Danielewski's *House of Leaves* twice and presented on it twice, but I've never finished the book. It would be easy for me to excuse myself critically by saying that the book, by its nature, can never be finished. But by that definition *and by any definition*, I haven't finished the book. I estimate that I've read about 40% of the words of the book, looked at 60% of the pages, and have read less than half of 1% of the marginalia the book has produced online.

Reading is not an accomplishment I take to the text. It's a dialogue, something I do to the text and something the text does to me. When I take a book into a classroom, reading and analysis become encounters I have together with a group of students. It is valuable to the encounter to have students in the room that haven't even cracked the book, even some arriving to the discussion having never felt the weight of it in their hands. For analysis, arrival and exactly not finishing is the goal, or at least a crucial part of it. Learning is a series of constant arrivals. And we should be just as willing to talk about and theorize our non-arrivals.

This is the exact sort of work I hope to inspire here — an *interactive criticism* that considers not only how our work engages a text but also the complicated ways that a text engages (and sometimes disengages) us. Interactive criticism: 1) recognizes that media is haptic and that we engage even seemingly intangible media in a visceral way; 2) is an encounter with a text in which we do something to the text and the text does something to us; 3) acknowledges that looking away and theorizing that looking away is a critical gesture; 4) is always unfinished, the start to a conversation not a reservoir. Roland Barthes calls this "applied reading." Laura U. Marks calls this "haptic criticism," a kind of reading that "presses up to the object and takes its shape."

I've spent more time not reading *House of Leaves* than I've spent reading other books. The same is true of *Moby Dick* and *Mrs. Dalloway,* which I've taught multiple times but "finished" only once. These books haunts me — hit me sidelong when I least expect it.

They bubble to the surface at inopportune moments. And there are holes in these texts I haven't yet fallen into. Holes in them I probably never will fall into.

This is my work, increasingly — to encourage students and other teachers to recognize that there is no genuine turn to a text that doesn't include both not knowing and not wanting to know as potential outcomes. There is no reading, analysis, or teaching that doesn't involve awe at the space in the text we haven't yet seen. For this reason, as a teacher, I sometimes even avoid reading myself as a tactical advantage, a way of knowing the text better through my own curiosity and surprise — a way of seeing the text better and more poignantly by looking away.

What I see when I'm not looking at the text are tangents, small cuts across its surface where leakage occurs. This is the part of the text I feel most viscerally, the part I fail to ever read, because my body stops me—because the words are difficult, sharp, or even empty. Sometimes, I'm not sure why I don't read. This too should be theorized. And recognized as part — and not a negative part — of what it is to learn. Pierre Bayard writes, "The key, in the end, is to reveal to students what is truly essential: the world of their own creation." Ultimately, pedagogy is less about required reading and more about copious piles of half-finished books and the stuff we build around them.

QUEEQUEG'S COFFIN: A SERMON FOR THE DIGITAL HUMAN

SEAN MICHAEL MORRIS

How I long for a time when text ended at the page. When it didn't follow. Me. Through the streets and the hallways and under the blankets of my bed.

~ Anonymous

The digital has breached the screen. Text fails to tell whole stories. We can no longer accept the division between our lived experiences and the texts we produce. Instead, the two now copulate — unfamiliar but desperate lovers — to create versions of stories that are both entirely not lived and only ever real.

Storytelling has changed. Stories are no longer told to audiences, but by audiences. And this goes way beyond collaboration. It's dissemination. It's the question Anna Smith asks in "Your Voice in Mine," "How can I hear my own voice unless it bounces off of yours?" It's a massive game of "telephone" played every day by every connected person in the world, reinterpreted and remixed, shared appropriately and inappropriately, NSFW and rated-T-for-teen, with every passage from one mouth to the next ear changing the message in sometimes imperceptible ways. This is Miley Cyrus's world now. We are all in her book. If we find that appalling, we shouldn't. Because as much as we are her audience, so too we are her authors. We make what we hear, we say what we're told, and we improvise endings, outcomes, characters, and love affairs in the time we have between red light and green.

You are what you write; and what you read, you write. You are the consumer and producer simultaneously, making the news by tweeting the news as you read it. The boundary between reading and writing has shifted. Editing is no longer enough to keep the leviathan under. Ratings, SafeSearch, and follower-blocking does nothing to keep the stories at bay. The digital will never echo the care you take with it. It's just around the corner always. The corner you'll turn. The corner you'll always turn.

We are at our most laughable when we imagine we have control over text. When we do that, we are twice foolish. Text is not what needs taming; it is the whole of the story which has slipped our grasp. We reach to amend our words, our phrases, our first-person present-tense; but in doing that, we overlook that form itself lies exposed. Genre is an aged lion, run down by his awful, lifelong predation upon authors who, rather than holding the whip, obeyed the tooth and claw to avoid an untimely censure. No longer able to discourage forays upon his territory, now genre falls prey in the open field. He was sleeping when the digital came. And we are he, standing upon the African veldt, wondering what's become of our invention.

The writing of academics is today among the most risible, for our genre has expired. Our own fierce, tamed beast has died the way all the lions have perished. The opportunity for a new digital scholarship has emerged, but it requires a determination and risk that writing has not demanded of us since the dawn of the university. Now to write as academics are accustomed is to copy by hand in the age of the printing press. Speed, movement, alteration, collaboration (in the moment, sirs, not in offices and coffee shops, but in the digital), these have killed the academic genre. The digital is personable, unique and individual. The cloning done in the labs of the academy fails to embrace the thriving, thrashing, teeming world of digital language, symbol, and sign. The lobotomized salmon does not spawn. Not in these waters.

And so there must be a change — in degree, in kind, in the hides we wear — if writing is to remain productive. To which I myself respond, "I've read my Derrida. You're saying what he's already said." Which would be true enough, but now the very hegemony of the page upon which Derrida wrote has ended. Dreaming there is a center does not make it so. Imagining ourselves the conquerers of a landscape wild and torn will not win us the prize. "Think, think of your whale-boat, stoven and sunk! Beware of the horrible tail!" The more we grasp at control of the words we disperse, the greater our folly. And this is why we can no longer accept the division between our lived experiences and the texts we produce. Do we pepper our conversations with citation? Do we not use contractions when we speak? Do we not all have holes in our socks?

The life an academic leads is not a life of genre, but a life of fear and mystery, a life of dread and discovery, insolence and compassion. But what of that drips into her writing?

It is the fiction writers, and the poets, and the manuscript illuminators, and the tellers of their own stories who may survive upon the digital writing landscape. Because it is they who remember: Writing is invented as it's done. The very best writers have never had a lesson. They do not know their grammars, their *see-spot-run*. They know the melodies of nursery rhymes and the musical language of fairy tales, and ghost stories improvised around a fire. Improvisation is key to writing in the digital. If you are not prepared to make it up as you go along, then you belong to a mustier party, where the cheese is old and the wine has breathed its last. Improvisation is key because play is the mode of digital writing.

Getrude Stein says in *Tender Buttons*, "Act so that there is no use in a centre. A wide action is not a width. A preparation is given to the ones preparing. They do not eat who mention silver and sweet. There was an occupation."

Kenneth Goldsmith responds, "words today are cheap and infinitely produced, they are detritus, signifying little, meaning less ... The blizzard of language is amnesia inducing; these are not words to be remembered." (*Uncreative Writing*)

Once, speech was irreversible, but today, it is exactly reversible. Erasure as common as speaking. So much so, that we can now consider the act of deletion a part of the act of writing. "The best-performing writers with the highest grades were massively more likely to use the backspace key," Clive Thompson notes. But erasure does not only happen in the mid-stream, mid-sentence edit made possible by word processing softwares, but afterward — after publishing, after upload, after dissemination. So that even that which has been heard and seen can be unheard and unseen. Relics may float, disembodied from their original textual and narrative relationships, bits and pieces of pages that remain cached somewhere else, but the original can be gotten rid of. And so when we write, we must consider we are writing in fragments and deletions. Self-conscious Sapphos, all. Constructing the de Milo with, but also without, her arms.

All this because the medium of our writing is impenetrable to us. Even if we are coders, even if we host our own sites and move image, music, text where we like, our efforts are the same as sailing the Pequod upon the world's seas. We cannot know when what storm will hit, we cannot know when we'll encounter the *Jeroboam*. The ocean has a will of its own, and so the digital, and so the texts we make and offer out to the waves.

What's the answer? How do we write? We write by admitting that our lives and our words are entwined. We make this that, that this, all things all things. And so I stare into my computer and I type these words, knowing one day they shall be divided like pennies, some of them erased, even as my fingers age and my bones grow more brittle. The screen no longer separates me from what I write. There it is, floating soft and dirge-like, but there it shall not remain.

DIGITAL HUMANITIES IS ABOUT BREAKING STUFF

JESSE STOMMEL

Many have argued that the digital humanities is about building stuff and sharing stuff — that the digital humanities reframes the work we do in the humanities as less consumptive and more curatorial, less solitary and more collaborative. I maintain, though, that the humanities have always been intensely interactive, an engaged dance between the text on a page and the ideas in our brains. The humanities have also always been intensely social, a vibrant ecosystem of shared, reworked, and retold stories. The margins of books as a vast network of playgrounds.

The digital brings different playgrounds and new kinds of interaction, and we must incessantly ask questions of it, disturbing the edge upon which we find ourselves so precariously perched. And what the digital *asks of us* is that every assumption we have be turned on its head. The digital humanities asks us to pervert our reading practices — to read backwards, as well as forwards, to stubbornly not read, and to rethink how we approach learning in the digital age.

In fact, the course itself is one of the central texts we must consider, a collection of stories about reading and writing that can be actively hacked and remixed. Sean Michael Morris writes in "Courses, Composition, Hybridity," "A course today is an act of composition," an active present participle and not a static container. This is more and more true of courses that live even partially online, demanding we thoughtfully examine the digital as a frame, while recognizing that the digital does not supersede and can never unseat the work we do in the world. In "The New Learning is Ancient," Kathi Inman Berens writes, "It doesn't matter to me if my classroom is a little rectangle in a building or a little rectangle above my keyboard. Doors are rectangles; rectangles are portals. We walk through." This is where learning happens, at the breaking point of its various containers. The semester is arbitrary. The course is breached. Canons must yield.

This is true just as well of the literary texts we analyze (and ask students to analyze) with digital tools. In the syllabus for a recent undergraduate seminar in the digital humanities, I pose the following questions:

> How is literature and our reading of it being changed by computers? What influence does the container for a text have on its content? To what degree does immersion in a text depend upon the physicality of its interface? How are evolving technologies (like the iPad) helping to enliven (or disengage us from) the materiality of literary texts?

Literature, film, and other media are changing, and the way we interact with them is also changing. As we imagine a digital approach to the humanities, we must look back even as we look forward, considering what media has become while we simultaneously examine the *hows* and *whys* of its becoming. We once watched film only in a darkened theater without the distraction of other external physical stimuli. Now, increasingly, we watch film on hand-held digital devices, many with touch screens that allow more and more interaction with the content. Our apparatuses for media-consumption juxtapose digital media, literature, and film: Now, we watch Ridley Scott's *Alien* in a window alongside *Twitter* and *Facebook*. Film no longer exists as a medium distinct from these other media.

The same is true of new modes of reading. Digital texts invite (or *allow*) us to do other things with our eyes, brains, and bodies while we experience them. As I write this, I have 9 windows open on my computer, each vying for my attention. Some of these windows have several frames in further competition. Advertisements. E-mail. Documents. Widgets. Social-networking tools. Chat interfaces. Each layer has an effect on how I engage the digital text. In spite of all these layers, I don't think we experience a *decreased* attention; rather, the digital text demands a different sort of attention. Even as my direct engagement is challenged, my brain is offered more fuel for making connections and associative leaps. A proactive approach to online and digital pedagogy asks us to put these associative leaps to work. So, *Twitter* and *Facebook* may be a distraction, but that distraction can be harnessed for good pedagogy.

Social media can also function as a potential site of resistance, a leveled playing field, a harbinger for another kind of engagement. The keenest analysis in the digital humanities is born of distraction and revels in tangents. The holy grail of this work is not the thesis but the fissure.

Breaking Stuff as an Act of Literary Criticism

The digital humanities is about breaking stuff. Especially at the undergraduate level, this is the work of the digital humanities that most needs doing. In "Notes Towards a Deformed Humanities," Mark Sample proposes "what is broken and twisted is also beautiful, and a bearer of knowledge. The Deformed Humanities is an origami crane — a piece of paper contorted into an object of startling insight and beauty." And, by the end of a class, if it's successful, this is what becomes of the syllabus, the texts, the assignments, and us. Sample continues, "every fact is a fad and print is a prison. Instructors are insurgents and introductions are invasions." In this way, all of my courses work to violently dismantle fact and print, instructors and introductions, and I revel together (and part and parcel) with students in both discovery and uncertainty.

In my undergraduate digital humanities course, the first assignment has students break something as an act of literary criticism. Specifically, I ask them to take the words from a poem by Emily Dickinson, "There's a certain slant of light," and rearrange them into something else. They use any or all of the words that appear in the poem as many or as few times as they want. What they build takes any shape: text, image, video, a poem, a pile, sense-making or otherwise.

Dickinson's poem is itself about troubling interpretation, about skewed perspective, and about frustrating the supposed neat-and-tidy signifying powers of language: "We can find no scar, / But internal difference / Where the meanings are."

In his response to the assignment, Timothy Merritt used the iPad app Simple Mind to create a mind map of his encounter with the poem.

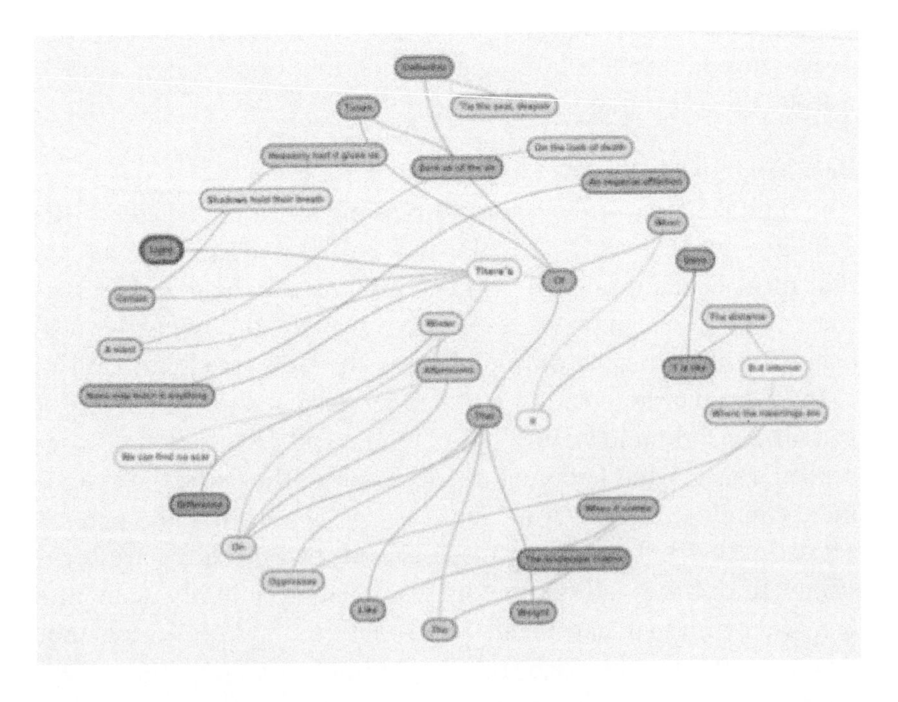

Having no clear beginning nor end, Tim's work asks the reader to consider the linearity of poetry, responding directly to Dickinson's call to read the poem (all poems) at "a certain slant." In her work, Rachel Blume plays with the metaphorical density of Dickinson's words, re-arranging them into a single haiku:

> Winter Oppresses
> Shadows the landscape like death
> Tis heavenly when it goes

Rachel constructed her poem by meditating carefully on the weight of each of Dickinson's syllables — both the ones she included in her haiku and the ones she left out. Finally, Lans Nelson Pacifico used TypeDrawing for the iPad to literally paint with words, turning Emily Dickinson's poem into the raw material for her own work, "A Certain Slant of Light, Typographically Speaking."

Even more compelling than the striking and solemn work itself are Lans's documents and videos describing the various layers of her process. She shows the progression of her work from annotations through rough notes, several sketches, coloring, and the final step in which she signed her name to the work in gold across the sky. The clarity of the layering of Dickinson's words in Lans's re-creation illustrates her understanding of the density of Dickinson's language. What we see in her account are the ways our work within the digital humanities becomes an archeological dig, a nibbling at the stratum of the digital to deconstruct what is tacit and to discover what is voraciously humane.

HYBRID PEDAGOGY

The promise of digital publishing is one that begins with the entrance of the written, and one that concludes with distribution, reuse, revision, remixing — and finally, redistribution.

WHAT IS HYBRID PEDAGOGY?

JESSE STOMMEL

In a broad sense, my own scholarly work is about the (sometimes wondrous, sometimes horrifying) relationship between bodies and technology. As our flesh is made intangible in the digital age, we find ourselves increasingly interested in bodies, dead and otherwise — in cadavers, crime scenes, bodily mutilation, and torture — in shows like *Six Feet Under* and *The Walking Dead,* films like *Saw,* video games like *Gears of War,* and novels like Cormac McCarthy's *The Road.* This is, by no means, a new-found fascination, but reflects a far more universal fear: a fear Shakespeare explores in *Hamlet,* beginning with the ominous words "Who's there?"; a fear Mary Shelley explores in *Frankenstein,* wondering about identity and physicality from the first phrase, "I am by birth"; and a fear Herman Melville explores in "The Tartarus of Maids," where he describes "blank-looking girls" working in a paper factory, slaves to a new-fangled machine. Each author wonders what constitutes a self, of what sort of matter are we made, what it is to be a body, to be human. Each wonders where our (technological and political) machines end and we begin.

The questions of my pedagogical work are inextricably bound to the questions of my literary scholarship. My hypothesis is that all learning is necessarily hybrid. In classroom-based pedagogy, it is important to engage the digital selves of our students. And, in online pedagogy, it is equally important to engage their physical selves. With digital pedagogy and online education, our challenge is not to merely replace (or offer substitutes for) face-to-face instruction, but to find new and innovative ways to engage students in the practice of learning.

At a philosophical level, my own thinking about hybridity is influenced, in part, by the heated discussion of hybridity among postcolonial theorists. In "The Commitment to Theory," a chapter from *The Location of Culture*, Homi Bhabha writes,

> The language of critique is effective because . . . it overcomes the given grounds of opposition and opens up a space of translation: a place of hybridity, figuratively speaking, where the construction of a political object that is new, neither the one nor the other, properly alienates our political expectations, and changes, as it must, the very forms of our recognition of the moment of politics.

Bhabha's use of the word "moment" is important here, because it calls attention to the urgency and suspense inherent in the sort of transformation he describes.

In "A Cyborg Manifesto," Donna Haraway makes an explicit connection between postcolonial theory and what she describes as the colonizing work of machines. She writes, "by the late twentieth century, our time, a mythic time, we are all chimeras, theorized and fabricated hybrids of machine and organism, in short, we are cyborgs." I begin by discussing these notions of hybridity because there is an important way in which our roles as teachers and learners are bound up in who we are as people (including our life experience, cultural background, race, gender, and sexuality). In a recent discussion I had on Twitter, I argued for the importance of us being vulnerable as teachers by risking failure and modeling that vulnerability in our interactions with students. For me, though, there's a delicate balance between being my performed, teacher-y self and being this more honest, vulnerable self. The same is true for myself as a student. This is just one of the many ways that I am hybrid.

In the book *Hybridity*, Marwan M. Kraidy writes, "hybridity has proven a useful concept to describe multipurpose electronic gadgets, designer agricultural seeds, environment-friendly cars with dual combustion and electrical engines, companies that blend American and Japanese management practices, multiracial people, dual citizens, and postcolonial cultures." For Kraidy, and for me, the term is powerful exactly because it resists easy signification.

At its most basic level, the term "hybrid," as I'm using it here, refers to learning that happens both in a classroom (or other physical space) and online. In this respect, hybrid does overlap with another concept that is often used synonymously: blended. I would like to make some careful distinctions between these two terms. Blended learning describes a process or practice; hybrid pedagogy is a methodological approach that helps define a series of varied processes and practices. (Blended learning is tactical, whereas hybrid pedagogy is strategic.) When people talk about "blended learning," they are usually referring to the *place* where learning happens, a combination of the classroom and online. The word "hybrid" has deeper resonances, suggesting not just that the *place* of learning is changed but that a hybrid pedagogy fundamentally rethinks our *conception of place*. So, hybrid pedagogy does not just describe an easy mixing of on-ground and online learning, but is about bringing the sorts of learning that happen in a physical place and the sorts of learning that happen in a virtual place into a more engaged and dynamic conversation.

The "hybrid" in *Hybrid Pedagogy*, though, does not just refer to hybrid learning. Our goal with this project is, rather, to think holistically about the various hybridities of the modern pedagogue, to think about how we live our real/digital lives in both academic and extra-academic spaces. *Hybrid Pedagogy*, then, is about the intersections of:

Physical Learning Space / Virtual Learning Space
Academic Space / Extra-academic Space
On-ground Classrooms / Online Classrooms
Permanent Faculty / Contingent Faculty
Institutional Education / Informal Education
Garden-walled Academia / Open Education

Scholars / Teachers
Academic Product / Learning Process
Disciplinarity / Interdisciplinarity
Performed (School-y) Selves / Real (Vulnerable) Selves
Teacher, Student, Scholar / Collaborative Communities
Learning in Schools / Learning in the World
Analog Pedagogy / Digital Pedagogy
Use of Tools / Critical Engagement with Tools
Machine and Machine-like Interaction / Human Interaction
Passive Learning / Experiential Learning
Teaching and Learning / Critical Pedagogy

Each of these binaries is currently being challenged by the evolution of educational technology. Our goal is to think critically about both sides of each binary (and not to neatly privilege either) toward the (perhaps distant) goal of a more thorough deconstruction of our pedagogies. Hybridity is about the moment of play, in which the two sides of the binaries begin to dance around (and through) one another before landing in some new configuration. Thus, this chapter (and the work of *Hybrid Pedagogy*) is not just about what will become of us in the wake of technological and cultural transformation, but also (and perhaps more predominantly) about the process of becoming itself.

PUBLISHING AS PEDAGOGY

JESSE STOMMEL

The idea for the name of *Hybrid Pedagogy* came from a job talk I gave in October 2011. The thesis of that talk now sits on the journal's homepage: "All learning is necessarily hybrid." The line is inspired by a blog post from February 2010, in which I write: "The teacher 2.0 must shift the focus from individual learners to the community of learners, drawing new boundaries that reflect a much larger hybrid classroom." This sentence also describes the work of new-form academic publishing, which draws new boundaries by upsetting the distinction between scholarship and teaching — between the work we do in journals and the work we do in classrooms.

When Pete Rorabaugh and I began discussing what would become *Hybrid Pedagogy* in early 2011, we wondered if what we were describing was a "journal" or something else entirely. At various points, we flirted with calling the project a "symposium," "colloquium," "collective," or "school." It was clear to us, from the start, that what we were creating was not a traditional academic publication. What we wanted to build was a network, a community for engaging a discussion of digital pedagogy, critical pedagogy, open education, and online learning. At the same time, we wanted to build a collection of resources to help facilitate conversations within that community.

We worked from the start to develop the journal openly, gathering together an advisory board that had virtual "meetings" on the web via the discussion forum on the site. The goal was to interrogate academic publishing practices by making them transparent — to lay bare our process while it was in formation. We published articles about peer-review before we had established our own peer-review process, inviting feedback and commentary. We crowd-sourced the majority of our initial decisions, down to the layout and design of the site.

Hybrid Pedagogy has become a publication that combines the best aspects of an open-access journal with the best aspects of a group blog (timeliness, a nimble publishing schedule, and direct engagement with readers). Through the articles we've published and events we've hosted (like MOOC MOOC and regular #digped chats), we've brought together higher education teachers, K-12 teachers, the open education community, students, and lifelong learners. We've worked to disrupt the conventions of academic publishing, while still maintaining a careful attention to detail, context, and critical engagement.

Based on input from our initial advisory board, we've developed what we call "collaborative peer review," in which editors engage directly with authors to revise and develop articles, followed by post-publication peer review. Once an article is accepted for review, we partner a new author with an editorial board member (myself, Pete, Sean, and Robin Wharton) and a guest editor (usually someone that has already published an article in the journal). Editorial work is done both asynchronously and synchronously in a Google Doc that evolves through an open dialogue between author and editors.

We fully expect our process will continue to evolve. Kathleen Fitzpatrick argues, "Peer review is extremely important — I want to acknowledge that right up front — but it threatens to become the axle around which all conversations about the future of publishing get wrapped." Going forward, I think it's vital that every academic publication continuously (and even publicly) interrogates its own practices. Given how rapidly education is changing, we need to keep pushing ourselves to innovate — to learn from our mistakes — and to stay nimble in our approaches. We need to actively overturn the existing hierarchies and power dynamics that fuel unethical practices like blind peer-review, the proliferation of overpriced and barely read monographs, closed-access publishing, and business models that rely insidiously on the free labor of contingent faculty.

I'm glad Pete and I ultimately decided to describe *Hybrid Pedagogy* as a "journal," exactly because this designation allows us to push on the boundaries of what, when, and how academic work gets published. The notion of an "academic journal" needs dismantling and reimagining. This isn't to say that we shouldn't continue to have traditional academic journals, but that we need to considerably broaden the landscape to make way for dynamic collaboration, new media, and participatory culture.

Since launching *Hybrid Pedagogy* in January 2012, we've published 94 articles by 17 authors. (As of this publication, there are nearly 500 articles by approximately 200 authors). The majority of these have been peer-reviewed by at least two reviewers (all but the earliest articles and #digped announcements). We've worked especially hard to encourage collaboration; 21 of the 94 articles we've published were written by two or more authors, including one article by five authors, one article by twelve authors, and one article by hundreds of authors. Articles have covered a wide range of topics, from MOOCs to digital writing, from intellectual property to personal learning networks.

Shortly after we launched *Hybrid Pedagogy*, Pete and I wrote "The Four Noble Virtues of Digital Media Citation," an article about the changing nature of citation in the digital age — an article in which we made nods to the various sources for our work on the journal. In that article, we write, "In digital space, everything we do is networked. Real thinking doesn't (and can't) happen in a vacuum. Our teaching practices and scholarship don't just burst forth miraculously from our skulls. The digital academic community is driven by citation, generosity, connection, and collaboration." I believe generosity is what will drive the future of digital publishing.

#

Since I first started teaching in 2001, I've spoken the words almost like a mantra, "my scholarship and teaching are married." And it isn't just that the academic writing I do is influenced by the work I do in the classroom, even though I've put some version of this statement in nearly all of the 200ish academic job applications I've submitted. Here it is, right out of my mouth (er, fingers), in the job letter that led to my being hired as an Assistant Professor at Marylhurst University: "My research has considerable influence on my teaching." To speak frankly, this line is bullshit, something I felt pressured to write by colleagues and in a half-dozen academic job search workshops.

And by "bullshit" I don't mean that what I said was false. I mean that the phrasing was disingenuous. Put simply, my research *is* my teaching. For me, the two practices are inextricable from one another. When I was finishing my PhD, I didn't "teach to my dissertation" as so many academics recommend. My dissertation was born out of my teaching, out of interactions I had with students and out of my witnessing countless interactions between students.

It would be an oversimplification, though, to say just that my teaching is a source (or even the primary source) for my published writing. I would go even further than this to say that teaching itself has become, for me, my most important act of writing and publishing. There is a way in which I author myself and my work in the classroom, but I also produce countless tangible artifacts in the service of (or as part of) the act of teaching. The syllabi I publish to the web are an example, living documents that evolve over the term (and hopefully even after the term is over).

I will even go so far as to say that my syllabi are peer-reviewed — not only approved by the various department chairs I've worked for, but also reviewed by the colleagues I share my work with and by the larger scholarly community that use (and sometimes cite) the work I've done. The syllabi I create also evolve through careful work with students (who I consider my closest learning community peers).

The scholarly work I produce in collaboration with students doesn't stop there. I create class projects that have students working closely with each other and with me. In 2011, while teaching multimodal composition at GA Tech (a required course for Freshman), I had classes of 25 students working together to produce a short horror film. One student, Ben Lambeth, chose to continue working on his class's film after the semester was over, and I worked with him as an assistant editor (not as his teacher but as an artistic collaborator). At the same time, I also worked on *GA Tech: It Gets Better*, a documentary film I co-produced with yet another former student, outside any assigned class project.

As I've continued to evolve as a scholar and teacher, I've become more and more concerned with thinking about ways to make what I do in the classroom and what I do in the safe confines of a word-processing window more public. The impetus for my scholarly work and publishing is to do my pedagogy in much larger and more open spaces. I teach because I have to, because it's in my bones. I write because it allows me to teach more and to teach more people.

One way I've worked to bring my teaching and scholarly lives into closer public conversation is to have my CV and Teaching Portfolio exist alongside one another on my personal homepage. I've also begun publishing more about pedagogy and my teaching practices, something I've formalized through *Hybrid Pedagogy*. Finally, I force myself to build my scholarly writing out of the work I do in the classroom and to share my scholarly work in the classroom. This is particularly possible when I've taught writing, where I am able to work with my students as part of (not just facilitator of) a community of writers. It is students in writing classes I've taught, in fact, that I credit for the completion of my dissertation.

It's important for me, as a teacher and scholar, to be open not just with my intellectual and pedagogical products but even more so with my academic process and pedagogical practices. This intention has been the driving force behind my most recent scholarly writing / pedagogical project, *Hybrid Pedagogy*. An open-access networked journal, *Hybrid Pedagogy* creates meaningful connections between discussions of critical pedagogy, digital pedagogy, and online pedagogy. The journal also invites its audience to participate in (and be an integral part of) the peer review process, and thus makes transparent (and interrogates) academic publishing practices. In this way, *Hybrid Pedagogy* is a journal about pedagogy while also taking a pedagogical approach to publishing, by allowing its readers to peek behind the proverbial curtain of the publishing machine. In the wake of rapid changes in publishing, education, and technology, this kind of openness and transparency is becoming less and less an experimental indulgence and more and more a brunt necessity.

COLLABORATIVE PEER REVIEW: GATHERING THE ACADEMY'S ORPHANS

SEAN MICHAEL MORRIS

Revolutionary leaders cannot be falsely generous, nor can they manipulate. Whereas the oppressor elites flourish by trampling the people underfoot, the revolutionary leaders can flourish only in communion with the people.

~ Paulo Freire, *Pedagogy of the Oppressed*

I am the editor of a peer reviewed online journal, and I care little for peer review. I care little for any evaluative, assessment practice. Grades have always been meaningless to me. People who speak about "acceptable" prose versus "unacceptable" prose turn my head like a dog's, hearing the far-off yip of a mutt who doesn't know better. Yet, *Hybrid Pedagogy* employs relentlessly a peer review process with the articles we publish. My resistance to assessment and the journal's insistence on excellence are reconciled in a pedagogy of publishing that seeks to give any author voice, especially marginalized ones who have been shut out of more traditional academic peer review processes.

Hybrid Pedagogy is an experiment in publishing that could be seen as a digital humanities venture, or a playful approach to new form scholarly publishing; and indeed I've talked with Jesse, the journal's innovator, about our trafficking in those terms. But there's something else at work within *Hybrid Pedagogy*. "It was clear to us, from the start," Jesse says in "Publishing as Pedagogy," "that what we were creating was not a traditional academic publication. What we wanted to build was a network, a community for engaging a discussion of digital pedagogy, critical pedagogy, open education, and online learning." And to do this, we worked to develop a novel approach, a pedagogy for discussing pedagogy. Building the journal as a forum necessarily meant working with authors in a more than "thumbs-up or thumbs-down" manner.

This means being open to submissions of all shapes and sizes, from academic to editorial, from research-driven exposition to personal narrative. Good dialogue doesn't discriminate. All voices are welcome; all perspectives are necessary. A journal run by teachers is — or should necessarily be — a classroom. And a journal run by critical pedagogues must work toward "educational movement, guided by passion and principle, to help [writers] develop consciousness of freedom [...] and connect knowledge to power and the ability to take constructive action" (the rascally Henry Giroux in "Lessons to Be Learned from Paulo Freire as Education Is Being Taken Over by the Mega Rich"). In fact, one of the core missions of *Hybrid Pedagogy* has been to act as a bridge, bringing previously isolated conversations freely into the same room.

There can be no thumbs-down in critical pedagogy. There can be no thumbs-down in publishing as discourse. Interestingly, there can also never be a thumbs-up. Discernment is different from judgement, valuation a hair's breadth from evaluation. We offer instead an open hand. Thumbs be damned.

Our editorial process is first and foremost collaborative. When I receive submissions from new authors, my initial consideration is not whether the piece should be published; it's *how can I work with this author to make her work publishable?* I never assume a submission is a final draft; instead, every new article is full of potential — potential that I, our other editors, and the author can explore together. Kathleen Fitzpatrick writes in *Planned Obsolescence: Publishing, Technology, and the Future of the Academy*, "Sometimes the result of these new conversational publishing practices might be productive coauthoring relationships."

Throughout the collaborative peer review process, the author's own feelings about his writing are as important as the opinions of the editors. We in the process are a fellowship, all editors, all writers. A typical review process includes discussion about the overall direction of the piece, its voice, as much as the specifics of its rhetorical strategy. This is done with the author in as cooperative and supportive a way as possible, with an insistence not on academic excellence or perfection of prose, but on deliberate choices, discernment, and a care for the work that goes tirelessly until the piece is complete.

This discussion runs sometimes a week, a month, even three or four months, while editors and writer alike hammer, strop, or carefully scrape away to polish the piece. As Kris Shaffer noted in "A New Way to Do Peer Review," the collaborative peer review process "ensured that my ideas were sound before publication, it made my writing better, and it helped my writing reach a larger audience than I could on my own." I've said many times in correspondence with authors that the goal is to make these articles not only ready for publication, but as good as they can be for their own purposes and life.

Before assuming the role of managing editor at the journal, I had published rarely, and mostly fiction and poetry. As my training is creative writing, I also always believed staunchly in the gatekeeping methodology of the publishing world. One chance, one editor making the decisions. One vote to rule them all. I had never been in this role, nor did I ever expect to be. Now that I am a "gatekeeper," I find that authority requires generosity.

In many ways, I am an orphan of the academy. Beached on the sand at the M.A., employed only ever as an adjunct instructor at two-year colleges, generally looked at askance in the heady company of academics, I am the horse that didn't make the derby. Five years ago, I stepped away, my head sore from the brick walls of credentialing, publishing, and otherwise proving that my little engine, indeed, could.

I left my position in the academy because I was put-off by hoop-crazy bureaucrats, the voicelessness forced on adjuncts, and the too-popular notion that students have to be convinced to want to learn. I believed that not only could classrooms benefit from turning more learning over to students, but that colleges would run better if they listened closely to their troops on the ground. I was sure there was knowledge lost at every turn, simply because no one was listening.

And listening is all.

My project at *Hybrid Pedagogy* is to run a sort of orphanage. To listen for voices that have something to say, but which may not find purchase in traditional academic venues. This is not to say that we'll always publish every article that comes our way. We are yet a journal with a clear ideological and pedagogical bent, and some authors may find more comfortable roost at another journal. But it will not be genre, voice, prestige, research, or other bureaucratic concern that has us turn an author away. Because I believe there is no such thing as writing that cannot improve, a voice that cannot be made strong, so long as a writer is willing to work with us.

The open, collaborative peer review process results in more than mere publication; a community of discourse and practice arises. As Adam Heidebrink wrote after his first *Hybrid Pedagogy* article published,

> The relationship that Hybrid Pedagogy invites us to participate in is not simply means to an end (the publication) but rather initiation into a lively community of educators who are dedicated to creating open-ended dialogues about a wide variety of pedagogical concerns.

Hybrid Pedagogy believes that a commitment to learners and learning is the prime directive of all education, all pedagogy.

People everywhere are educating themselves on the Internet, through MOOCs and other online resources, and in digital communities and networks of all varieties. All this education is taking place all over the place... And yet so many of those trained to teach persist in doing their scholarly work inside the academy, lending their voices only to academic debates and publications. What is needed are rampant teachers, and a rampant education that permeates and infuses itself everywhere.

To foster such a teeming community of teachers requires a pedagogy that stretches beyond the bounds of academic culture, one that is hybrid — both germanely academic, and incessantly human — that encourages vociferous engagement and dialogue, and that offers genuine, productive hospitality.

HYBRID PEDAGOGY, DIGITAL HUMANITIES, AND THE FUTURE OF ACADEMIC PUBLISHING

SEAN MICHAEL MORRIS AND JESSE STOMMEL

Hybrid Pedagogy has been accused of being Pollyanna, our work too blithe and easy, our seriousness not nearly serious enough. Our editors on the tenure track have been reminded to publish with traditional journals, lest their academic work wither under the glare of rigor and double-blind peer review. But there is nothing casual about *Hybrid Pedagogy*, just as there is nothing casual about other digital work. What digital work does is change the landscape of all work. When we write in the digital, our words behave differently; when we broadcast our ideas, the reception re-broadcasts and re-purposes those ideas. Digital publishing, digital writing, digital humanities, digital literacy, digital citizenship — these are not terms à la mode, but rather they are new components of very real human communities, very real human craft. We may approach them with equal part suspicion and exaltation, but approach them we must.

It is not enough to write monographs. It is not enough to publish. Today, scholars must understand what happens when our research is distributed, and we must write, not for rarified audiences, but for unexpected ones. New-form scholarly publishing requires new-form scholarly (digital) writing. Digital academic publishing may on the surface appear as a lateral move from print to screen, but in fact it brings with it new questions about copyright, data analysis, multimodality, privacy, curation, archiving, and how scholarly work finds an audience. The promise of digital publishing is one that begins with the entrance of the written, and one that concludes with distribution, reuse, revision, remixing — and finally, *re*distribution.

Digital publishing is a field worthy of rigorous research and deep discourse. In a post-print environment, for example, social media — Twitter, Facebook, Pinterest, WordPress, or Tumblr — have supplanted the static page as the primary metaphors for how we talk about the dissemination of information. Digitized words have code and algorithms behind them, and are not arrested upon the page; rather they are restive there.

Traditional academic publishing is aimed at a scholarly process that is private and gradual, deliberate and uninterrupted by the memes and news of the day. Digital publishing is public work, packaged and poised for ready distribution. Post-print publishing keeps its focus on moving objects: digital artifacts and networked conversations that can be plumbed at the level of the code behind them, tracked in their progress through the web, or catalogued next to works beside which they would not normally sit. It happens as quickly and as prominently as rumor and gossip, but is rigorous in its play and tenable in its rapidity.

Hybrid Pedagogy models sustainable digital practices that work to represent the variety of tools, platforms, processes, and scholarly voices working in the field of Digital Humanities. But that's the tip of the iceberg: in fact, we are a group of humanists (mostly writing teachers) who run a peer-reviewed digital journal as part of a project that stretches well beyond the digital humanities into educational technology, composition studies, labor advocacy, and critical pedagogy. In truth, we see digital publishing as a form of digital pedagogy as much as a digital humanities project.

We believe that, at its best, digital humanities is the practical application of an experiment — and a deeply political one. At the center of the digital humanities should be an emphasis on individual and collective agency. What stirs at the foundation of

Hybrid Pedagogy is a desire to find in digital scholarship something fundamentally humane. There is a clear and present danger in the way our journal insists on not gatekeeping. It flies in the face of perhaps the most dearly held academic value of all: the hierarchy of reputational control. Our belief is and always has been that seniority, reputation, academic or social capital, should only be used in service to those without them. As a journal, we have *never not made clear* that we were founded in order to make a space for those voices the academy doesn't include.

Our goal is pedagogical: to share models that can be duplicated — and, in the manner of things open source, modified, reconfigured, and reworked — by other digital publishing projects. The journal is an entry point for scholars into a digital community, and for scholarship that is yet chrysalid.

Which is not to say that post-print publishing and digital writing and teaching are entirely novel. Rhetoric and Composition scholars have long investigated the shift from print to digital. The field of Computers and Writing and its companion conference create spaces for dialogue on the ground between those who are teaching, researching, and learning in digital environments. Cheryl E. Ball describes her editorial pedagogy as one that "builds on the recursive and reciprocal nature of professionalization through editing, writing, mentoring, and teaching – student and teacher, author and editor, reader and scholar learn from each other (and the lines between those roles blur in an editorial pedagogy)." More and more, scholars have sought to expound upon the digital within the digital, using the writing environment as both publishing platform and subject matter.

Hybrid Pedagogy provides a platform upon which participants can engage in meta-level thinking about teaching and learning. We focus less on building an archive for the preservation of ideas, and more on building networked communities of inquiry consisting of scholars, pedagogues, alt-academics, post-academics, activists, and students. We aren't interested in fortifying the walls around academic publishing, but rather making important scholarly work open and shareable. Together, our community has helped chart the journal's course, while also helping to imagine new directions for the field of critical digital pedagogy.

In this way, the journal itself, along with all of its articles are products of collaborative peer review. Collaboration is not just part of our review process, but part of our investigation and modeling of the digital humanities experiment. For our purposes, the collaborative process necessitates that every article be more than a reservoir of information. We encourage co-authored and multiple-author submissions; we invite the public into conversation around articles; we link articles directly to their sources, creating a web of influence and dialogue; and we hold Twitter chats (using #digped) which are curated and published as exemplars of critical work in process.

Bonnie Stewart points out in her article "What Counts as Academic Influence Online?": "The work of research that is not legible to others always feels, rhetorically, like lifting stones uphill: constantly establishing premises rather than moving on to the deep exploration of that one particular thing." Thus, one goal of the journal is to offer scholars strategies for making their pedagogical, editorial, and design work legible as scholarship to tenure committees, job search committees, and the discipline as a whole. Kathleen Fitzpatrick argues that "peer review is extremely important [...] but it threatens to become the axle around which all conversations about the future of publishing get wrapped." The notion of the "academic journal" needs to be rigorously hacked. This isn't to say that we should abandon traditional academic journals, but we need to broaden the landscape to make way for marginalized voices, dynamic collaboration, new media, and participatory culture. One of our central goals is to push on the boundaries of what, when, and how academic work gets published.

Our collaborative peer review process is aimed less at intellectual gatekeeping, and more at creating conversations and fostering new thinking about critical and digital pedagogies. Editorial work is done both asynchronously and synchronously in evolving Google Docs. In "Collaborative Peer Review: Gathering the Academy's Orphans," Sean writes,

> A typical review process includes discussion about the overall direction of the piece, its voice, as much as the specifics of its rhetorical strategy. This is done with the author in as cooperative and supportive a way as possible, with an insistence not on academic excellence or perfection of prose, but on deliberate choices, discernment, and a care for the work that goes tirelessly until the piece is complete.

Hybrid Pedagogy itself enacts a hybrid pedagogy. The journal is more than just another online academic journal because it seeks to practice that which it espouses: that all learning is necessarily hybrid. We are concerned as much with the writer as her words, as much with the online as with the on-ground, as much with the person as with the tech, and as much with rigor as with imagination. The journal is a hybrid between a blog and a journal; and our editors reside in a space somewhere between traditional peer-reviewers and educators.

Scholarly research is no longer a solitary activity. Reading, writing, and publishing in the digital must and always already do take place in public, collaborative spaces. This is the great project of the social Internet and an imperative for the digital humanities: to make space for thoughts and ideas — even our most scholarly and esoteric — to be made relevant. The journal's work, then, is less focused on publishing articles as content repositories and more on reimagining scholarship as pedagogical, publishing as a way to create conversations and bridge academic and non-academic communities.

CALL FOR EDITORS

SEAN MICHAEL MORRIS

The place of the editor is not above the writer, but beside. Editors are not meant to correct but to suggest, not to admonish but to inspire, not to coerce but to collaborate.

To write is to enter a unique space of potential. To enter that writerly space as an editor requires that we recognize the fragility of the ecosystem of those words on the page. The first draft is a learning environment, a classroom for writer and reviewer alike — and all drafts are first drafts. No words nor any writer should ever be sacrificed upon the pointed pen of an editor protecting his reputation. The editor's work is to preserve and refine, to shine and polish, not to sanitize, circumcise, or amputate. No words nor any writer should be left outside the gates. The editor need not guard the gate, for there are no gates worth guarding. The miscreant has a voice. The dropout has a voice. The insolent silent one in the back of the room, too, has a voice. The adjunct is a teacher when she writes. The undergrad, the grad student, the alt-ac and the post-ac — all teachers when they speak. The artist is a teacher; the poet, the musician, the anarchist, too.

Every voice is needed within academe, within education. The more we leave out, the less we have to offer. Gatekeeping corrupts — it does not fortify — ethos.

I have written before about the approach I've taken as an editor at *Hybrid Pedagogy*. During my tenure, I have insisted that the journal be a place for any writer with something to say about teaching and learning. The only merit a writer needs is a determination to work their craft upon the page, to listen, to speak, and to reflect. My inclusive approach has been born out of my time teaching Creative Writing and the critical pedagogy that our editors practice. My iron determination to offer authors publication is dogged. I prowl the gates of this journal, I do — but to keep them open, not closed; to invite in rather than keep out.

The more, in our case, does not only mean the merrier — the more is necessary.

In my time with *Hybrid Pedagogy*, I have run into and read many geniuses. Audrey Watters, Jonan Donaldson, Pat Lockley, Kate Bowles, to name just a very few. Bonnie Stewart I also count among that group. She recently posted "Open to Influence: Academic Influence on Twitter," a radical abridgement of the first paper of her thesis. She begins her post with these four sentences:

> I am the sort of person who was born to be elderly and didactic. Deep in my nature lurks the spirit – if not the vocabulary – of a teeny, slightly melancholic sixth cousin of Marcel Proust hankering to wax pensively about the eternal nature of change and What Once Was. Inside my head, it's all Remembrance of Things Past, all the time. Not because I'm nostalgic – je ne regrette rien! – but because this appears, even at midlife, to be my only wayfinding strategy; reflective recall is how I make sense of the world.

For comparison, here are the first four sentences of her thesis:

> Within the academy, signals of a scholar's academic influence are made manifest in indices like the h-index, which rank output. In open scholarly networks, however, signals of influence are less codified, and the ways in which they are enacted and understood have yet to be articulated. Yet the influence scholars cultivate in open networked publics intersects with institutional academia in grant-required measures of "public impact," in media visibility, and in keynote and job opportunities. How do scholars within open networks judge whether another scholar's signals are credible, or worthy of engagement?

At least to a degree, her point in publishing her abridgement was to offer up the ideas of her thesis *in her own voice,* rather than the academic voice her profession expects. What's interesting about this to me is that I came to know Bonnie through the voice of her blog — smart, witty, insightful, deliberate, balancing compassion as much as intellect, sting as much as salve. Both of the excerpts above are exceptional examples of good writing; but what the first offers me more than the second is a taste of what makes Bonnie *Bonnie,* a bit more of the whole of this scholar who is also a mom and Canadian, "elderly and didactic."

What I long for from academia are more *entirely legible* voices, emotionally resonant and intellectually vital. Your teeth do not chew without your tongue. The intellect cannot be incisive without the muscle of the heart.

The writers who have published on *Hybrid Pedagogy* have had their work cited in research and other publications, and not a few of their articles have found their way into classrooms and conference presentations. But they have also joined the #digped community, rallied under five iterations of MOOC MOOC, and formed networks within networks as a result of their participation. The work of our editors, then, is the work of community leaders, thought leaders, liaisons, and Pied Pipers.

The editors we seek are those with a commitment to the voices of others, editors who will enjoy championing growing writers, who read empathically as well as critically, and who understand the precarity of the act of writing itself.

ACTION

Every day, we participate in a digital culture owned and operated by others — designers, engineers, technologists, CEOs — who have come to understand how easily they can harvest our intellectual property, data, and the minute details of our lives. To resist this (or even to more consciously participate in it), we need skills that allow us to "read" our world (in the Freirean sense) and to act with agency.

WE MAY NEED TO AMPUTATE

SEAN MICHAEL MORRIS

The ability or inability of a group or culture to progress is in direct relationship to the proliferation of aphorism within it. General statements of fact and abbreviations of great wisdom are misleading in that they censure further inquiry and discussion. The brilliance of our predecessors was never meant to be carved into stone monuments, but as a point from which our own meditations should depart. When we rest on their laurels we languor, we enjoy a tenure of torpor. We cannot attend old leadership any more than we can wait for new leaders. We must take the lead.

I talk to leaders every day. Because every day I am in contact with teachers who have an array of backgrounds, an array of pedagogical stances, an array of fears and beliefs. I hear teachers write about their students — encouraging them, disparaging them, condoning and cursing them — and I hear teachers write about their profession, usually from a perspective of discontent, of everything being not-quite-right. Teachers are spooked by their institutions, they're intimidated by men and intimidated by women, no one is paid enough, and the list of crises in education seems impossibly long. Tenure and money are not solutions, online education is fraught, every single person deserves better treatment than they receive. Sisyphus had it easy.

But I talk to leaders every day. Teachers are among the most educated of any population. No one receives an education without solving some problems — from dorm roommates who store dead pets in the freezer to plumbing the depths of pre-Modern mathematics, our educations have been about untying knots — and no one comes to teaching without solving even more. We are more skilled than Sisyphus, cleverer, and not nearly so doomed.

I am in favor of speaking plainly. And more and more, bold outcry has become the norm. There is no use in being surreptitious on the internet; nor is there in education. We are not only educators in our classrooms. We are educators at lunch. We are educators at dinner parties. We are educators when we shop, volunteer, and raise our children. We are educators when we write. In "Academic Cowards and Why I Don't Write Anonymously," Tressie McMillan Cottom writes that: "this moment in time is woefully thin on leaders. I hope they emerge soon. And in numbers plentiful and intersectional enough that it ends highered's history of the most marginalized risking the most for the benefit of the many." Though her article ministers with a forthright compassion to those who are afraid to express themselves, her call to speak out is none too subtle. And she is right. Leaders must emerge. Or, perhaps more to the point, leaders must begin to recognize themselves.

There are a lot more leaders than we think. We are each better leaders than we give ourselves credit for. And it will be in bold speech, voices in the desert, that we'll recover our community of problem-solvers.

In the introduction to her MOOC about the future of higher education, Cathy Davidson says that "Far too little has changed inside our educational institutions, in the US and internationally, to prepare us for the demands, problems, restrictions, obstacles, responsibilities, and possibilities of living in the world we inhabit outside of school." She calls for us to begin rethinking the way we educate, to return to the blank page, the beginner's mind, to rediscover how learning happens. Education needs different objectives than it did when the current system was invented; and so, just as we would for a course with an evolving set of outcomes, we must continually rewrite the syllabus of education.

Cathy's MOOC proposed one space for that revision to begin — and it is a branching, disparate, distributed space, not localized inside her course alone. It is, as she said, *not a MOOC, but a movement.*

I dislike MOOCs. I have lain abed with them too long and we are both tired from the intimacy. But there is one thing I cannot deny about our copulation: it has been far from ordinary. I've said many things about MOOCs during our affair, ending with this from "What is MOOCification?":

> The MOOC has created debates about the ownership of ideas, the sharing of resources, the role of the teacher and learner, the notions of authorship and collaboration, the sticky mess of FERPA, and much more ... In these ideas, notions, messes, and themes lie new pedagogies waiting to wake up. In them lie the potential to change the way we teach to better match what is really going on in learners' lives and in our hybrid culture.

Andrew Ho and Isaac Chuang, of Harvard and MIT, have learned something similar from their intercourse with the MOOC. According to reporter Michael Patrick Rutter, they hold that "the rise of MOOCs has sparked and encouraged experimentation in teaching and in pedagogical research, benefiting both teachers and students." Most important here is the idea nascent in these observations: that education has become a place of experimentation on a grand scale, for good or bad, and that our classrooms, our journals, our conferences are transformed into a surgical theater.

If higher education is ailing, it is only because its many doctors have not applied themselves to its resuscitation. This is not a system that will care for us forever. It is a relationship that requires nurture and aid. The stacks of books upon which our universities have been built molder and decay. The digital makes walls into screens and debates into tweets, yet is less hale than our hallowed halls. Neither the analog nor the digital will preserve us. We are not a university unless we are colleagues, unless we care for the adjunct among us, unless we elevate the student, and unless we make friends as an act of radical political resistance.

Josh Boldt has said, speaking specifically of the decline of tenure, that "as of right now, things are not looking good. While we worry about the erosion of tenure (which affects a very small proportion of academic labor), the entire profession is crumbling. It's like painting your living room while the house burns down." He goes on to insist that collaboration will be essential to solving higher education's problems, that we cannot worry about hereditary hair loss when the victim's in a wheelchair. And he calls for help (if sardonically), when he offers "tell me how we can accomplish tenure for all and I will shake your hand. The person who figures out a way to make this happen would be a true hero."

Education's new leaders won't be heroes, though, they will be field medics. Jesse reminds us, in "A User's Guide to Forking Education," that we must "let the voices of authority proliferate rather than congeal." And we're going to need many opportunities for training, safe places with warm bodies, where new procedures can be tested and learning can occur. I'd characterize that MOOC of Cathy Davidson's as valorous because it advocates a pragmatic optimism that is the only remedy for what ails higher education. Davidson is not a Pollyanna. She knows we may need to amputate. If what needs to change ever will, it will ride on the shoulders of hard work, determined effort, and not a few more disappointments.

Being a leader will not be easy. It will take effort to begin rolling up our sleeves and bending our intellects to the matter at hand. It will no longer be enough to point out the leaky faucet; we must forge the wrench that will fix it. And if anyone can, we can.

Hell, we could run this place if we wanted to.

I talk to leaders every day. I publish leaders upwards of three times a week. Read them. Write your own words here. But be mindful: one day, you will be excerpted, so make your aphorisms discontent. You will write brilliant things. Let those things raise hell.

I WOULD PREFER NOT TO

JESSE STOMMEL

Assessment and standards are elephants in almost every room where discussions of education are underway. My goal here is not to demonize assessment but to dissect it — to cut right to its jugular: Where does assessment fail? What damage can it do? What can't be assessed? Can we construct more poetic, less objective, models for assessment? In a system structured around standards and gatekeeping, when and how do we stop assessing?

A while back, I tweeted, "Education needs more conscientious objectors," and I want to build upon that.

Taking a cue from my mentor Martin Bickman, I've chosen never to grade, or at least almost never. While I still submit grades at the end of a term, I've foregone grades on individual assignments for over 12 years, relying on qualitative feedback, peer review, and self-assessment. In "Ranking, Evaluating, and Liking: Sorting Out Three Forms of Judgment," Peter Elbow writes, "assessment tends so much to drive and control teaching. Much of what we do in the classroom is determined by the assessment structures we work under." My goal in eschewing grades has been to more honestly engage student work rather than simply evaluate it. Over many years, this has meant carefully navigating, and even breaking, the sometimes draconian rules of a half-dozen institutions. And I've brought students into meta-level discussions about these choices and have encouraged the same sort of agency among them. I tell students they should consider our course a "busy-work-free zone." So, if an assignment doesn't feel productive, we find ways to modify, remix, or repurpose its instructions. And when our assessments fail us (as they often do), we don't change our learning, we find new tools for assessment.

This is but one example. In "Bartleby, the Scrivener," Herman Melville writes, "Nothing so aggravates an earnest person as a passive resistance." More than just assessment, this is where our discussions must increasingly aim: the ways we respond (both actively and passively) in the face of institutional demands we find unethical or pedagogically harmful. The reference to Bartleby here is more than a coy nod. With its incessant refrain, "I would prefer not to," the story critiques the change in labor at the turn of the industrial age, the same age still attempting to drive a very different educational landscape.

The answer to Bartleby today is not to throw up our hands, but rather to ask: "Okay, what would you prefer to do?" How can we work together to make a guide — a how-to manual for saying "I would prefer not to..." in a grander and more collective way? How can we turn a simple act of civil disobedience into a rallying cry? And when we put our tools down and stand back from the furnace, the letter press, or the paper mill, what will we turn to build instead?

If we object to the increasing standardization of education, how and where do we build sites of resistance? What strategies can we employ to protect ourselves and our students? What workarounds can we employ as we build courage and community for revolt? What systems of privilege must we first dismantle? Finally, what kinds of assessment can or should we bring to our own strategies? If we write manifestos as a form of active resistance, how do we determine if they're working? As we organize, how do we measure the impact of our assembly? When we muster our pedagogy as a form of activism, how do we decide what counts as talk and what counts as action?

NOT ENOUGH VOICES

SEAN MICHAEL MORRIS

I do my best to stay quiet. It's only on Jesse Stommel's insistence that I'm here. It's not that I don't like to talk. My family will tell you I like to talk plenty. It's that when I speak, you listen to *me*. You listen because I have a podium. I have slides. I have this script in front of me. All your training tells you to listen to me.

I do my best to stay quiet because when I'm quiet, I can hear *you*. And it's you I'm interested in. Your stories. Your efforts. Your insights.

Over a year ago, I was having dinner with a friend of mine. He does social justice work related to small businesses. Unions. Minority business owners. Underdeveloped neighborhoods. Very worthwhile work. He told me that when he sits down with a group he's facilitating — made up largely of people of color, and LGBTQ business owners — he starts by saying that everyone has stories they want to tell, but at that table, everyone is equal.

That, of course, is not quite right. We've heard something like it before. It's the "all lives matter" argument.

All stories are equal. All stories matter. This is not how we get to hear stories we need to hear. This is not how we amplify silenced voices.

We amplify silenced voices by listening. By making space for them to speak. Not safe space, necessarily, daring space. Because it's never safe to speak.

This week, I've been working with a group of teachers designing space for themselves and their teaching on the Web, each picking through what they know and what they don't know, trying to decide what to say there. It's hard work. It's good work, but it's hard work.

Like learning.

I would echo this question from Martha Burtis: Why did we end up with courses in boxes instead of Domains of One's Own?

If I'm honest, I blame instructional design.

For too long — really, since its inception — instructional design has been built upon silencing. Instructional design generally assumes that all students are duplicates of one another. Or, as Martha says, standardized features, standardized courses. Standard students.

Despite any stubborn claims to the contrary, instructional design assigns learners to a single seat, a single set of characteristics. This is for efficiency. But it enacts an erasure that, taken to the extreme — say, to the massive — is unconscionable.

To understand how that erasure occurs, let's look at the origins of instructional design.

Today most students of online courses are more users than learners. The majority of online learning basically asks humans to behave like machines. This comes out of the fact that most online courses today are written around instructional design principles, which in turn were written around research in computer-aided instruction (CAI). The relationship fostered by instructional design is not one of learner to learning, it's one of learner (or, more to the point, student) to mechanized instruction.

I say this now, even as I bear the mantle of Instructional Designer.

A very long time ago, I wore that mantle for a small start-up firm in Colorado whose nearly sole client sold courses to human resources administrators in the banking industry; and whose primary foundation for instruction was Bloom's Taxonomy. Quite literally, software for corporate training was designed around the cognitive domain of the Taxonomy of Educational Objectives. All learning, in this case, boiled down to five component objectives:

- Remembering
- Understanding
- Applying
- Analyzing
- Evaluating

And every course we wrote scaffolded learning along the ladder of these objectives, almost always resting at application-level work... Doing what you've learned to do. Because that's all that was expected of our clients' workers. To be considered knowledgeable, all you need to do is remember what you learn, understand what you learn, and then apply what you learn.

Remember. Understand. Apply.

Knowledge.

But Bloom and his team defined knowledge as involving "the recall of specifics and universals, the recall of methods and processes, or the recall of a pattern, structure, or setting." Which means that by this definition, knowledge is the same as recall.

Remember. Understand what you remember. Apply what you remember.

New experiments in digital learning — personalized learning, adaptive learning, competency-based learning — raise the banners of education revolution, but what principles are they founded on? What relationship do they encourage between learner and learning, or learner and computer? In many cases, the methodology hasn't evolved from a critical pedagogy, but rather from the same CAI principles of traditional instructional design.

What's really scary here is that, due to the ubiquity of LMS adoption at colleges around the world, classroom teaching has started to change. CAI has entered the classroom, turning students into pigeons, teachers into dumb terminals. Now we must produce quantifiable data from our on-ground teaching, designing in-person learning from the same foundation as online learning.

When online learning has yet to get it right.

See, knowledge isn't the same as recall. It's more than that. For starters, we know that learners can create knowledge, that they can be their own best resources outside of a teacher or content. If we look at complexity theory, for example, we discover that knowledge is the result of inquiry, experimentation, feedback, and emergence. As well, the relationship of the learner to the computer can be more nuanced than the kind of "banking education" CAI demands.

Seymour Papert offered this challenge:

> Most honest Schoolers are locked into the assumption that School's way is the only way because they have never seen or imagined convincing alternatives to impart certain kinds of knowledge ... almost all experiments in purporting to implement progressive education have been disappointing because they simply did not go far enough in making the student the subject of the process rather than the object.

The hard truth is that instructional design — nay, teaching —

needs to start imagining convincing alternatives, needs to go "far enough".

In contrast, B.F. Skinner, one of the granddads of educational psychology, wrote that:

> The application of operant conditioning to education is simple and direct. Teaching is the arrangement of contingencies of reinforcement under which students learn.

In other words, the secret to efficient learning is a controlled environment, a managed environment, a place where the correct behavior results in the desired outcome. Later, Skinner would forward an idea about teaching machines which could guarantee that learners would reach desired outcomes, regardless of the presence of a human teacher.

Operant conditioning and the manipulation of response to stimuli are at the heart of theories that support instructional design. But more, they form the foundation of almost all educational technology—from the VLE or LMS to algorithms for adaptive learning. Building upon behaviorism, Silicon Valley—often in collaboration with venture capitalists with a stake in the education market—have begun to realize Skinner's teaching machines in today's schools and universities.

And there's the rub. When we went online to teach, we went online almost entirely without any other theories to support us besides instructional design. We went online first assuming that learning could be a calculated, brokered, duplicatable experience. For some reason, we took one look at the early internet and forgot about all the nuance of teaching, all the strange chaos of learning, and surrendered to a philosophy of see, do, hit submit.

The problem we face is not just coded into the LMS, either. It's not just coded into Facebook and Twitter and the way we send an e-mail or the machines we use to send text messages. It's coded into us. We believe that online learning happens this way. We believe that discussions should be posted once and replied to twice. We believe that efficiency is a virtue, that automated proctors and plagiarism detection services are necessary—and more than necessary, helpful.

But these are not things that are *true*, they are things that are *sold*.

In the time since I was an instructional designer building training courses for corporations, the digital landscape has changed so radically as to be unrecognizable from 1999. We've seen the advent of social media, wiki spaces, crowdsourcing, and Connectivism, a resurgence of Constructivist pedagogies, the Massive Open Online Course, and more. Instead of the relatively sterile, humorless environment of the early LMS, now across the internet, we are exposed afresh to the idiosyncrasies of culture, and also the deep-seated problems of racism, misogyny, xenophobia, homophobia... and on many fronts we're seeking ways to challenge these issues using digital media. There have been hashtag revolutions, fake news, cyberbullying, and the rise of micro-celebrity.

And yet, instructional design at its core, has not changed much. Neither has the technology upon which it floats.

When I left instructional design and entered graduate school, I was immersed in teacher training founded upon the critical pedagogy of teachers like Paulo Freire, John Dewey, Maria Montessori, bell hooks, Peter Elbow, and Henry Giroux. Here I learned about an approach to education that involved helping students develop an epistemological relationship to reality, to encouraging them to be "readers of their world" so that they could better grasp the oppressive forces and institutions that controlled their society, and could develop a knowledge of their ability to make change. Bloom's Taxonomy disappeared as an approach, replaced by student-centered learning, collaboration, and problem-based education.

Starting in 2005, fresh out of graduate school, I found myself again teaching in fully online environments, only now in higher education settings. Immediately, I found it a challenge to bring the principles of critical pedagogy into a digital classroom space designed against them. The learning management system sought to do just that: manage learning; and I was hard put to find ways to perforate the baked-in pedagogies of the interface so that a more critical learning could take hold.

Matthew Kruger-Ross writes that "Computer-Aided Instruction redefined learning as driven by clear and concise objectives that could be easily quantified and measured." And quantifying learning — that thing that administrations want us to do and for which so many functions of the LMS exist — depends on right answers. And right answers are based on recall of content.

You remember to sit or you don't. You remember to stay, or you don't.

This is learning reduced to a game of Simon.

Ira Shor writes, "At the heart of my lecture was my search for a presentation that could unveil a compelling reality to the students."

We must ask, is instruction bent on this same unveiling? Can a course whose content circles around objectives, assessments, and recall pull back the curtain on anything? Can it, as Paulo Freire suggests, invite learners into an epistemological relationship to reality?

Do all our lectures reveal a compelling reality?

Does this keynote?

There is something insidious about the way we talk about learning. Something insidious in the keynote format. Something pretty horrendous happens when we assume all ears are the same ears. And that all ears are trained to listen in the same way to the person at the podium. When we do that, we're silencing voices that might speak.

And we do this because the alternative is too complex. Too difficult.

D Watkins, a writer for Vice and Salon, wrote about a visit to his 13-year-old nephew's school. His nephew was having trouble communicating with one of his teachers, and Watkins thought he might be able to help. Here is how he described the scene he came upon:

> This school seemed like a jail, and level two ... was the psych ward. Students bolting up and down the hallways, desks taking flight, a trail of graded and ungraded papers scattered everywhere, fight videos being recorded on cellphones, Rich Homie Quan turned to the highest level, crap games and card games going down ... everywhere — all bottled up and sealed with that same shitty smell, so bad it was loud enough to hear, a shit stench I hoped wouldn't stick to my flannel.
>
> 'So this is it,' my sister says with an uneasy smirk. This is her only option.

According to Watkins, this scene is too common in inner-city schools. It's a deeply troubling scene, and one that threatens to rip us out of the joy and collegiality we've enjoyed here this week.

But I offer it because I don't believe we can afford to silence any voices. I offer it because when we're talking about designing for outcomes, designing for skills, or designing for emergence, we are not talking about this. And we must. Where is learning happening in this scene? What good are objectives and assessments going to do for these kids? Are the answers that Vygotsky offers, that Skinner offers, or even that Freire offers going to help us here?

There is no inner city LMS. And if we make the mistake to think that we don't teach inner city kids, let me remind you that children grow to be adults and they carry with them the circumstances under which they received an education. Your students have fought, your students have hidden from bullies, your students have been hungry, they have passed for straight, they have held their tongues, and they have been broken.

In many cases, the students you work with have had to subvert a system that sought to oppress them in order to make it to your classroom. Or to show up as a name inside your LMS.

Learning is a subversive act.

It is not an act of recall. It's not an act of imitation, regurgitation, repetition. It's never passive.

Learning is a subversive act, and so must teaching be — not out of compulsion, but from logical necessity. If learners are to move from what-we-know into what we do not yet know—from recall to emergence—or more importantly, from oppressed to liberated — then teaching must also deal in what we do not yet know. It must deal in the stuff of real struggle.

Emergence isn't pretty. It's not a flower opening. It's rough, complicated, unruly, embarrassing... and in that way full of wonder.

> To teach in a manner that respects and cares for the souls of our students is essential if we are to provide the necessary conditions where learning can most deeply and intimately begin. ~ bell hooks

Learning is not safe. In fact, to learn is to take a risk, to become an aerialist, to put your head in the lion's mouth. Learning is a death-defying act. And though it takes place largely within the confines of silent classrooms and sterile learning management systems, within the mind of the learner, riots can occur.

Take, for instance, Frederick Douglass:

> As I writhed under it, I would at times feel that learning to read had been a curse rather than a blessing. It had given me a view of my wretched condition, without the remedy. It opened my eyes to the horrible pit, but to no ladder upon which to get out. In moments of agony, I envied my fellow slaves for their stupidity. I have often

> wished myself a beast. I preferred the condition of the meanest reptile to my own. Any thing, no matter what, to get rid of thinking!

We need to remind ourselves that learning is the single most important act in human life; and to treat it ever so lightly through conversations about objectives and outcomes and alignment and — for goodness' sake — educational psychology, to entrench it within a discourse permeable only to the institutionally educated, is to not just do it a disservice, but is to reduce it so far that passion, drive, need are all emptied from it.

How could we scaffold the learning Frederick Douglass did? What objectives would we set before him? What outcomes would we expect?

By the end of this course, you will:

- Give tongue to interesting thoughts of your own soul;
- Gain from dialogue the power of truth;
- Abhor and detest your enslavers;
- Understand how the silver trump of freedom rouses the soul.

Funny, right? But these should be the concerns of a critical instructional design.

I want to thank you for listening to me. I'm not an experienced keynote speaker. I'm not a professor. I have no advanced degree. But because I look like I do, people quiet to hear what I have to say. With this gray beard of mine, I am the institution. I am the LMS. I may be gay, but I can pass as someone who carries all the cards of privilege. And privilege is authority, it's a podium. And when each of us steps behind any podium, we are positioned to be listened to, when really we need to be listening.

It's difficult, I admit, to go through 20-plus years of education listening and listening to the person at the front of the room only to be told by all us well-meaning pedagogues that listening is also the key to teaching. Making space for others to speak. Making space for invention, for backchannels, for tangents. It sorta sucks. When will we get to speak?

The answer doesn't lie in turn-taking, but in changing what it means to speak. Make speaking a collaborative event. Join your voice with the voice of students. Join your voice with the voice of other teachers. Join your voice — and this one is really essential if we're to make any headway — join your voice with the voices of educational technology.

Annemarie Pérez wrote in her teaching statement, which she posted on her blog this morning:

> There are not enough voices engaged in Chicana/o studies in this university, in this state, in this country, in this world. Our artists, our people are under attack and it has pretty much ever been so. Yet there is so much that is significant in Chicana/o thought, in literature, art and in our own lives. I teach what I do the way I do because I want us to see it and talk about it together. I want my classes to add to and be part of this collection, to hear the voices from our past and amplify them. I want your voices to be amplified, your word to be read, your art seen.

I would agree. There are not enough Chicana voices. There are not enough Black voices. There are not enough First Nation voices. There are not enough trans voices. There are not enough women's voices. There are not enough queer voices.

We need to change our minds about speaking as coming from a single mouth, a single amplified signal. We must learn to hear the patterns in the noise... And we probably shouldn't call it noise any more — all those blogs, all those domains of your own, all those sites where educators get angry or get sad or begin the long path toward empathy.

Do we need single voices to rise above the others? Do we need keynote speakers? Do we still need podiums at all?

Let's build an education where professors and their looka-likes—old white men with gray beards — listen more, and women, people of color, trans folk, and others whose voices and wisdom have been omitted for so long become our collaborators.

Let's design that classroom, that learning experience. Let's make that the world we occupy.

VULNERABILITY, CONTINGENCY, AND ADVOCACY IN HIGHER EDUCATION

JESSE STOMMEL

I find myself increasingly unwilling to rest on my own privilege. In August of 2013, I accepted a tenure-track position at University of Wisconsin-Madison. From 2013 - 2015, I worked in the Division of Continuing Studies, advocating for lifelong learning and what I call the "public digital humanities."

In my previous position, I was Faculty and Director of a new Digital Humanities degree program at Marylhurst University, a small liberal arts institution in Portland, OR. I had taken the job with the belief that it would be my career for 10 years or more. It was a full-time position with benefits, not tenure-track but within a system that was described to me as "tenure-equivalent." My colleagues seemed collegial, the campus was lovely, and the students are some of the best I've worked with in my 15 years of teaching.

Ultimately, though, I discovered that my position was, in fact, deeply contingent. As the financial woes of the institution mounted, the mistreatment of faculty, and especially adjunct faculty, increased. What I discovered was that as people got scared for their own welfare, they began to more tightly guard their perceived territory, whether administrative or scholarly. The work I value most — collaboration and interdisciplinarity — suffered and was at times even actively discouraged. The treatment of adjuncts was downright appalling. Tears were not unusual at committee meetings.

This was the environment in which I wrote my proposal for this MLA 2014 panel. My goal in this piece is to unsettle assumptions about how academia should operate in the wake of widespread exploitation of contingent laborers. For me, every aspect of higher education is either suspect or somehow implicated: hiring practices, administrative bloat, disciplinarity, traditional academic publishing, double-blind peer review, the notion of a terminal degree, and the tenure system itself. Too much of the system is designed to defend the status quo and reinforce the mistreatment of a 75% majority (AAUP) of the academic labor force. This is, quite frankly, not healthy for any of us, whether on the tenure-track or not.

In December 2012, the academic journal I founded, *Hybrid Pedagogy*, hosted a Twitter chat about "The State of Higher Education and Its Future." During the discussion, I tweeted: "We need more tenure-track & full-time faculty willing to advocate for their colleagues & students. #highered needs more bravery." Within a couple days, the tweet had been retweeted 41 times and favorited 10 times, which is telling, calling attention to the need for not only adjunct faculty, but full-time faculty, to rise up in active resistance. The best pedagogues take risks, and we need curricula, hiring practices, and protections for contingent faculty that encourage those risks.

During another Twitter discussion, I tweeted: "Higher education pushes out the exact wrong people. Those wrong people are about to rise up. We need more right leaders of wrong." Educators need advocates and need to be advocates. We can't just notice the problems, but must take specific action to solve them individually and institutionally. There are various stakeholders in this conversation (including students, administrators, and faculty), various folks we need in the room as we make and implement strategies for resisting the spread of business models for education that rely insidiously on contingent labor. And full-time faculty must be willing to take risks in support of their adjunct colleagues and students. In many cases, this kind of advocacy looks less like marching, writing, or speaking, and more like listening.

Throughout Fall 2013 and Winter 2014, *Hybrid Pedagogy* published a series of articles focused on our role as pedagogues in a system wherein education does not always lead to opportunity. In the first article from the series, "A Lecturer's Almanac," Katie Rose Guest Pryal offers a harrowing account of her experiences as a contingent laborer, a litany of seemingly mundane grievances, the collective weight of which becomes quickly oppressive. Tiffany Kraft, in her article "Adjunctification: Living in the Margins of Academe," describes her experiences in "extreme adjuncting," hoping with her story "to tip the elephant in the room."

From its beginning, one of the goals of *Hybrid Pedagogy* has been to create these sorts of conversations, which build bridges across systemic divides in education, making connections to facilitate productive action. The issue of academic labor is deeply interwoven with any project that attempts to promote good pedagogy. We simply can't create an environment that enables *student agency* as long as our educational institutions do not support *the agency of teachers*.

Our work in the humanities is a scholarship of resistance, predicated on our being humans, not mere cogs in a machine. We need to support (financially, politically, and emotionally) the faculty most passionate about teaching and learning, while making alliances across disciplines and between community college teachers, K-12 teachers, contingent faculty, tenure-track faculty, academic staff, and students. Being tenure-track doesn't mean we should wait seven years to speak out on adjunct labor conditions. We need to take risks and speak out now. The current hierarchies and political economies are becoming, more and more, at odds with a humanist ethic. We must make the humanities — and higher education — viable for the digital age in ways that value the work of teaching and learning. The bravery we need right now is to champion the people doing that work.

The text of this talk is drawn from a motley crew of sources. Parts of it appeared in a co-authored article by myself and Lee Skallerup Bessette, her voice inside of mine, and my voice in hers. This story can't be told by one person, and not by a small panel of people, but only by a cacophony of voices, a gathering together — of sounds, of ideas, of intentions. Some of this work is loud, a rage against the dying of the light, and some of it is quieter like the space between this sentence and the next. This work is not and can never be faceless. We no longer have the luxury of resting on the privilege of our own anonymity. Real bodies — bodies that ache and bruise and die — are doing this work, fighting in classrooms, online, and at institutions — institutions that don't always fight for them.

So *I can't give this presentation by myself.* As a single body. These words require many more voices than just my own to make them go.

Chuck Rybak writes, "The emotional terrain of the higher ed workplace, or any workplace for that matter, is real. How we treat people matters."

Tressie McMillan Cottom writes in "Dude, Where's the Race in Your Class Analysis of HigherEd?," "Many of our most strident debates of highered's labor system do not speak as eloquently about how that labor system intersects with institutional racism, if they speak about it at all."

Sean writes in "Collaborative Peer Review," "I am an orphan of the academy. Beached on the sand at the M.A., employed only ever as an adjunct instructor at two-year colleges, generally looked at askance in the heady company of academics, I am the horse that didn't make the derby."

And Brian Croxall at MLA in 2009: "I'm sorry that I can't be delivering these comments in person."

What scares me most are my deeply contingent colleagues —

adjuncts, staff, and students — who aren't or soon won't be able to *deliver their comments in person* for more distinctly physical reasons, because their bodies — all our bodies — are fragile. Limbs break. Organs give way. Cancers go untreated. Bile and pus and blood refuse to be contained. This is our humanity, the humanity our talks about labor must acknowledge.

And it isn't that we should build harder and harder armor around ourselves. Advocacy should not look like an impenetrable phalanx. Just the opposite. We must work together, and not *just* from a place of politics or administration. This is as much about how we are made professionally vulnerable by the corporatization of education, as it is about how making ourselves *even more vulnerable* — by taking risks and being honest — will help us find a way forward. We need to actively ensure that academia is a safe place for the contingent among us to speak openly about their professional lives without fear of losing their livelihood. We need to gather together in number so our pedagogies and politics can be safely laid bare.

I recently tweeted, "If bigger and bigger bits of our 'wellbeing' is what makes it go, I suddenly feel like all of education is contingent." This in response to a blog post by Kate Bowles, "Irreplaceable Time." In that post, Kate describes the physical burden of academic labor and what it has literally wrought upon her own body. She describes "the corporate culture of team-building that is so reckless with people's time and trust." And she concludes, "*you don't have my consent to use my remaining time in this way*." If we're contingent, we labor. If we're tenure-track, we labor. And rarely are we called on to labor for each other's mutual benefit.

As I write this, Kate Bowles is my hero. Tiffany Kraft is my hero. Katie Rose Guest Pryal and Lee Skallerup Bessette are my heroes. They've said to me what I can't always say to myself. We must be brave. But we must also take care. "What we need," Kate writes, "is the courage to put work itself at risk." For her — for myself — I will, if necessary, fight to the death of my own tenure.

A MANIFESTO FOR COMMUNITY COLLEGES, LIFELONG LEARNING, AND AUTODIDACTS

SEAN MICHAEL MORRIS

As some are raised a Catholic or an atheist or a vegetarian, I was raised an academic. The university always had about it a mystique, a cloud of mystery and veneration. Lauded in my household were the values of objectivity, critical thinking, close reading. As early as the fourth grade, my mother took me to her college Shakespeare classes, introduced me to her professors, and indulged me with lunch at the student union. I attended classes with her throughout her undergraduate study; and for years after, I'd walk through campus simply to absorb the essence of the place. Today, I am as much in love with the endeavor of higher education as I am disappointed by its outcomes.

The reformation of higher education is under way. Whether we agree or not, the vast credentialing system of universities and colleges, the importance placed upon expertise, the value of the degree and the Ph.D., the political economies that oppress those that form the backbone of the system, the administration of learning, the rights of students, and even the act of learning itself are all under scrutiny. It is a scrutiny that's been in play for years, and has been exacerbated most recently by the advent of the MOOC (massive open online course), the corporatization of education, and the exportation of pedagogy to technologists and private entrepreneurs. Sadly, little is coming forward from this inquisition of education that's hopeful. Academics and administrators are afraid for their careers, and students and learners of all ages are looking openly at other options (other options that enterprising speculators are at the ready to provide).

I have read and written about the way that learning is changing. Learners today are taking matters of education into their own hands. DIY education practices proliferate. MOOC providers, now in cahoots with university systems, are doing both a service and a disservice to higher education by offering creditable courses far and wide for low cost. The new culture of learning (as imagined by Douglas Thomas and John Seely Brown) is one where learning takes place all the time, everywhere, and according to learners' own preferences and motivations. Disappearing quickly are the rigor, expectations, and outcomes provided by the structures of a traditional education; and coming to the fore is an autonomous learner, who is her own authority on what's relevant, germane, vital to her own education. Wide and resounding is the call: "The learner has changed! And so has learning changed!" And it follows that if they wish to survive, institutions of learning must change, too.

Learning, we know, is something a person can do on her own, and something that should (does) take place throughout her life. An education is something she must be granted. The institutions of higher education, as they have been established and maintained, are primarily credentialing services. Four-year institutions and those offering advanced degrees are diploma-makers, stamp-affixers, magic wand-wavers. Pay your dues (and tuition), write your theses, and walk out the door you came in with extra letters on the end of your name, and the verification that you have completed your education.

But I am unconvinced by the primacy of the Ph.D., or the degree in general, as currency. While it is impossible to deny the Ph.D. holds sway over the M.A., which is much preferred to the B.A., it is not true that any of these achievements develops in a person a greater or lesser ability to do their own thinking. The degree grants the student her hard-earned credential, but it does not make a person more herself, more productive, more capable, or more sustainably successful. In fact, the political economy of the Ph.D. has overtaken the benefits of receiving it. Audrey Watters speaks to this in her article, "The Real Reason I Dropped Out of a Ph.D. Program":

> I quit because I'd lost the stomach for being part of the institution of higher education — one that wasn't sustaining me intellectually, financially or spiritually; one that wanted me to teach classes for very low wages — as a grad student and then likely as an adjunct faculty member ... I quit because far from that so-called Ivory Tower being a place of solace and contemplation, it had become a nightmare of bureaucracy and politics. I quit because I didn't want to be a cog in that machine.

We have — we participate in — a system of education that works against the learner. The university is a place where students must abandon their passions and hopes to tread instead the minefield of mimetic professionalism, canonized assignments, and stringent (though often highly subjective) assessment in order to be granted a degree which may have dehumanized their study and disabled, rather than empowered, their critical thinking skills. It's completion, not learning, that's key to getting an education.

But I want to return learning to this endeavor. I want to restore the high gloss image of the university as a vibrant campus of engaged learners. I want to free learning from the grip of education. The learner has changed, evolving before our eyes into the autodidact, and so our institutions and pedagogies must cooperate (or at least compensate) by becoming responsive, flexible, and decentered. And I see the way through to this lodged in the convictions of the community college.

I believe that community colleges are situated best among all institutions of higher education to open education to the lifelong, autonomous learner. Four-year institutions are limited by their own biologies, and the ossification of values of expertise, specialization, exclusivity, reputation, and relevance. But the anatomy of the community college gives it much greater flexibility, and therefore greater resiliency in the face of the challenges of new learning. The community college is based on far more humanistic, and more open source, values: personal achievement, complementarity between learning and life skills, diversity, citizenship, and autonomy. There are no "research one" community colleges; every one of these two-year institutions is founded on teaching, and on leading students into a greater understanding of their own intellectual potential.

According to the American Association for Community Colleges (AACC), "Most community college missions have basic commitments to:

- serve all segments of society through an open-access admissions policy that offers equal and fair treatment to all students
- a comprehensive educational program
- serve its community as a community-based institution of higher education
- teaching
- lifelong learning".

Service to the learner is written into the constitution of the community college. This is fundamentally different from an institution focused on research, and on granting advanced degrees. The Carnegie Classification of Institutions of Higher Education listed the following criteria for a doctoral/research university ("R1" in 1994 when the criteria were named):

- Offer a full range of baccalaureate programs
- Are committed to graduate education through the doctorate
- Give high priority to research
- Award 50 or more doctoral degrees each year
- Receive annually $40 million or more in federal support

These, then, are institutions interested in the products of learning and research, less so the learner herself. There are no mentions of service, nor of teaching, nor of lifelong learning. Indeed, the learner appears left out of the equation entirely — except as she is an implied producer and consumer of knowledge and research (who she is not until late in her advanced academic career) — which may be why so many bemoan the university as a relic of the industrial age.

But today's learner is a lot more than simply a producer and consumer of research and information within the confines of the academy. Today's learner is a doer and a maker of content — of artifacts personal, professional, academic, and anthropologic — developed and shared communally within relatively disorganized collectives... and usually entirely outside institutions of higher education. Lifelong learners do not restrict themselves to learning from instructors, from texts, nor even from information available on the Internet. They learn from a multitude of sources, and from each other.

The notion of the learning collective is key to discovering why the approach of the community college may be the best one for the emerging autodidact population. In "A New Culture of Learning", Thomas and Brown predict that learning collectives will take over the landscape of adult learning in the immediate future. They say that:

> Collectives are not solely defined by shared intention, action, or purpose ... Where communities can be passive (though not all of them are by any means), collectives cannot. In communities, people learn in order to belong. In a collective, people belong in order to learn. Communities derive their strength from creating a sense of belonging, while collectives derive theirs from participation.

We may be tempted to consider other communities outside of higher education as better fitted to the lifelong, autonomous learner. The learning collective as Brown and Thomas' describe it sounds suspiciously like the community inside a MOOC, for example. MOOCs offer the opportunity for learners in any location in the world (assuming reasonable access to the Internet) to study and discuss alongside learners everywhere else, forming collectives of learners whose only qualification is participation. Likewise, other communities have begun to spring up. MOOC Campus, a residential retreat-like campus that offers advising for a MOOC-based education, emphasizes the centrality of community in the educative endeavor.

The problem with MOOCs and MOOC campuses is that they're primarily derivative of undergraduate education at research-intensive institutions, and therefore generally rely on the most vacuous of pedagogies. As well, the paroxysmal growth of MOOCs (especially those built to replace baccalaureate classes) overlooks pedagogy in favor of credentialing, thus falling into the same woeful rut as most of higher education. So, I am not here talking about MOOCs or other online monstrosities offered in place of higher education. I am talking about scooping the collective, about bringing onto campus the type of learning that learners are doing without us — in a partnership that looks a lot like college, and nothing like college at all.

David Staley says in his article, "Autonomous Learning and the Future of Higher Education", that autonomous learners will change the way learning happens, even in on-ground campuses.

> What will a physical campus mean to autonomous learners? These students, I suspect, will still wish to meet with faculty, who will serve more as personal tutors than as traditional instructors ... In such a learning environment, classrooms will inevitably be altered. Large theater-style lecture halls might go unused, whereas the faculty office, seminar room or laboratory becomes the preferred physical venue for interactions between teacher and learner. Communities of self-learners might gather for mutual benefit.

As higher education stands on the precipice of its own temerity and demise, here we see a way out. A new learning environment that does not do away with the college campus, but that embraces without ambivalence communities of learning that do not rely upon the resources of that campus. The community college, preconditioned as it already is to serve the student, is in a unique, favorable position to cater to this new culture of learners... simply by doing what it does best, yet aiming its students not at four-year and advanced degree credentialing, but at autonomous lifelong learning.

I am not doe-eyed about this. The community college suffers under many of the same restrictive expectations that doctoral/research-driven institutions do. The community college is just as liable for its completion rates, just as answerable for its curricula, and just as eager for its share of educational funding as four-year institutions (if not more so). The community college has long been under pressure to prove itself to its older brothers, to validate itself through participation in the culture of expertise, specialization, and relevancy. Add to this the diverse nature of the community college student — many of whom must begin their academic careers in developmental courses, and most of whom are otherwise employed and obligated — along with the heavily contingent faculty workforce, and the ambition to be itself credentialed can imperil the community college's mission.

Daring is necessary. As Jesse Stommel and Lee Skallerup Bessette urge us in their article, "Scholarship of Resistance: Bravery, Contingency, and Higher Education",

> Higher education needs more bravery. Digital pedagogy, or any experimental critical pedagogy, is necessarily dangerous, often with real risks for both instructors and students, much of which can be valuable for learning. But when we experiment with our pedagogies, we confront an establishment that can be hostile to anything new — an establishment that often punishes rather than rewards innovation — that increasingly enforces the standardization of curriculums and classroom practice.

Even the community college, always ready and ripe for experimentation, and built as it is upon the notion of community, will face an enormous challenge making room for the new culture of learning. But as practiced as it is at seeking recognition and relevance, the community college can, if it is daring enough, become an institution of collective learning.

Ultimately, what must happen is the development of a pedagogy, and an institution supporting that pedagogy, that is resilient in the face of the most rapidly-evolving learner in history. We must have pedagogies (and pedagogues) that are as responsive and flexible as our technologies. We must do more learning and teaching on the fly, collaborating with rather than corralling learners.

And if it is not the community college that will lead the charge in the new educational model, someone must. Someone who is willing to stand back from the authority-driven dispensation of learning and create a pedagogy from what happens already, what happens now. A pedagogy based on the way people are learning, teaching themselves; rather than a pedagogy of leading, it is a pedagogy of fine-tuning, a syntonic pedagogy. And, by its own enactment, it is a pedagogy that spreads pedagogies, rippling outward like soundwaves.

FREE COLLEGE; FREE TRAINING FOR COLLEGE TEACHERS

JESSE STOMMEL

I am a huge proponent of free college. Especially free community college. Especially free community college for returning non-traditional students.

There is much to read on this front. You could start in the *New York Times,* where Sara Goldrick-Rab writes, "How we finance public higher education is a matter of political will. Universal public higher education recognizes that college must be affordable for all if it is to help drive our economy and our democracy." You could also read this piece by Tressie McMillan Cottom in *Dissent Magazine,* where she writes, "I do not care if free college won't solve inequality ... Today's debate about free college tuition does something extremely valuable. It reintroduces the concept of public good to higher education discourse."

The gist: free college is possible, it is a political decision, it is not a solution to all the inequalities of education, but it is an opening to an important conversation.

I am also strongly in favor of free Bachelor's degree "finishing" programs designed and suitable for "continuing" adult students. Many of these students have attended multiple colleges in several states and have amassed a degree's worth of credits in all manner of disciplines. The moniker "continuing" has an almost Orwellian ring, since many of these students are struggling hard to finish but finding their path frustrated by bureaucracy, accreditation standards, or curricular inflexibility. In fact, the *continuing* students most determined to finish are often the same ones finding themselves unable to finish (or deterred from finishing by inadequate curricula, course formats, and scheduling) within traditional 4-year institutions. Those most likely to take ownership of their own education also seem more generally unwilling to suffer the absurdity of mindless box-checking and hoop-jumping.

And the students most dedicated to finishing their degrees frequently end up in online / hybrid courses where they face the worst of what Sean describes in "Critical Instructional Design" as the "monkey see, monkey do, monkey hit submit" of bad instructional design. I have worked with these students at the community college level and in a 4-year liberal arts program for non-traditional adults. I currently have one of these students among the very close circle I call my "family." Every one of these students is brave, brilliant, and persistent. They deserve the best possible education we can collectively muster.

What I would propose.

If we are to make higher education a public good, and I think we should. If we are to open education to those for whom it might not otherwise be available, and I think we should. **If we are to make college free, we must also offer free training for college teachers** — as part of and also beyond graduate degree programs.

Adjunct teachers must no longer be required to attend unpaid required job training, as they are by many institutions. Any required training should be subsidized. Kathi Inman Berens takes this one step further, in "Want to 'Save the Humanities'? Pay Adjunct to Learn Digital Tools," "Don't just make tools freely available. Pay adjuncts and other teaching-only faculty for their *time* to learn them."

And if graduate programs and employers of faculty are currently unable to offer free pedagogical training (or to pay adjuncts for participating in this training), how about offering *any pedagogical training at all*?

Graduate programs should incorporate more courses focused explicitly on pedagogy. If teaching is 40 – 90% of most full-time faculty jobs in higher ed., **pedagogical study should constitute at least 40% of the work graduate students do toward a graduate degree**. I was recently laughed at by someone in a traditional academic discipline when I offered this as a provocation, but it feels hardly provocative to me. For some programs, even requiring a single graduate course in pedagogy would be a step in the right direction, but 40% of coursework seems an incredibly reasonable bar (even if also well out of current reach for many programs).

It would mean offering more courses (or components of required content-focused courses) dedicated to pedagogy. It would also mean discipline-specific pedagogies would be a significant component of comprehensive or qualifying exams. It would mean 40% of the dissertations or research projects in a field would focus (at least in part) on pedagogy. And it would mean the culture of every department would acknowledge pedagogy as a respected sub-discipline (as well as a discipline in its own right).

And, **if 75% of university faculty are adjunct, graduate programs should be helping prepare students in very specific ways for this work**. Or, even better, helping prepare "future adjuncts" to resist the increasing adjunctification of higher education.

Through my work with *Hybrid Pedagogy*, I have engaged many folks at many different kinds of institutions across the country and around the world. I have myself taught at a community college, three public R1s, one public liberal arts institution, and one private liberal arts institution. What I have heard most commonly from other college instructors is that they received *zero* training in pedagogy as part of their graduate degree programs or upon starting a faculty position at another institution. What I have heard less frequently are accounts of one or two seminars, courses, or workshops incorporated at some level during their work as a graduate student. I recognize that the culture and conversations are different at different kinds of institutions and in different disciplines. And, of course, there are outliers we should hold up as models.

I myself took one required pedagogy course in my own graduate program, two elective graduate courses, and also a handful of workshops that added up to a graduate teaching certification. I certainly wouldn't diminish the amazing work already being done at a few institutions to offer training in pedagogy for future or current college teachers.

But it isn't enough.

Digital Pedagogy Lab, which I co-direct, has begun offering low-cost opportunities for professional development including online courses and in-person institutes. We give significant discounts to adjuncts and full fellowships. We have also offered entirely free professional development opportunities since 2012 as part of the outreach mission of the Hybrid Pedagogy 501(c)3 non-profit. There are a few other groups offering similar opportunities, some for-profit, some not-for-profit, some within institutions, some peripheral to them.

But it isn't enough.

Until 40% or more of the courses in graduate programs are pedagogically focused, I would argue we are doing a disservice to graduate students.

Until continuous, not continuing, education in pedagogy becomes the norm for college teachers, we are doing a disservice to all college students.

By "pedagogy," I mean something much broader than just preparing graduate students to teach in university classes. I also mean preparing graduate students and new faculty for outreach, activism, work in libraries, instructional design, public scholarship, educational journalism, etc. Work that moves beyond content to consider how our study of that content gets shared with others or inflected in the world.

Training college teachers can't be an afterthought or an add-on (and by "training" I mean engaging future teachers thoughtfully in praxis-focused pedagogical work).

Ultimately, this work is for the public good and should be supported by our public educational institutions.

If college is ever to be "free" in any broad or expansive sense of the word, we must start by fostering pedagogical work as an ethic.

TEXTBOOKS, OER, AND THE NEED FOR OPEN PEDAGOGY

JESSE STOMMEL

Textbooks are a social justice issue. The cost of textbooks has increased over 1000% in the last 40 years (3 times the rate of inflation). Over a shorter frame of 10-20 years we've seen other non-academic books actually go down in price while textbook prices have continued to go up.

This steady rise in cost is driven by the fact that students are being required to buy these books. And commercial textbook companies are adding insult to injury by bundling textbooks with other (often digital) course materials so that the cost of a single "textbook" can be as much as $400 or more. In many classes, the stuff that's bundled with the textbook goes unused.

When I was an undergraduate student in the 1990s, I would budget around $250 each semester for all my books. Now, students find themselves commonly paying more than that for a single book.

The push toward **Open Educational Resources** is fueled, at least in part, by the steady rise in textbook costs. And there is a lot of good intentions behind the OER movement. But, increasingly, commercial textbook companies are confusing the movement by pushing high-cost digital alternatives to textbooks. Students are offered limited licenses to these books and so they are, in a sense, only renting access to a digital file that is much less flexible than a print book.

Many of these supposed OER initiatives are framed in terms of access. Because they appear to lower the cost for individual classes. But with these models students are paying less and also getting less, because they have only limited access to the material. Either they get access for a limited period, they get the material in a proprietary format, or they have to use restrictive platforms to engage the material.

And the textbook companies are also banking on the fact that digital books can't be resold. But a student's right to resell their own property is part of what they are buying when they buy a physical book.

For all of these reasons, I find the increasing use of the phrase "**inclusive access**" by textbook publishers incredibly problematic. The phrase is marketing spin designed to make institutions think signing profit-driven deals with massive corporate publishers is actually in the best interest of students, when it usually (almost always) isn't. There is very little that is inclusive or accessible about the materials being marketed like this. According to Lindsay McKenzie in Inside Higher Ed., "The 'inclusive' aspect of the model means that every student has the same materials on the first day of class, with the charge included as part of their tuition." As the story goes, publishers can charge less, because students have to opt out, and only 2% choose to (Douglas-Gabriel). But the need to bundle course materials with tuition points to a larger problem: why are students often unwilling to buy these course materials in the first place?

Textbooks are also a pedagogical issue. I would like to shift the conversation about textbooks more toward choice, so the question for teachers becomes not just how much will the required texts for a class cost, but is it necessary that I require specific materials at all? Why would I choose these texts before even meeting the students and understanding their needs? Is there a better way to allow students multiple points of entry to a course? Can I use free online readings instead? Recommended print books? And only require students buy materials those students see as having value beyond a single semester?

I also think it's important for teachers to realize that students have to make incredibly difficult decisions around the economics of college. For example, students should never have to decide between buying a textbook for a class or eating. But they often do. This means when educators design courses or academic programs, we have to start from a place of trusting students to make important decisions about their own education. And we have to start from a place of empathy.

What I'm most interested in is the shift toward freely available open educational resources. And especially ones that students have a hand in creating. An OER is not just a (hopefully) free resource but also an opportunity. Open pedagogy pushes, in fact, on the very notion of static "resources" in favor of tools that emphasize student contribution and dialogue. In their chapter from *A Guide to Making Open Textbooks With Students,* Robin DeRosa and Rajiv Jhangiani write, "Knowledge consumption and knowledge creation are not separate but parallel processes, as knowledge is co-constructed, contextualized, cumulative, iterative, and recursive." (See more examples at their Open Pedagogy Notebook.)

The way forward is more agency for teachers and students and fewer back-alley deals with corporate publishers. I'm inspired by projects that push hard against the idea of knowledge as static and hierarchical—like the Equality Archive from Shelly Eversley and a collective of over 25 feminist authors, artists, and teachers. And I'm inspired by projects that invite a much larger audience into their continued creation, like the Open Music Theory interactive "textbook" published free and open-source by Kris Shaffer and others.

At University of Mary Washington, our Domain of One's Own program gives students a domain name and space on the Web where they can develop their own digital identity and contribute to knowledge in their field. There is so much knowledge openly available on the Web. And having students work with OER gives them opportunities to think critically about that information and about who controls what is "true" in a given discipline. Ultimately, I want education to make space for students to be creators of knowledge not just consumers of it. Traditional textbooks become resources, in this kind of approach, rather than doctrine. And, no matter how difficult it's become, **the Web has to be a place of constant and active interrogation** of what and how we know.

Our work at UMW is less about thinking through how students consume content on the Web and more about how they can be inspired to build and rebuild the Web. My work in faculty development has always been focused on helping teachers think beyond content—to imagine ways for students to co-construct their own educations.

The emphasis of open pedagogy can't be on how we copyright, license, and share content. That can be one tiny piece, but it's a mostly metaphorical one, and an offshoot of the deeper and more necessary social justice work: seeing students as full humans, as agents, not customers. The cost of textbooks needs to be addressed, especially when students increasingly face basic needs insecurity—but through a reconsideration of when and how we use textbooks altogether, rather than by simply changing how they are monetized. In this, **open pedagogy is the thing**.

A GUIDE FOR RESISTING EDTECH: THE CASE AGAINST TURNITIN

SEAN MICHAEL MORRIS AND JESSE STOMMEL

> *Students often find themselves uploading their content — their creative work — into the learning management system. Perhaps they retain a copy of the file on their computer; but with learning analytics and plagiarism detection software, they still often find themselves having their data scanned and monetized, often without their knowledge or consent.*
>
> ~ Audrey Watters, "Education Technology's Completely Over"

A funny thing happened on the way to academic integrity. Plagiarism detection software (PDS), like Turnitin, has seized control of student intellectual property. While students who use Turnitin are discouraged from copying other work, the company itself can strip mine and sell student work for profit.

For this bait-and-switch to succeed, Turnitin relies upon the uncritical adoption of their platform by universities, colleges, community colleges, and K12 schools. All institutions that, in theory, have critical thinking as a core value in their educational missions. And yet they are complicit in the abuse of students by corporations like Turnitin.

The internet is increasingly a privately-owned public space. On April 3, 2017, Donald Trump signed into law a bill overturning Obama-era protections for internet users. The new law permits Internet Service Providers (ISPs) to access, without permission, data about our internet use patterns — from the sites we visit to the search terms we use. And this data isn't restricted to the work we do on computers. Thanks to the "internet of things," all our various connections can be monitored by our ISPs — from our physical location to the temperature we keep our homes to the music we ask Alexa to play for us. (In fact, Alexa processes all of our speech when it is on, even when we are not addressing it.)

Every day, we participate in a digital culture owned and operated by others — designers, engineers, technologists, CEOs — who have come to understand how easily they can harvest our intellectual property, data, and the minute details of our lives. To resist this (or even to more consciously participate in it), we need skills that allow us to "read" our world (in the Freirean sense) and to act with agency.

CRITICAL DIGITAL LITERACIES

Tim Amidon writes in "(dis)Owning Tech: Ensuring Value and Agency at the Moment of Interface",

> Educational technologies, as interfaces, offer students and educators opportunities to discover and enact agency through strategic rhetorical action. Yet, realizing this agency is complex work ... [that] requires an increasingly sophisticated array of multiliteracies.

Developing these critical multiliteracies is vital if we want scholars and students — and all the digital citizenry — to retain ownership over their intellectual property, their data, their privacy, their ideas, their voices. Even tools we love — that have potential to do good work in the world — need careful scrutiny. It is, in fact, part of our care for those tools and students who use them that demands we approach educational technology critically. There is no good use in tool fidelity. For example, uncritical belief in the superiority of the Mac OS over Windows or Linux may lead us to overlook how single-platform solutions exclude those without access to them. Tools (and software) are not something we should ever be "loyal" to. Even when a company's ideology is sound, the execution of that ideology through the platform may be flawed. For this reason, it's important to understand how to look deeply at any digital tool.

This isn't, as Howard Rheingold writes in *Net Smart*, "rocket science. It's not even algebra. Becoming acquainted with the fundamentals of Web credibility testing is easier than learning the multiplication tables. The hard part, as always, is the exercise of flabby think-for-yourself muscles." There is no special magic to digital literacies, whether we're assessing information or which word processing tool to use — and no pre-defined set of "transferrable skills" that can only be drawn upon by "experts" in the field. Rather, the work involves a shift in orientation and acknowledgement that the Web works upon its objects and people in specific and nuanced ways.

At the Digital Pedagogy Lab Institutes where we've taught, there's one exercise in particular we return to again and again. In our "crap detection" exercise (named for Rheingold's use of the term), participants use a rubric to assess one of a number of digital tools. The tools are pitted, head to head, in a sort of edtech *celebrity deathmatch*. Participants compare Blackboard and Canvas, for instance, or WordPress and Medium, Twitter and Facebook, Genius and Hypothes.is.

We start by seeing what the tools say they do and comparing that to *what they actually do*. But the work asks educators to do more than simply look at the platform's own web site, which more often than not says only the very best things (and sometimes directly misleading things) about the company and its tool. We encourage participants to do research — to find forums, articles, and blog posts written about the platform, to read the tool's terms of service, and even to tweet questions directly to the company's CEO.

This last has led to some interesting discussions on Twitter. One CEO, for example, wondered defensively what his own politics had to do with his tool. Others have been incredibly receptive to the conversations this activity has generated. We would contend that this is the exact kind of work we should do when choosing what tools to use with students. (Jesse has also done the activity with a group of digital studies students at University of Mary Washington.) Educators should be looking under the hood of edtech tools and talking more directly with technologists. Meanwhile, edtech CEOs should be encouraged (and sometimes compelled) to better understand what happens in our classrooms. Otherwise, we end up with tools — like ProctorU and Turnitin — that not only try to anticipate (or invent) the needs of teachers, but ultimately do damage by working directly at odds with our pedagogies.

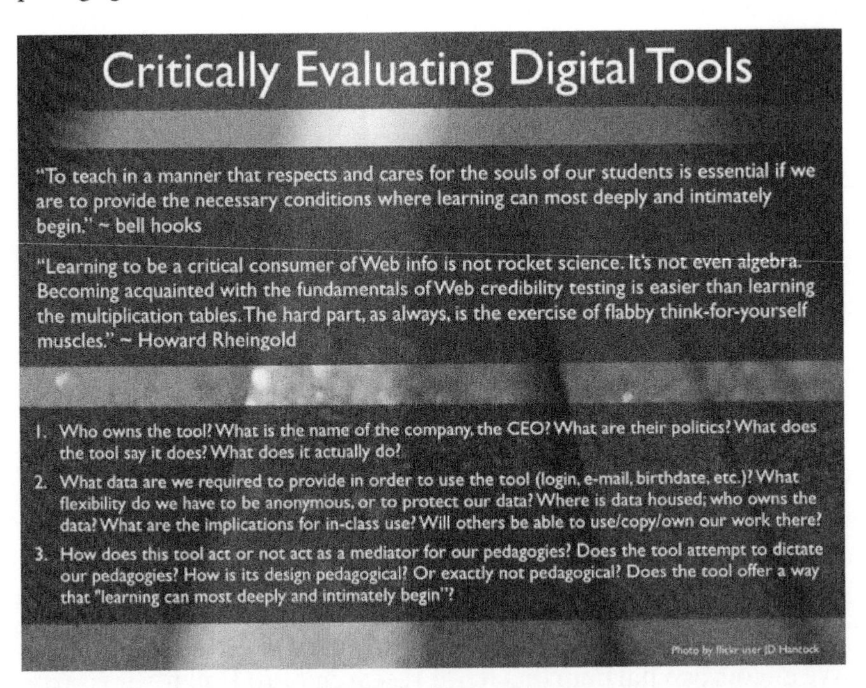

The goal of the exercise is not to "take down" or malign any specific digital tools or edtech companies, but rather for participants to think in ways they haven't about the tools they already use or might consider asking students to use.

Here's the rubric for the exercise:

1. Who owns the tool? What is the name of the company,

the CEO? What are their politics? What does the tool say it does? What does it actually do?
2. What data are we required to provide in order to use the tool (login, e-mail, birthdate, etc.)? What flexibility do we have to be anonymous, or to protect our data? Where is data housed; who owns the data? What are the implications for in-class use? Will others be able to use/copy/own our work there?
3. How does this tool act or not act as a mediator for our pedagogies? Does the tool attempt to dictate our pedagogies? How is its design pedagogical? Or exactly not pedagogical? Does the tool offer a way that "learning can most deeply and intimately begin"?

Over time, the exercise has evolved as the educators we've worked with have developed further questions through their research. Accessibility, for example, has always been an implicit component of the activity, which we've now brought more distinctly to the fore, adding these questions: How accessible is the tool? For a blind student? For a hearing-impaired student? For a student with a learning disability? For introverts? For extroverts? Etc. What statements does the company make about accessibility?

Ultimately, this is a critical thinking exercise aimed at asking critical questions, empowering critical relationships, encouraging new digital literacies.

In "Critical Pedagogy and Design," Sean describes these kinds of literacies as a vital component of teaching and learning in digital spaces:

> What lies at the heart of these literacies also forms the primary concern of critical digital pedagogy: that is, agency. The agency to know, understand, and thereby be able to act upon, create, or resist one's reality. For the student, this can mean anything from knowing how and why to read terms of service for a digital product or platform; recognizing the availability of networks and community

> in digital spaces, even in the LMS; understanding the multitude of ways that digital identity can be built, compromised, and protected; discovering methods for establishing presence and voice, and the wherewithal to reach out to others who are trying to discover the same.

This is ethical, activist work. While not exactly the Luddism of the 19th Century, we must ask ourselves when we're choosing edtech tools who profits and from what? Audrey Watters reminds us that, for the Luddites, "It was never about the loom per se. It's always about who owns the machines; it's about who benefits from one's labor, from one's craft." Because so much of educational technology runs on the labor of students and teachers, profiting off the work they do in the course of a day, quarter, or semester, it's imperative that we understand deeply our relationship to that technology — and more importantly the relationship, or "arranged marriage," we are brokering for students.

Because what's especially problematic in all of this is that instructors compel students to comply with the terms of these software and tools. And administrators or institutions compel faculty to compel students to comply. Meanwhile, everyone involved is being sold a "product," some of which, like Turnitin, are designed to eat our intellectual property and spit out control and hierarchy on the other end. When adopting new platforms, we shouldn't invest in or cede control to for-profit companies more interested in profit than education. And, when our institutions (or teachers) make unethical choices, we must (if we are able) find ways to say "no."

In "Bartleby, the Scrivener," Herman Melville writes, "Nothing so aggravates an earnest person as a passive resistance." We must become conscious of, as Jesse observes in "I Would Prefer Not To,"

> the ways we respond (both actively and passively) in the face of institutional demands we find unethical or pedagogically harmful … And if we object to the increasing standardization of education, how and where do we build sites of resistance? What strategies can

> we employ to protect ourselves and students? What work-arounds can we employ as we build courage and community for revolt? What systems of privilege must we first dismantle?

Critical analysis is resistance. Questions are our sabots.

TURNITIN: ACADEMIC INTEGRITY AT $2 PER STUDENT

Some platforms are not agnostic. Not all tools can be hacked to good use. Critical Digital Pedagogy demands we approach our tools and technologies always with one eyebrow raised. Some tools have good intentions squandered at the level of interface. Some tools have no good intentions at all. And when tools like these are adopted across an institution, the risks in mounting a resistance can be incredibly high, especially for contingent staff, students, and untenured faculty.

Turnitin isn't selling teachers and administrators a product. The marketing on their website frames the Turnitin brand less as software and more as a pedagogical lifestyle brand. In fact, the word "plagiarism" is used only twice on their home page, in spite of the fact that the tool is first and foremost a plagiarism detection service. The rest of the copy and images are smoke and mirrors. They are "your partner in education with integrity." They are "trusted by 15,000 institutions and 30 million students." (We feel certain they didn't ask those 30 million students whether they "trust" Turnitin.) The "products" most prominently featured are their "revision assistant" and "feedback studio." For the teachers and administrators using Turnitin as a plagiarism detector, these features function like carbon offsetting. When asked whether their institution uses Turnitin, they can point to all the other things Turnitin can be used for — all the other things that Turnitin is not really used for. The site even attempts to hide its core functionality behind a smokescreen; in the description for the "feedback studio," plagiarism detection is called "similarity checking."

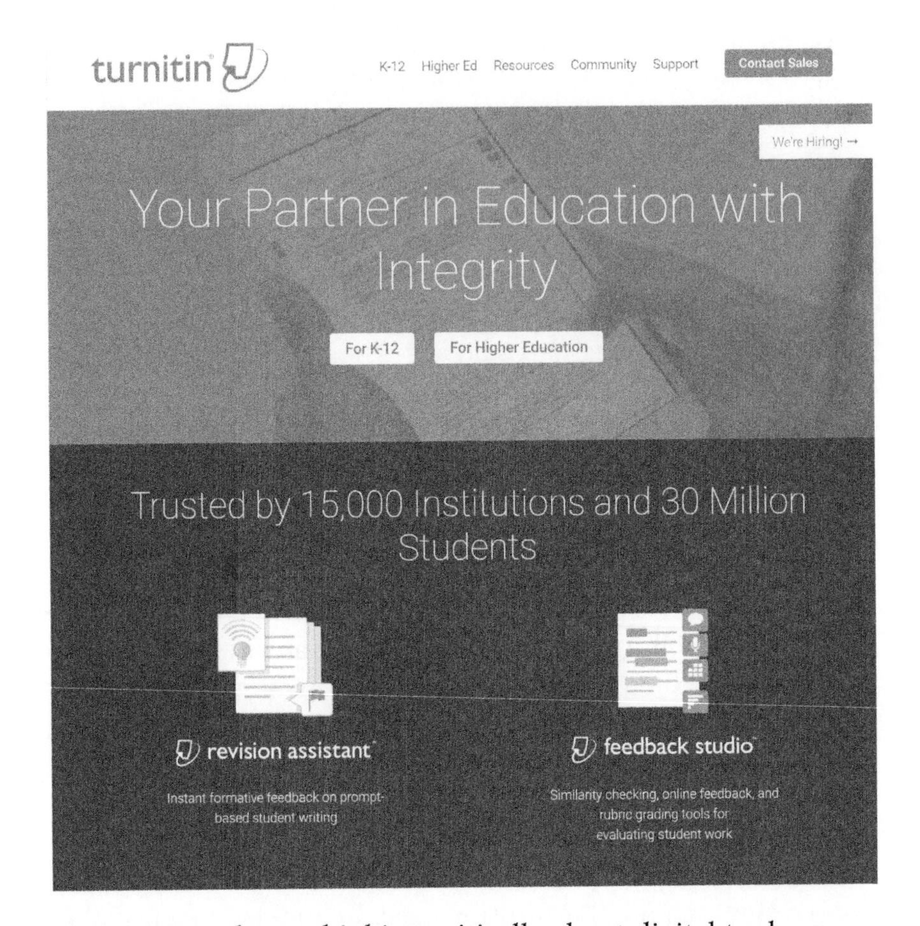

As we wrote above, thinking critically about digital tools means *weighing what the tools say they do against what they actually do*. In the case of Turnitin there are some marked discrepancies. For example, at the top of Turnitin's Privacy page (which they grossly call their "Privacy Center"), a note from the CEO declares, "Integrity is at the heart of all we do; it defines us." Then later, Turnitin declares that it "does not ever assert or claim copyright ownership of any works submitted to or through our service. Your property is YOUR property. We do not, and will not, use your intellectual property for any purpose other than to deliver, support, and develop our services, which are designed to protect and strengthen your copyright." Even if it is true that Turnitin doesn't assert *ownership* over the intellectual property it collects, their statement is misleading. They are basically saying *our brand*

is your brand — that by helping them build their business we all simultaneously protect our own intellectual property. This is absurd.

Robin Wharton encourages educators, at the end of her 2006 piece "Re-Thinking Plagiarism as Unfair Competition," "to take a long hard look at how their own practices may foster an environment in which students are disenfranchised and relegated to the status of mere consumers in the education process."

In a recent conversation where he tried to explain why Turnitin's violation of student intellectual property was a problem, Sean's argument was countered with a question about whether that intellectual property was worth protecting. After all, most student work "isn't worth publishing." Ignoring for a moment this flagrant disregard for the value of student work, the point to make here is that Turnitin actively profits (to the tune of $752 million) from the work of students.

Let's look closer at Turnitin's terms of service, keeping in mind that complying with these terms is not optional for students required to submit their work to Turnitin.

> **Any communications or material of any kind** that you e-mail, post, or transmit through the Site (excluding personally identifiable information of students and any papers submitted to the Site), including, questions, comments, suggestions, and other data and information (your "Communications") **will be treated as non-confidential and nonproprietary. You grant Turnitin a non-exclusive, royalty-free, perpetual, world-wide, irrevocable license to reproduce, transmit, display, disclose, and otherwise use your Communications on the Site or elsewhere for our business purposes**. We are free to use any ideas, concepts, techniques, know-how in your Communications for any purpose, including, but not limited to, the development and use of products and services based on the Communications. [emphasis added]

As Jesse writes in "The Dissertation in the Age of Mechanical Reproduction: "What we see there is a blur of words and phrases separated by commas, of which 'royalty-free, perpetual, world-wide, irrevocable' are but a scary few. The rat-a-tat-tat of nouns, verbs, and adjectives is so bewildering that almost anyone would blindly click 'agree' just to avoid the deluge of legalese. But these words are serious and their ramifications pedagogical." Note also that this rather crucial paragraph is currently buried in the middle of Turnitin's TOS, over 5000 words in.

For papers submitted to the site specifically, the Turnitin TOS states "You hereby grant to Turnitin, its affiliates, vendors, service providers, and licensors a non-exclusive, royalty-free, perpetual, worldwide, irrevocable license to use such papers, as well as feedback and results, for the limited purposes of a) providing the Services, and b) for improving the quality of the Services generally." The gist: when you upload work to Turnitin, your property is, in no reasonable sense, YOUR property. Every essay students submit — representing hours, days, or even years of work — becomes part of the Turnitin database, which is then sold to universities. According to the company's website, as of this writing, Turnitin has a "non-exclusive, royalty-free, perpetual, worldwide, irrevocable license" to more than 734 million student papers.

734 million student papers.

Turnitin doesn't reveal its pricing on its website, going instead for a "get a quote" model, but Financial Times reported in 2012 that the cost per student was around $2 per year. So, that means an institution of 10,000 students will pay Turnitin $20,000 per year so the company can build its business. But Turnitin does not do a large chunk of the labor it sells. Students do. And even if students don't actively object to donating that labor, educators should never be in the business of removing student agency.

The abuse of student labor and intellectual property is only the beginning of the problem with Turnitin. If the company's financial and legal model isn't troubling enough, consider then how the application of its services affects the pedagogical relationship between students and teachers.

Tim Amidon observes:

> iParadigms' Turnitin employs a rhetoric of fear to turn educators away from, as Rebecca Moore Howard puts it [in "Understanding 'Internet Plagiarism'"], "pedagogy that joins teachers and students in the educational enterprise [by choosing] ... a machine that will separate them," but also leaches the intellectual property students create within educational systems only to sell it back to schools.

Turnitin supplants teaching. Whereas intellectual property is a multivalent issue in the academy (especially in a digital age when authorship and ownership are mutable and contested), Turnitin's solution is writ in black and white. "Students uploading their work to Turnitin are turned from learners into potential plagiarizers," Jesse writes in "Who Controls Your Dissertation?," "and the teaching moment (about attribution, citation, and scholarly generosity) is given away to an algorithm." To an issue of academic integrity that has been the project of teaching for decades, educational technology answers with efficiency. Plug it in. Add it up. Point a finger.

Behind this surrender to efficiency over complication, Turnitin takes advantage of the perennial mistrust of students by teachers. Turnitin relies on suspicion of plagiarism as an assumed quantity in the teacher-student relationship, and it feeds that polemic through its marketing. In their "Plagiarism Spectrum" infographic, for example, student writing is reduced to quaint icons and graphics. Plagiarism comes in flavors — from CTRL-C to Hybrid, from Remix and Recycle to 404 Error — which assign students to 10 discrete types. Easily managed, simple to define, less than human.

Rebecca Moore Howard writes in "Arguing Against Turnitin":

> Many of our colleagues are entrenched in an agonistic stance toward students in the aggregate: students are lazy, illiterate, anti-

> intellectual cheaters who must prove their worth to the instructor. Turnitin and its automated assessment of student writing is a tool for that proof...

There's something terribly parasitic about a service that plays on our insecurity about students and our fears of cheating. And it's not just leaching student intellectual property, and reinforcing teachers' mistrust of students, it's actually handicapping teachers from exercising their pedagogical agency. Inside Higher Ed reported in 2015 that:

> The Council of Writing Program Administrators has noted that "teachers often find themselves playing an adversarial role as 'plagiarism police' instead of a coaching role as educators." As a result, the "suspicion of student plagiarism has begun to affect teachers at all levels, at times diverting them from the work of developing students' writing, reading and critical thinking abilities," the organization wrote in a statement on best practices from 2003.

So, if you're not worried about paying Turnitin to traffic your students' intellectual property, and you're not worried about how the company has glossed a complicated pedagogical issue to offer a simple solution, you might worry about how Turnitin reinforces the divide between teachers and students, short-circuiting the human tools we have to cross that divide.

These arguments and others led the CCCC Intellectual Property Caucus to issue a statement about Turnitin and other plagiarism detection services. In short, the statement cites five irreconcilable problems with Turnitin (none of which even begin to mine its problematic business model):

Plagiarism detection services

1. "undermine students' authority" over their own work;
2. place students in a role of needing to be "policed";
3. "create a hostile environment";
4. supplant good teaching with the use of inferior technology;

5. violate student privacy.

RESISTING TURNITIN

How does a student push back against the flood of a tool like Turnitin, especially when that tool has been adopted across an institution? Resistance has to be on multiple fronts, offering individual students ways to respond when they are asked to compromise their intellectual property, while also addressing the systemic issues that leads to the institutional adoption of Turnitin in the first place. Many students instinctually understand the problems with a tool like Turnitin. Many have told us both how it feels to hit submit, turning over their work to an algorithm, and how helpless they feel to challenge a system that has distrust at its core. As educators, we can advocate and work to educate others about the problems of tools like Turnitin, but we find ourselves wanting better solutions, in the moment, for students who find themselves staring down the requirement of submitting to Turnitin.

Toward that end, we've put together a draft letter that students can send to faculty, that faculty can send to administrators, to help them better understand the problems with Turnitin. The tone of the letter is intentionally non-combative, and it includes a list of further resources. **We encourage anyone to fork, remix, re-imagine this letter at will. Help us by offering suggestions on how we can continue to revise. And, if you send some version of it, let us know.**

Dear [Name]:

In 2014, the Conference on College Composition and Communication, a branch of the National Council of Teachers of English, concluded that plagiarism detection services, like Turnitin by iParadigm, "create a hostile environment" in classrooms, "undermine students' authority" over their own work, and violate student privacy. Despite this fact, I am asked to submit my work frequently through Turnitin in the name of academic integrity. Unfortunately, the use of student intellectual property and labor for profit by a third party is neither academic in practice or spirit, nor does it model integrity.

Plagiarism detection services rely upon the labor of students as their business model. Although Turnitin markets itself as a "partner in education," "trusted by 15,000 institutions and 30 million students," in fact the service does what no collaborator should do—forces me to license to them my intellectual property and makes it impossible for me to reclaim my full rights to that work. Turnitin's terms of service state very clearly:

> **If You submit a paper or other content in connection with the Services, You hereby grant to Turnitin, its affiliates, vendors, service providers, and licensors a non-exclusive, royalty-free, perpetual, worldwide, irrevocable license to use such papers**, as well as feedback and results, for the limited purposes of a) providing the Services, and b) for improving the quality of the Services generally.

This means that, not only do I surrender the license to use my work in perpetuity to this plagiarism detection service, but Turnitin *sells my work* back to you.

I've gathered together a few resources on the matter for your consideration:

- What Is Detected? by Carl Straumsheim, from Inside Higher Ed (https://www.insidehighered.com/news/2015/07/14/turnitin-faces-new-questions-about-efficacy-plagiarism-detection-software)
- Understanding "Internet Plagiarism" by Rebecca Moore Howard (https://pdfs.semanticscholar.org/2fe4/f4c5e372d280c9b4cad07b15d0206dda9ef1.pdf)
- CCCC-IP Caucus Recommendations Regarding Academic Integrity and the Use of Plagiarism Detection Services (http://culturecat.net/files/CCCC-IPpositionstatementDraft.pdf)

- McLean Students File Suit Against Turnitin.com: Useful Tool or Instrument of Tyranny? by Traci A. Zimmerman (http://www.ncte.org/cccc/committees/ip/2007developments/mclean)

Please stop using Turnitin at our institution. Choose instead to keep academic integrity a human problem with human solutions. Or, at the very least, allow me to individually opt out. Should I ever unintentionally plagiarize, I would rather have the opportunity to speak with my instructor about my mistake than receive a machine-generated report. Please put teaching back in the hands of teachers, where it belongs.

There is no reason to surrender this institution's tradition of teaching and academic integrity to a third-party technology solution. Thank you for your support.

Sincerely,
[Name]

DEAR CHRONICLE: WHY I WILL NO LONGER WRITE FOR VITAE

JESSE STOMMEL

Dear Chronicle–

I recently accepted a job as a columnist for Vitae from the Chronicle of Higher Education, where I've published two columns in the last two months. A draft of my third column is due today. I won't be submitting it.

Unfortunately, Vitae continues to publish "Dear Student," its student-shaming series, also referred to as "professorial tough love."

Here's some tough love of my own.

The concerns the series has focused on are petty and pedantic, and nobody is being well-served by the content on display (not students, not professors, editors, the Chronicle, the other writers for Vitae, the job seekers visiting the site, or the job advertisers using the service).

The great concerns of teachers featured in this series:
"it's February and you didn't buy your textbook,"
"no I won't change the grade you deserve,"
"my class began two weeks ago and you just show up now,"
"your 'granny' died and I have absolutely no compassion."

On textbooks. Education should be about dialogue, conversation, community. We do not invite students into an educational environment by admonishing them. Our classes should have more valuable tickets for entry than textbooks.

On grades. They're a red herring. Any teacher that regularly gets caught up in power and control struggles with students over grades has missed the point.

On a student showing up for a class that started two weeks ago. The work of gatekeeping is anathema to the work of education. Our classrooms should have more doors and windows, not less.

On grandmothers. The statistics are compelling: "grandmothers are 20 times more likely to die before a final exam." Here's a better statistic: it is 100 times kinder to err on the side of giving students the benefit of the doubt when it comes to dead grandmothers. And we need to consider whether there is something about the educational system that has put students in the awkward and uncomfortable position of feeling like they have to lie to their teachers.

Everyone that comes into even casual contact with Vitae's "Dear Student" series is immediately tarnished by the same kind of anti-intellectual, uncompassionate, illogical nonsense currently threatening to take down the higher education system in the state of Wisconsin.

The word "entitlement," used pejoratively about students in two of the four articles, needs to die a quick death. College students ARE entitled — to an education and not the altogether unfunny belittling on display in the "Dear Student" series.

This series is not effective satire, not a useful kind of venting. This series plays to the insecurities of its audience in a way that feels opportunistic. Academic job seekers are concerned about their current and future livelihood. They are oppressed by a system that calls 75% of its labor-force "unnecessary," "contingent," "adjunct." The "Dear Student" series turns that oppression, and the most snickering part of it, upon students.

What everyone working anywhere even near to the education system needs to do:

- Treat the least privileged among us with the most respect.
- Recognize that the job of a teacher is to advocate for students, especially in an educational system currently under direct threat at almost every turn.
- Laugh at ourselves and not at those we and our system have made most vulnerable.
- Rant up, not down.

Giggling at the water cooler about students is one abhorrent thing. Publishing that derisive giggling as "work" in a venue read by tens of thousands is quite another. Of course, teachers need a safe place to vent. We all do. That safe place is not shared faculty offices, not the teacher's lounge, not the library, not a local (public) watering hole. And it is certainly not on the pages of the Chronicle of Higher Education, especially in Vitae, the publication devoted to job seekers, including current students and future teachers.

I won't stand beside this water cooler. I won't encourage anyone else to come near to it. Until "Dear Student" has ended its run and the Chronicle has published a public apology to students, the words right here (in this "Dear Chronicle" letter) are the only words of mine the Chronicle has my permission to publish on Vitae.

DEAR STUDENT

JESSE STOMMEL

Almost a year ago, I wrote a blog post responding to a series of student-shaming articles published at the *Chronicle of Higher Education*. The post was ultimately read by 50,000 people and spawned more than a dozen responses, some from the darker corners of the web. I hadn't intended my little 750-word piece as a massive public pillory and didn't expect it to be read by such a large audience. As I wrote in several places over the days following its publication, my piece was not meant as an attack on any specific individuals and was certainly not an attack on teachers. I wrote,

> This series plays to the insecurities of its audience in a way that feels opportunistic. Academic job seekers are concerned about their current and future livelihood. They are oppressed by a system that calls 75% of its labor-force 'unnecessary,' 'contingent,' 'adjunct.' 'Dear Student' turns that oppression, and the most snickering part of it, upon students.

The Chronicle profits directly by encouraging a culture that pits vulnerable students and teachers against each other. The "Dear Student" series was not the first of its ilk, and not the last. What I see are teachers with genuine anxieties being asked to put themselves in a compromised position from which they are very publicly belittling students. Nobody wins. Not the students. Not the teachers. Not education in the eyes of its detractors. The fact that this kind of shaming often gets encouraged and defended by teachers is a structural problem. The fact that the Chronicle promotes it and profits from it is a decidedly corporate one.

What I listened to most intently during the aftermath of "Dear Chronicle" were the student voices, a number of whom commented anonymously on my piece:

"Part of the reason why I never asked for help was because I saw what my professors thought of those who did."

"I dropped out of college, in large part due to the hoops I had to jump through to get my disabilities recognized. I was always so tired of having to justify myself and I didn't want to have to argue 'but I'm not like *those* students' because then I'd be no better than the people judging me."

"It's a lot easier to stay motivated when you're not made to feel like you're stupid or a liar. It's a lot easier to focus on studying when you're not focused on having to justify yourself."

This is where the conversation starts. By listening seriously to the voices of students and recognizing that students can be drivers of the conversation about the state of education. Teachers have anxieties. Teaching is one of the most emotionally difficult jobs I have done and can imagine doing. Of course, we need to vent. But it is not productive for us to continue creating spaces for teachers to vent that students can eavesdrop on but feel excluded from. I agree that we need to talk openly about real concerns, but there are better ways to have those conversations than by stereotyping, mocking, and shaming.

Some stats from a few recent studies of bullying in higher education:

- 62% of professionals stated they had been bullied or witnessed bullying in higher education vs. 37% in the general population. Women, African Americans, and members of the LGBT community are disproportionately bullied. (Hollis)
- 51% of students claimed to have seen another student being bullied by a professor/instructor at least once and

> 18% claimed to have been bullied themselves by a professor/instructor at least once. (Marraccini)

These statistics are definitely in sync with my anecdotal experience. I have heard stories or seen students mistreated by faculty (and faculty mistreated by faculty) at every institution where I've worked. If you haven't seen this bullying running rampant, you may be the bully. And it may be unintentional, because the problem is systemic.

The Milgram experiment famously put its participants in three roles: "experimenter," "learner" (an actor), and "teacher" (the subject of the experiment). It was as much an experiment about education as it was an experiment about compliance. In short, the experimenter would order the teacher to give shocks to the learner, for getting a wrong answer, and more often than was expected the teacher complied. This was not a *nice* experiment, and I've found the videos genuinely harrowing. The results were compelling but flawed.

In the epilogue to *Obedience to Authority*, Stanley Milgram argues,

> Each individual possesses a conscience which to a greater or lesser degree serves to restrain the unimpeded flow of impulses destructive to others. But when he merges his person into an organizational structure, a new creature replaces autonomous man, unhindered by the limitations of individual morality, freed of humane inhibition, mindful only of the sanctions of authority.

Milgram was ultimately denied tenure because the ethics of his experiment were rightfully questioned. Still, Milgram's experiment has been continually re-created. Perhaps, what is most telling is not Milgram's results, but the fact that the experiment continues to be repeated and debated and supported and refuted. When faced with an oppressive authority figure, we wonder how we'll act, what we'll do, who we'll obey. The answers, unfortunately, aren't clear. Even good teachers, *kind* teachers, given an oppressive hierarchical system, will misuse their authority.

Milgram concludes his book with this line, "the condition of freedom in any state is always a widespread and consistent skepticism of the canons upon which power insists." Whatever else we might say about Milgram and his experiment, there is something useful here. His call was for a constant vigilance, flushing at any onset of unthinking, uncaring obedience. And yet his call was couched within an experiment that was itself *mean*, callous even, desperate for results — the same sort of educational system we see today in K-12 and Higher Ed. A precarious labor force is an obedient one. And ill-fitting cogs do not make for better machines. A system of standards, outcomes, and measurement (in which assessment drives learning) is well-served by adjunctification, casualization, and corporatization — a well-oiled experimenter demanding the intimidated teacher abuse hapless learners.

Who in this system is most vulnerable?

It's important to think about intersectionality when talking about power and hierarchies. Teacher / student is a binary that needs deconstructing but never at the expense of the other identities in play (race, class, gender, sexuality, ability, etc.). No binary exists in a vacuum.

If a straight white male student harasses a gay teacher, *that* is an example of homophobia. If the same teacher gives the student an "F" in retaliation, *that* is an example of misused institutional authority. If the gay teacher has a conversation with the student or all the students about systemic gender and sexuality bias, *that* would be a direct response to those dynamics without an abuse of the student / teacher hierarchy.

When we talk about "ranting up," as I did in my "Dear Chronicle" piece, students are not "up." If a teacher is targeting a student publicly, *calling out their student-ness from a position of authority*, and belittling them, I'd call that "ranting down," no matter the other positionality involved. And too often it is the most vulnerable students (the ones facing multiple oppressions) who get the least compassion in our educational system.

Kindness does not mean sugarcoating. But neither should "professionalism" excuse cruelty. Being frank and honest is essential. Students are not undifferentiated masses of positivity. Each of them is unique and worth my acknowledging and engaging individually and respectfully. Some of those interactions are difficult. None are easy. We have to approach our interactions with students from a place of care. Like when my dad let go of my bike for the first time even though he said he "had me..." It was a loving gesture. And he did have me. Just not the seat of my bike. As a teacher, I want students to "show up" because I value their contributions — because I (and the other students in class) learn as much from them as they learn from me. Advocating for students doesn't mean being blindly permissive. It doesn't mean having no expectations.

Marty Bickman writes, "We often ignore the best resource for informed change, one that is right in front of our noses every day — our students, for whom the most is at stake." And, to that, I responded in "The Public Digital Humanites," "We have built an almost ironclad academic system — and I acknowledge myself as one of its privileged builders — a system which excludes the voices of students, which calls students 'customers' while monetizing their intellectual property, which denigrates the work of learning through assessment mechanisms and credentialing pyramid schemes." This is not a system that empowers students.

We can't get to a place of listening to students if they don't show up to the conversation because we've already excluded their voice in advance by creating environments hostile to them and their work. Listening to students is not a gimmick. Sean Michael Morris writes in "Collegiality as Pedagogy,"

> At some point, we need to stop blaming students for the state of education. If, after so many years of controlling student behavior, analyzing their data to understand and curtail that behavior, we are

> still unhappy with their performance, perhaps it's time we turn education over to them.

We can't get to a place of listening to students if we continue to create us/them dichotomies — as I have done in this very sentence — that position teachers and students against one another.

The work of educating from a place of care might seem abstract, or might be dismissed as *touchy-feely,* but if our goal is truly to resist the corporatization and standardization of education, we must recognize the ways that the failure to acknowledge students as full agents in their learning is a process that runs immediately parallel to the failure to acknowledge teachers as full agents in the classroom. The process that makes teachers increasingly adjunct is the same process that has made students into customers. And the gear that makes this system go depends on the pitting of students and teachers against one another.

The gear that makes this system go is obedience — mere compliance at the expense of critical engagement and complex human understanding.

For education to work, there can be no divide between teachers and students. There must be what Paulo Freire, in *Pedagogy of the Oppressed,* calls "teacher-students." Specifically, he writes, "no one teaches another, nor is anyone self-taught." So, "teacher" becomes a role that shifts, and learning depends upon a community of teacher-students. Any authority within the space must be aimed at fostering agency in all the members of the community. And this depends on a recognition of the power dynamics and hierarchies that this kind of learning environment must actively and continuously work against. There is no place for shame in the work of education.

WIDE-AWAKENESS AND CRITICAL IMAGINATION

SEAN MICHAEL MORRIS

I have a tradition of getting really sick to my stomach before every presentation. Every keynote. Every opening remark at Digital Pedagogy Lab. Every lesson taught in a classroom. Every first video filmed for an online class.

Rolling Stones lead singer Mick Jagger used to eat a special banana before every performance. Sting did yoga.

I make references that age me. And I get sick in my stomach.

Right now, if you were close enough to tell, you'd see that I'm shaking. You might hear my voice quaver. You might get the sense that my eyes are darting back and forth, looking for a friendly face, a smile, eye contact.

It's uncomfortable for me to speak in front of people. And yet I've chosen a life of teaching—teaching students, teaching teachers—and I founded Digital Pedagogy Lab... which means I've spoken in front of people on three continents. In vastly different cultures. And every time... I guess it's like my own special banana before every talk. A good luck charm.

I bring this up because nervousness—shaking, quavering, nauseated nervousness—is exactly what critical pedagogy actually feels like.

Maxine Greene says that "experiences of shock are necessary if the limits or the horizons are to be breached." It is therefore unwise to sit in our comfort when what we hope to do is unseat, to shrink when what we want is to grow.

So, I stand up and speak. And students attend school.

I first attended a college class when I was 10. It was a Shakespeare course taught by Reg Saner at the University of Colorado-Boulder. My mom had returned to school only a few years before to complete a bachelor's degree in English, and she decided to take me out of school that day. To go to her school. To see what teachers and discussions and classes were like at the far end of my education.

Here I was accustomed to weekly vocabulary drills, reading books checked out from my elementary school library. I'd never read Shakespeare (though my mom had read me Dickens, Poe, and Frost at that point). But I'd grown up in Boulder, where so many of the roads literally lead to the university. College was a fixture in my life, a geographical one as much as an ideological one. My mother had battled her own fear of speaking to attend her first classes at Metro State University, later transferring to CU Boulder; and there was simply nothing more aspirational in my family than getting a degree.

So, one sunny morning, my mom took me to her Shakespeare class. They were discussing Hamlet. We walked across the campus—a wonder of imported Tuscan architecture, and so green in the springtime before the Colorado heat has baked the landscape. I marveled at the adult children at play on the quad, at the long, silent hallways that felt at once serene and deeply judgmental, the ancient chalkboards and the one particular wooden desk I sat in beside my mom.

She opened her book. She bent her head to take notes. The professor entered. And he spoke.

It was theatre. And I loved every minute of it. Professor Saner's preoccupation was poetry—writing as much as reading—and so his lecturing voice rolled across the classroom, speaking in longer words than I'd ever heard, and handling the English language so expertly that I was at once envious and inspired.

My mother also adored Dr. Saner, and visited him in office hours often. She purchased his books of poetry. She signed up for every one of his classes that fit her schedule as a mom of three. But when it came time to approach him for a letter of recommendation for her application to CU's graduate program in English, he told her:

> "I'll write you this one. But I wouldn't recommend you for the doctorate."

In "Not Enough Voices," I write:

> "Your students have fought, your students have hidden from bullies, your students have been hungry, they have passed for straight, they have held their tongues, and they have been broken. In many cases, the students you work with have had to subvert a system that sought to oppress them in order to make it to your classroom."

What happens when they find out, upon entering the classroom, that this oppressive system is alive and well there? What happens when a student who loves to learn is told they are not qualified to to so? And yet, how many of us in this room could, without much effort, identify a student we felt wasn't built for our field, or for education at all?

Students live in a space of imagination. They have to, if for no other reason than that they are learning. They have come to school at cross purposes with society's reasons for schooling: for the student, learning—the ache to do it, not necessarily its realization in school—is spurred by a desire to claim their agency, which they can only do through critical thinking and critical imagining; for society, the student will become a bundle of fulfilled outcomes, a set of data which can be applied to a task in the marketplace.

What is particularly interesting about this conflict of interests is that the student, in seeking agency, autonomy, and the ability to see things as if they were otherwise, must front with the expectations of society, which precisely fuel and always also threaten to overturn their agency.

Which is why when they come to school, they are not only learning mathematics, physics, anthropology, English, the world of business, or whichever, they are also slowly learning—through our rubrics, policies, grades, assessments, our delivery of content—not to mention the culture of student shaming and distrust that rolls like the professorial voice does across the room through our halls, across our campuses, into our social media—that they must accept education as it is, to cease questioning it for its greater possibilities.

This is the kind of oppression that Maxine Greene writes about when she says, "The oppression and the domination that I have in mind are the kind that breed 'false consciousness' … the kind that subject human beings to technical systems, deprive them of spontaneity, and erode their self-determination, their autonomy."

It is not, in other words, the oppression we believe our liberal politics or our inclusive approaches, our concern with open educational resources and open pedagogy address. It is the oppression of the letter of recommendation, the oppression of the grade, the oppression of an authority who determines whether or not we are fit to learn, fit to explore, fit to exercise our agency and autonomy.

And yet students have fought, hidden, gone hungry, held their tongues so that they could enjoy the privilege to imagine for themselves something different than the taken for granted, something otherwise.

Let me put it another way: When we turn to learning, we are making a choice to express an interest in things, an action that social philosopher Alfred Schutz might call a move toward wide-awakeness, "a plane of consciousness of highest tension originating in an attitude of full attention to life and its requirements." This interest in things is what propels learning, it is what propels education. Most of us have arrived here today because we have an interest in things, a desire to become more wide awake.

Henry David Thoreau tells us in *Walden* that "We must learn to reawaken and keep ourselves awake, not by mechanical aids, but by an infinite expectation of the dawn, which does not forsake us in our soundest sleep."

Infinite expectation of the dawn. Imagine if that's what each new semester felt like. Imagine if that's what a dissertation defense felt like. Or the five paragraph essay. Or your syllabus.

But of course we have built machines and systems designed for slumbering—those "technical systems" that Greene points out deprive us of our spontaneity. She writes that "attentiveness, this interest in things, is the direct opposite of the attitude of bland conventionality and indifference so characteristic of our time."

We have created best practices "to guard us against the incalculable difference of students." We have created the learning management system to parse learning into discrete moments and sections, all interrelated through the will and capacity to grade and assess. We have filled the university with processes and committees and an economy of reputation which rewards us for our compliance exactly as it blunts our wits and bores us to tears.

These are the machines we've designed for slumbering, for exactly not staying awake. And when we don't challenge them, when we shrug and say "It is sad, but what can be done. This is what reality is," then we are surrendering to the conditions we see around us, to indifference—instead of saying "Reality is not inexorably that."

"The opposite of morality," Greene writes, "is indifference—a lack of care, an absence of concern. Lacking wide-awakeness...individuals are likely to drift, to act on impulses of expediency."

And what is more expedient than the rubric, the grade, the standardized assessment, the LMS? I propose that when we notice that our systems and tools are built for efficiency, we choose to recognize not their time-saving features, but the way they encourage indifference, the way they lull us to sleep.

Critical digital pedagogy isn't this:

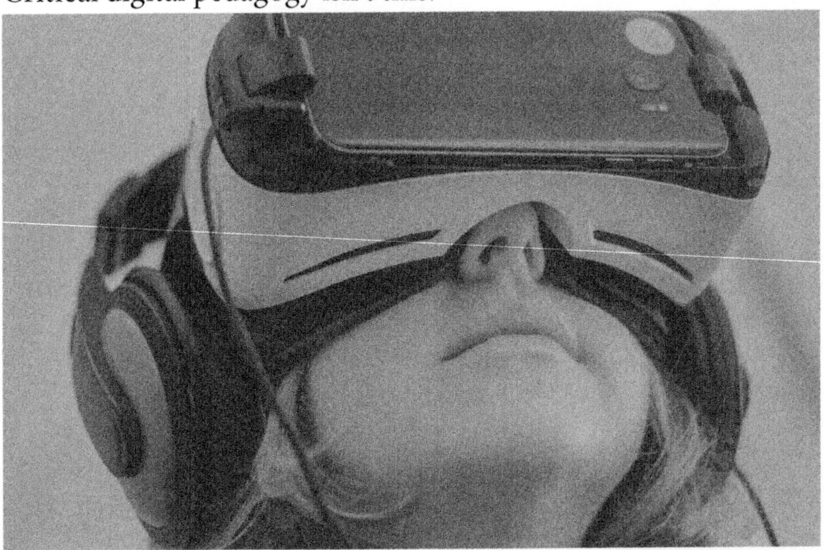

It's not the wonder of a new Canvas LTI. But it's also not the thrill of taking a tool down a notch.

Critical digital pedagogy is this.

And this.

And this.

The whole point of everything I'm saying is that we have not only a right to imagine education as if it were otherwise, but we have the responsibility to do so. A responsibility as educators to students, to the very systems of education, to the tools we use in class, to the mechanisms we employ to assess, and the approaches we use to include, validate, and keep human students.

But also a responsibility as educators to ourselves. To the very curiosity that has brought us here today, that took us through the humbling of our dissertations, the long nights of little food and much scholarship, the weird bantering arguments of grad school, and the doubt. Always the doubt.

Freire insists that the future is not inexorable. We can intervene. On a small scale, but no less important, we can say that grades are not inexorable, learning objectives are not inexorable, the rubric, textbooks, the lecture, all those component parts of education which have been passed down to us and which we pass down because "This is what reality is"—even the keynote—none of these things are anything more than interpretations of reality. We have the agency to change them, no matter what they are.

Agency is nothing more complicated than our ability to intervene in reality as historical subjects. Which means things can change, can be otherwise.

This is why we're here today. Or, I think so. To practice agency. To look at what we may have become inured to and to raise our heads and think (with a q) about new possibilities—possibilities made available through critical digital pedagogy, new thinking about design, and remixing pedagogies.

We have to be careful when we talk about remixing pedagogies, though, that we're daring ourselves to invent something, to push farther forward on the long arc of justice, rather than holding onto that which we have always known and are unwilling to let go of. Things as they are. Things we take for granted. A submergence in the habitual.

But let me back away for just a moment from all of this high-falutin' language. There's a constant threat with critical pedagogy that it can become so purely theoretical. But, as I wrote to a friend recently,

> "There are times when a critical pedagogy refuses to be merely theoretical. It is a tradition that comes out of a concern for labor, for the agency of those doing labor, and the perspicacity inherent behind that agency. The imagination is not an impractical facility at all, not a dreamer's tool only, but a precision instrument that delivers a certainty that things can be otherwise."

And so let's take a look at one particular innovation that works to address the problem of student agency in education:

Domain of One's Own, or "Domains" (or, Ms. Domains, if you're nasty). The Domains project started at the University of Mary Washington as an extension of the digital storytelling course,

DS106. According to the Division of Teaching and Learning Technologies web site, Domains allows

> "students, faculty, and staff to register their own domain name and associate it with a hosted web space, free of charge while at UMW. With their Domain and corresponding web space, users will have the opportunity and flexibility to design and create a meaningful and vibrant digital identity."

According to one of its originators, Martha Burtis, there are four goals embedded in Domain of One's Own:

- Provide students with the tools and technologies to build out a digital space of their own
- Help students appreciate how digital identity is formed
- Provide students with curricular opportunities to use the Web in meaningful ways
- Push students to understand how the technologies that underpin the Web work, and how that impacts their lives

In short, Domains allows students to create a space on the web that they can call their own, upon which they can write their digital identities, and through which they learn about digital technologies and tools, the affordances and limitations of both, and what it means to have a digital fingerprint.

According to Martha, the Domains project rose out of a moment of critical looking, followed shortly on by imaginative thinking.

> "We've doubled-down on courses and the LMS, we've bought into the notion that what technology afforded us for teaching and learning was standardization of experience and pedagogy, and we've abandoned the nascent spaces that might have let us continue to explore the Web as a flexible, open, and powerful platform for teaching and learning.
>
> "And we've spent so many years going down this path that there are

> now powerful monetary investments and administrative processes and expectations pounding on our backs, pushing us further and further.
>
> "How do we make it stop?"

Domain of One's Own rose out of the kind of practice that Greene and Freire both advocate for, the kind of practice which is at the core of critical pedagogy: the recognition of a reality that's less than desirable, a further recognition that that reality isn't inexorable, and the determination to intervene.

Domain of One's Own is as fraught as it is successful. And every step of the way—even now, after six years—working with Domains is anything but simple. It is that nervous, shaking, quavering experiment which is what critical pedagogy is all about. Questions abound: what do we do about assessment? should Domains even be curricular? what do we do with old Domains after students graduate? what sorts of freedoms should be encouraged, what sort of ethics should be maintained? what are the skills we're teaching with Domains? what skills is the Domains project teaching us?

There are the practical considerations about archiving and storage, assessment and grading, and the place of Domains in the curriculum. And there are the theoretical questions: is a student's domain really their own? does Domains hark or not hark back to Virginia Woolf's "A Room of One's Own", and her refusal of an unendurable reality, her demand for a space of reflection and self-ownership?

The cool thing is that the problems with Domains are also its joys, for to work with Domains requires a wide-awakeness to the project itself, and to the students and teachers and others who use it, explore it, defy its immediate constrictures. In other words, the very best part of Domains has nothing to do with the web at all; it has to do with how we as humans encounter the questions it raises.

The Domains project should make us nervous. It should leave us a little bit scared. We should look at it every year, every semester, and wonder if it can or should continue. Because this is the work of battling expediency and the machines made for slumbering.

And so perhaps there's a measure for whether a project is truly critically digitally pedagogical in its intention, execution, and practice: that if we're not just a little bit scared, if we're not just a little bit nervous, a little bit pukey, then it's likely we're not pushing far enough.

But let me take a quick step back from that, and question even what I've just said. This idea of pushing far enough, of turning it up to eleven, can have some pretty rank repercussions.

Back in 2014, I attended the INACOL conference in Palm Springs. At that conference, which was largely for a K12 audience, and was sponsored by the deep pockets of Silicon Valley, I initiated a small, spontaneous unconference with a few participants who all found themselves unhappy with the mostly vendor-centered presentations, the commercializing of elementary education, and the zeal for personalized learning which they recognized as an iteration of B. F. Skinner's teaching machines.

It's always great to have a dark side conversation about educational technology. There's nothing quite like it to keep your fervor going. But it's hard to maintain a balance of optimism alongside the disgruntle. What's more, advocates of critical digital pedagogy can become a feisty bunch. And this little unconference was no exception. Amid the delight and haranguing, out popped the question:

"But how do we drag our colleagues into the digital? How do we bring them into the 21st century?"

Those of us who have spent the last many years hashtagging our insights and relationships do have a desire to bring others into the fold. And part of that impulse is generous: we want for them to see what we see, to experience what we experience. This is a reason for teaching, it is a reason for wide-awakeness, for pedagogies of hospitality, openness, agency, freedom, kindness.

As well, in critical pedagogy, there is an impulse toward change. As I said earlier, we have not only a right to imagine education as if it were otherwise, but we have the responsibility to do so. If that's true, do we also have a responsibility to drag others along with us?

My answer at the time was "no". If one of our colleagues already finds the fax machine overwhelming, then introducing WordPress will not only not be productive, it will likely shear in half what relationship we have with that person. For me, what is most important to the practice of a critical digital pedagogy is... well, this.

Critical pedagogy, and its digital counterpart, are practices obsessed first and foremost with liberation, with freedom, and with agency. And to that end, the very best thing we can do is to support those whose interest draws them to this work, and thus spread the work where it will grow most rapidly. The caution here is that when we become insistent that our colleagues follow along our desire lines—and not their own—we run the risk of oppressing them.

We can be the judge of our own work, but we cannot hold sway over the work of others. We cannot deny them access, we cannot make them dependent on our blessing.

At the beginning of this year, I wrote:

> "Critical pedagogy, digital pedagogy, #digped—none of these is our community. Increasingly, I recognize that there is no "us" when "us" means "our." Should we find ourselves saying that someone is a good fit for our community, we are also saying that someone else is not. Some have seen me as a poor fit for their communities; and so how could I turn around and guard the gate in that fashion? Generosity of spirit, generosity of dialogue, generosity of justice, cannot be exclusive."

Here at the end, I want to return to my mother. Because she is not here, though I invited her. She is not here because she would not feel like she belonged. And she's not here because Reg Saner wouldn't recommend her to the highest degree.

My mother is in her 70s. She's on a fixed income. And she teaches as an adjunct for the Colorado Community Colleges Online. Every semester for the last ten years, she has worried about whether she would get enough courses to make ends meet.

But none of this keeps her from taking risks for students. None of this keeps her from caring for her students. She shared with me some encouragement she offered one of her students recently, one who felt they had failed to do well, failed to meet the expectations of the Developmental English course my mom teaches. She wrote:

> "I have pretty vivid memories of when I started college. I was sooooo anxious. Even when I made it through the first semester, I kept thinking, 'How am I going to be prepared for 200-level, 300-level, and oh goodness, 400-level classes?'

> "Well, the odd thing is that I seemed to somehow absorb knowledge from one semester to another. It was not conscious; but somewhat mysteriously, it happened...And, honestly, when I grade, I sense this. Final drafts may still be a bit rough, but there is learning happening even when the thoughts may not seem to come together as hoped.
>
> "So, I guess what I'm trying to say, is: Trust in the learning process."

A lifetime later, my mom is encouraging students to believe in themselves, to hold fast to their agency, and to be incredibly patient with what Freire might call the "long march" of critical pedagogy. The progressive task "to encourage and make possible, in the most diverse circumstances, the ability to intervene in the world—never its opposite, the crossing of arms before challenges."

With that, I encourage you all to step into our work today with open arms, with insistence and care, with imagination, and with the idea that things can be otherwise.

LEAVING WISCONSIN

JESSE STOMMEL

Increasingly, I think the work of education is activism not teaching.

I was born in Madison in 1976. I left Wisconsin when I was 6 years old and grew up in Colorado. I came back to Madison in 1999. After a year working at a bookstore and living on Blount st. near James Madison park, I decided to turn down an offer from the UW-Madison English graduate program and went back to Colorado for my Ph.D. I was offered more funding at CU Boulder, more teaching, and (most importantly) more opportunities for training in teaching.

Two and a half years ago, I moved back to Wisconsin for a tenure-track faculty position at UW-Madison.

It has been fraught. And now I find myself leaving again.

For anyone following the news about the gutting of public education in the state of Wisconsin, this announcement probably doesn't come entirely out of the blue. But I'm surprised at how quickly I've found myself surrounded by cardboard boxes.

I've accepted a non-tenure-track position as Executive Director of Teaching and Learning Technologies at University of Mary Washington, a public liberal arts institution in Virginia. I will be starting in October. Taking this job was an easy decision. I'm challenged by the shoes I'll fill and excited about the people I'll work with. Because of them, I knew within one hour of the start of the campus visit that I would accept the job if it was offered.

But leaving Wisconsin is still hard. Some of the first words I wrote to a close colleague in May when the dominoes here began to fall: "I'm intensely loyal. I don't abandon ship, but I looked around today and just saw water — no ship."

There are many reasons I'm deciding to go:

- In a few short months, Wisconsin has gone from being the only state to protect tenure and shared governance in state law to being the only state to limit tenure and shared governance in state law. I've been less disheartened by the fact of this and more by the lack of response from University of Wisconsin leadership, in spite of nationwide calls for active resistance.
- Our leaders have insisted we're "safe." It is one thing to take down tenure. It's another thing to take down tenure while insisting tenure is "safe" and "nothing will change." And it's yet a third thing to take down tenure while saying tenure is "safe" and have people actually believe it. We are in George Orwell territory in the state of Wisconsin. I am concerned for UW-Madison, and I am even more concerned for how this will impact other UW institutions, the state system, and public higher education as a whole.
- I have said before that I believe tenure is a red herring. This is a politically-motivated attack on the values that underlie tenure at the University of Wisconsin: job security, academic freedom, and shared governance.
- About six months ago, when UW started to feel pressure, I was told to "be careful." Since then, I've been advised many times to compromise my work for tenure (or to just do different work altogether).
- The institutional climate at UW-Madison has suffered.

It has become, quite frankly, an unfriendly environment, and my own efforts at collaboration have been repeatedly frustrated. Public scholars have come under direct attack. In our work as educators, we must leave no stone unturned, and suddenly there are snakes under some of the stones. And, in order to do our work, we now have to put our jobs at risk.

- The Wisconsin Idea, the principle that the work of UW extends beyond its own borders, is what brought me to this institution, but the commitment to it is being directly challenged. Again, the harder part has been the lack of a strong and collective outcry. Many have been caught up in abstraction, guarding the words — ones like "tenure" and "truth" — while their meaning has been stripped.
- My work — the work I was hired to do — has not been supported. While I was initially assured that digital work for broad public audiences would *count*, I was later told I should wait to do that work until after tenure and focus on traditionally peer-reviewed publications for academic audiences. In January, the following bolded words were sent to me in a letter for my official file: "**The Committee wants to send a clear message that what matters is tenure, what matters for tenure is peer review, and work posted on the web is not considered peer-reviewed.**"
- Finally, because of the current budget cuts, my husband is being laid off from the spousal hire position he has held at UW-Madison. He was officially notified about his impending layoff in the subject line of a calendar invite: "layoff meeting."

This is not what I expected when I moved my family to Wisconsin two and a half years ago. When I took this job, I thought I'd be here for life. I was born in this state, my closest mentor was born in this state, and I have some of the most daring and brilliant colleagues here. We have collaborated in spite of systems that have made that increasingly difficult. I remain awed by what we've built together.

I'm awed by Sage Goellner's resolute calm. Sage is doing the kind of outreach scholarship and teaching that brought me to UW-Madison. Few understand the Wisconsin Idea as deeply as she does. I'm awed by Sarah Marty's ability to keenly balance what would drive anyone else into a frenzy. She has taught me to build things bigger than I thought I could build. I'm awed by Chuck Rybak's resolve and moved by his sadness. He has spoken words I couldn't find. I'm awed by Sara Goldrick-Rab's willful optimism. I'm awed by Brianna Marshall, Joshua Calhoun, Lisa Hager, Jason Lee. I'm awed by every single one of the students I've met and worked with. These people are the reason leaving is hard.

Still, the community of UW has changed, and the changes will have a direct effect on the learning that can happen here. The attacks on shared governance, tenure, and academic freedom are part of a divide and conquer mechanism that deters all of us from advocating for each other. I am in favor of lifting up non-tenure-track faculty, students, and staff so that universities are not caste systems with an oppressed contingent labor class. I am not in favor of making everyone and everything in education adjunct.

I keep seeing the word "unfortunate" used to describe the situation at UW. This is not the right word. What's become of education in the state of Wisconsin is not fate, accident, or misfortune, but has been carefully coordinated and calculated. How about instead we use words like "horrific," "appalling," "insidious," "treacherous"? There is nothing strategic about understating what's happening to the UW System.

This announcement is more anthemic than I intended it to be. I've been incredibly passionate in my love of this place, and so I find myself equally passionate now as I think about my next steps.

Many of my UW colleagues are fielding similar offers or are also thinking about next steps. Some will make the decision to leave. Some will have that decision made for them. Students will be left without mentors. Faculty will be left without collaborators. Education will be left without advocates. Not everyone will leave. Not everyone *can* leave. And, hopefully, all of us that do leave — and those that stay — will keep fighting.

EPILOGUE: HOSPITALITY AND AGENCY

SEAN MICHAEL MORRIS

In most cases, the future of higher education is being written by those who can participate in the dialogue; and as generous as that dialogue might be, there are always conspicuous omissions.

I learned early and quick that academic life operates on an economy of prestige and opportunity. The more prestige one has or gains, the more opportunities; and more opportunities lead to greater prestige. Publishing moves toward tenure. Promotion leads to speaking gigs. Speaking gigs move toward greater capital in the economy. Prestige and opportunity. If you're a director of something, you are more likely to be acknowledged than if you're an assistant director. If you're a professor, you have more clout than an adjunct. If you earn your PhD, doors will open to you that MA-level students don't know exist. At every level, there's somewhere we're struggling to rise from, and a level further we hope to rise to.

This economy of prestige and opportunity makes less room even for people of color, women, queer folk, people with families, and people with disabilities. Cisgender, straight, white men have more ease in this economy than any other demographic.

Despite our best efforts to bring others into the conversation, higher education is notorious for keeping its gates closed, and for building labyrinths within its walls — mazes so unnavigable that many cannot thrive in their complexity, and seek open spaces for their ideas. Communities of change can never be insular.

There are accidental pedagogues everywhere, teachers without classrooms who left the academy but kept their ears and eyes open for when a discussion of a new future for higher education might take place. These are the optimists and introverts, the radicals, the truly deeply irrevocably fringe. And they are most often lurkers in our MOOCs, precarious voices in our Twitter chats, lingerers in rooms at conferences.

Derrida wonders.

> It is as though we were going from one difficulty to another. Better or worse, and more seriously, from impossibility to impossibility. It is as though hospitality were the impossible: as though the law of hospitality defined this very impossibility, as if it were only possible to transgress it, sa though the law of absolute, unconditional, hyperbolical hospitality, as though the categorical imperative of hospitality commanded ... that the 'new arrival' be offered an unconditional welcome. Let us say yes to who or what turns up...

I have never found much comfort in Derrida. Even in his speaking about hospitality, his language is inhospitable, hard to read, concerned with theory that demands action; but that action never comes, unless delivered as a lecture. I do love Derrida. I find his ideas stirring and his perspective on the world off by just the right fraction so that it challenges us and sheds light. But I struggled to find the compassion behind his intellect. Do these words of his inspire the handshake, the embrace, the hospitable abandon they demand?

I wrote recently, in a blog post called "Tobacco and Patchouli: Writing about Teaching", that:

> To teach, we must believe in the potential of each person in the room. Unwaveringly. This is not to say we don't get to have our bad days, our off days, the days when we really can't stand to talk to another student or plan another lesson. But it does mean that we teach for a reason, and that reason lies in what lies in the heart of a student. What lay in our hearts when we were students. Hope despair melancholy desire passion hunger confusion. All the things

it takes to learn to walk. All the things it takes to learn to do anything.

Critical pedagogy demands a lot of us. It demands we walk away from our assumptions about how teaching and learning happen. It demands that we question the teaching we received. It demands we listen. Sometimes, it demands we step aside from our own identity to make room for the identity of a student struggling far more than we are—but just as hard as we once did—to find their identity. Critical pedagogy requires a radical hospitality.

And yet the very notion of hospitality implies a host, someone who is offering space, someone who makes the plan, invites, sets the table. Hospitality requires that a center be established before anything else can happen. It requires occasion, and to some degree, authority. A classroom requires a teacher because the teacher understands, to quote myself from earlier in this volume, "more in its entirety the circumference of the community." The host knows the occasion from which transpires hospitality. Saying "yes to who or what shows up" requires first that a place be determined for that showing up.

In education, that space is most usually the classroom, and today, the learning management system. But what has happened in the classroom is something beyond sending the invitation and setting the table. Education has become a party game with too many rules.

I wish we would suspend our need for learning objectives. I wish we would suspend the temptation to align lessons and assessments to outcomes. I wish we would stop talking about scaffolding. Maybe these apparatuses have something to do with learning and teaching (by my own principles, I have to admit they may). But I wish we could step aside from them—because they prevent discovery, they sanitize and make learning predictable in ways that make us deeply comfortable. Best practices such as these orchestrate learning over much.

But we must recall: "hope despair melancholy desire passion hunger confusion." Learning is uncomfortable. It exposes our soft underbellies. And teaching must address this. If our rubrics can account for whomever shows up, if our learning objectives can do that, then we should employ them. If they do not, if they cannot, they must be reconsidered.

No one likes it when I say that. We are tied to our way of doing things, our way of seeing education. We are bound to these, and having been bound to them for so long, we've grown used to them. But being accustomed to a thing does not make it useful.

If he is adamant about anything, Paulo Freire is adamant about refusing the notion that our situations are unchangeable, that our systems are not only complete but also that they determine the outcome of our work, our histories, and our identities. If I say that I am a teacher who uses the LMS, if I say I am a teacher who must create learning outcomes, who must grade, if I say I am a teacher whose students do not trust him or who only learn from lectures or who do not want to take ownership for their learning—and yet I want to do or believe differently—then I am settling for a reality that is not just. And that is distinctly *un*critical.

When we do because we are told to do, or because we have inherited a kind of doing from our teachers or parents or from society, or we assume that doing it this way or that way has been proven to be most effective, or, worse, we wait upon the news of what is best to do coming from our governments, our administrations, Silicon Valley, the keynote at a conference, then we surrender our agency to learn for ourselves the material substance and nature of our reality and can no longer take it upon ourselves to change, to do, as best suits our wisdom and identity. And if teachers surrender their agency, they can only teach students to do the same.

Over and over we have surrendered our agency—to the modern myths of behavioral psychology, neurology, "learning styles," and more. Audrey Watters writes, in "The History of the Future of Learning Objects and Intelligent Machines,"

> What we know about knowing is not settled. It never has been. And neither neuroscience nor brain scans, for example, move us any closer to that. After all, "learning" isn't simply about an individual's brain or even body. "Learning" – or maybe more accurately "learnedness" – is a signal; it's a symbol; it's a performance. As such, it's judged by and through and with all sorts of cultural values and expectations, not only those that we claim to be able to measure. What do you know? How do you know? Who do you know?

Learning is complicated, multivalent and multi-layered, and our understanding of it should always be evolving. But not evolving toward an understanding that can claim mastery, not toward an understanding that will define learning finally and for the last time and perfectly. Our first mistake is to assume that because something sounds reasonable, sounds like it will work, rings true of the ways we've seen students behave, that it is reasonable, will work, is the way students behave. And we make that assumption, we choose to believe what research tells us about learning because we have forgotten the original lie: that students are a population to control.

When we choose to believe that lie, we do not only surrender our agency to actually teach, we erase agency from the conversation altogether. We no longer have freedom, nor can we any longer assume accountability.

Agency lies in the balance between freedom and accountability. It is not wholly one, nor the other. It does not, cannot discount the relationships we maintain of respect, confidence in another's knowing, or the responsibility that comes with authority. But it also does not yield the capacity of critical inquiry that is the hallmark of liberated life. And so agency is more than choice, but not always more than collaboration. It is rebellion, but it is always also nurture. Freire says directly that the oppressed must free the oppressor as much as themselves in order to overcome oppression. An unwillingness to do so, an inability to make real the balance of criticality and kindness, results in another oppression, and no one is freed.

Critical inquiry, then, is a conversation always, an hospitable one.

Hospitality may begin with a host, but it continues with those who show up. But not in actions of politeness and etiquette—in critical inquiry. When we find ourselves at an occasion, or in the presence of an authority who has laid out the ground rules for our time together, we must ask: Where have we arrived? What is the occasion? What is expected of me, and what is fair? Is this a space where I am free, or is this a space where control has overwhelmed collaboration? Who will I show up as, and am I ready to welcome whomever else shows up? Will I become a model for participation—whether by joining the games, changing their rules, or disrupting them—and how does my agency as a participant affect and balance with the agency of everyone else?

These are questions students should ask when they see a syllabus, when they are invited to complete an assignment, when they enter the LMS, agree to use a digital tool, or when they are considering a university for study. And educators should ask these questions of their professional organizations, the conferences we attend, the committees we belong to, and even of the profession itself. Elision of these questions, or the space to ask these questions, is oppressive, and does not lead to the kind of critical collaboration that frees agency to take the floor.

Let us, then, move from impossibility to impossibility together, rather than move together with side-eyes and rubrics. We must recognize the spaces we occupy, the occasions we act from, and the communities that accompany us in the work we do. We must make our conversations critical inquiry, our collegiality liberatory, and our respect for one another impressive and irresistible, excited and sanguine.

BIBLIOGRAPHY

Almereyda, Michael, director. *Experimenter*. BB Film Productions, 2015.

American Association for Community Colleges. "About Community Colleges." aacc.nche.edu/AboutCC/Pages/default.aspx. Accessed 1 May 2013.

American Association of University Professors. "New Report on Contingent Faculty and Governance." aaup.org/news/new-report-contingent-faculty-and-governance. Accessed 21 August 2018.

American Association of University Professors. "Statement on Online and Distance Education." aaup.org/report/statement-online-and-distance-education. Accessed 21 August 2018.

Amidon, Tim. "(dis)Owning Tech: Ensuring Value and Agency at the Moment of Interface." *Hybrid Pedagogy*, 8 September 2016. hybridpedagogy.org/disowning-tech-ensuring-value-agency-moment-interface

Aronowitz, Stanley. *Against Schooling: For an Education That Matters*. Routledge, 2008.

Ball, Cheryl. "Editorial Pedagogy, Pt. 1: A Professional Philosophy." *Hybrid Pedagogy*, 5 November 2012. hybridpedagogy.org/editorial-pedagogy-pt-1-a-professional-philosophy

Barthes, Roland. "Death of the Author." *The Rustle of Language*. Translated by Richard Howard. University of California Press, 1989, pp. 49-55.

Barthes, Roland. *The Pleasure of the Text*. Translated by Richard Miller. Hill and Wang, 1975.

Bhabha, Homi. *The Location of Culture*. Routledge, 2012.

Bickman, Martin. "Returning to Community and Praxis: A Circuitous Journey through Pedagogy and Literary Studies." *Pedagogy*. Vol. 10, no. 1, 2010, pp. 11–23.

Blikstein, Paulo. "Travels in Troy with Freire: Technology as an Agent of Emancipation." *Educação e Pesquisa*. Vol. 42, no. 3, 2016, pp. 837-856.

Bloom, Benjamin Samuel, David R. Krathwohl, and Bertram B. Masia. *Taxonomy of Educational Objectives: The Classification of Educational Goals. Handbook 2: Affective domain*. David McKay, 1956.

Boldt, Josh. "99 Problems But Tenure Ain't One." *Chronicle Vitae*, 21 January 2014. chroniclevitae.com/news/283-99-problems-but-tenure-ain-t-one

Bouchardon, Serge and Davin Heckman. "Digital Manipulability and Digital Literature." *Electronic Book Review*. 2012.

Bowles, Kate. "Irreplaceable Time." *Music for Deckchairs*, 24 November 2013. musicfordeckchairs.wordpress.com/2013/11/24/irreplaceable-time

Brooks, David. "The Campus Tsunami." *The New York Times*, 3 May 2012. nytimes.com/2012/05/04/opinion/brooks-the-campus-tsunami.html

Burtis, Martha. "Making and Breaking Domain of One's Own: Rethinking the Web in Higher Ed." *Hybrid Pedagogy*, 19 August 2016. hybridpedagogy.org/making-breaking-rethinking-web-higher-ed

Byrnes, Jesse. "Obama hits 'coddled' liberal college students." *The Hill*, 15 September 2015. thehill.com/blogs/blog-briefing-room/news/253641-obama-hits-coddled-liberal-college-students

Campbell, Andy. "Spawn." *I <3 E-Poetry.* iloveepoetry.com/?p=300. Accessed 21 August 2018.

Carnegie Foundation Foundation for the Advancement of Teaching. *Carnegie Classifications of Institutions of Higher Education, 2010 Edition.* Stanford, 2011.

Carr, Nicholas. "Is Google Making Us Stupid?" *The Atlantic Monthly,* July/August 2008. theatlantic.com/magazine/archive/2008/07/is-google-making-us-stupid/306868

Cavanaugh, Joseph K. "Are Online Courses Cannibalizing Students From Existing Courses?" *Journal of Asynchronous Learning Networks.* Vol. 9, no. 2, 2005, pp. 3-8.

Cohen, Jeffrey Jerome. "Monster Culture (Seven Theses)." *Monster Theory: Reading Culture.* University of Minnesota Press, 1996, pp. 3-25.

Collier, Amy. "Not-yetness and Learnification." *Red Pincushion,* 1 April 2016. redpincushion.us/blog/teaching-and-learning/not-yetness-and-learnification

Cook, Lloyd Allen. *Community Backgrounds of Education: A Textbook in Educational Sociology, Volume 6.* Taylor & Francis, 2006.

Cormier, Dave. "Explaining Rhizomatic Learning to My Five Year Old." *Dave's Educational Blog,* 18 November 2011. davecormier.com/edblog/2011/11/18/explaining-rhizomatic-learning-to-my-five-year-old

Croxall, Brian and Adeline Koh. "'Digital Pedagogy'?" *A Digital Pedagogy Unconference.* briancroxall.net/digitalpedagogy/what-is-digital-pedagogy. Accessed 21 August 2018.

Croxall, Brian. "The Absent Presence: Today's Faculty." *Brian Croxall,* 28 December 2009. briancroxall.net/2009/12/28/the-absent-presence-todays-faculty

Crystal, David. *txtng: the gr8 db8.* Oxford University Press, 2009.

Daly, Jimmy. "11 Enlightening Statistics About Massive Open Online Courses." *EdTech*, 5 February 2013. edtechmagazine.com/higher/article/2013/02/11-enlightening-statistics-about-massive-open-online-courses

Danielewski, Mark Z. *House of Leaves*. Pantheon, 2000.

Davidson, Cathy N. "Access Demands a Paradigm Shift." Modern Language Association Conference, 4 January 2013, Sheraton Boston, Boston, MA.

Davidson, Cathy N. "Let's Talk about MOOC (online) Education–And Also About Massively Outdated Traditional Education (MOTEs)." *HASTAC*, 20 July 2012. hastac.org/blogs/cathy-davidson/2012/07/20/lets-talk-about-mooc-online-education-and-also-about-massively

Davidson, Cathy N. "Year of the MOOC: Rsp to NY Times, A Student-Made MOOC by Dan Ariely and me." *HASTAC*, 3 November 2012. hastac.org/blogs/cathy-davidson/2012/11/03/year-mooc-rsp-ny-times-student-made-mooc-dan-ariely-and-me

Davidson, Cathy N. "Year of the MOOC: Rsp to NY Times, A Student-Made MOOC by Dan Ariely and me." *HASTAC*, 3 November 2012. hastac.org/blogs/cathy-davidson/2012/11/03/year-mooc-rsp-ny-times-student-made-mooc-dan-ariely-and-me

Davidson, Cathy. "Collaborative Learning for the Digital Age." *The Chronicle of Higher Education*, 26 August 2011. www.chronicle.com/article/Collaborative-Learning-for-the/128789/

Davidson, Cathy. "History and Future of (Mostly) Higher Education." YouTube, uploaded by Duke Learning Innovation, 3 February 2015. youtube.com/watch?v=8KWeOuqXty8

Davidson, Cathy. "Shifting Attention." *YouTube*, uploaded by Duke University, 16 August 2011. youtube.com/watch?v=eG3HpEN9Y8E

Davidson, Cathy. *Now You See It*. Penguin Books, 2012.

DeRosa, Robin and Rajiv Jhangiani. "Open Pedagogy." *A Guide to Making Open Textbooks with Students. REBUS Community.* press.rebus.community/makingopentextbookswithstudents/chapter/open-pedagogy. Accessed 21 August 2018.

Dewey, John and Evelyn Dewey. *Schools of To-morrow*. Dent, 1915.

Dickinson, Emily. "From all the Jails the Boys and Girls." *The complete poems of Emily Dickenson.* Edited by Martha Dickenson Bianchi. Little, Brown, 1924.

Dillon, Sam. "Troubles Grow for a University Built on Profits." *The New York Times.* 11 February 2007. nytimes.com/2007/02/11/education/11phoenix.html

Dimeo, Jean. "Improving Instructor-Student Engagement Online." *Inside Higher Ed,* 27 September 2017. www.insidehighered.com/digital-learning/article/2017/09/27/instructors-suggest-digital-tools-improving-engagement-online

Douglas-Gabriel, Danielle. "Battle Over College Course Material is a Textbook Example of Technological Change." *The Washington Post.* 14 April 2018. washingtonpost.com/local/education/battle-over-college-course-material-is-a-textbook-example-of-technological-change/2018/04/14/fb3d0394-0db5-11e8-95a5-c396801049ef_story.html

Douglass, Frederick. *Narrative of the Life of Frederick Douglass, an American Slave*. Bedford/St. Martin's, 2003.

Edmundson, Mark. "The Trouble with Online Education." *The New York Times.* 19 July 2012. nytimes.com/2012/07/20/opinion/the-trouble-with-online-education.html

EDUCAUSE Learning Initiative (ELI). "7 Things You Should Know About the Internet of Things." *EDUCAUSE*. 6 October 2014. library.educause.edu/resources/2014/10/7-things-you-should-know-about-the-internet-of-things

Elbow, Peter. "Ranking, Evaluating, and Liking: Sorting Out Three Forms of Judgment." *College English*. Vol. 55, no. 2, 1993, pp. 187-206.

Emerson, Ralph Waldo. "The American Scholar." Phi Kappa Beta Society, Cambridge University, 31 August 1837. Oration.

Fitzpatrick, Kathleen. "On the Future of Academic Publishing, Peer Review, and Tenure Requirements (Or, Remaking the Academy, One Electronic Text at a Time)." *The Valve*. 6 January 2006. thevalve.org/go/valve/article/on_the_future_of_academic_publishing_peer_review_and_tenure_requirements_or

Fitzpatrick, Kathleen. "On the Future of Peer Review in Electronic Scholarly Publishing." *If:book*. 28 June 2006. futureofthebook.org/blog/2006/06/28/on_the_future_of_peer_review_i

Fitzpatrick, Kathleen. *Planned Obsolescence: Publishing, Technology, and the Future of the Academy*. NYU Press, 2011.

Freire, Paulo. *Pedagogy of Indignation*. Paradigm Publishers, 2004.

Freire, Paulo. *Pedagogy of the Oppressed*. Translated by Myra Bergman Ramos. Penguin, 1970.

Fyfe, Paul. "Digital Pedagogy Unplugged." *Digital Humanities Quarterly*. Vol. 5, no. 3, 2001, digitalhumanities.org/dhq/vol/5/3/000106/000106.html

Giroux, Henry. "Lessons to Be Learned from Paulo Freire as Education Is Being Taken Over by the Mega Rich." *Truthout*, 23 November 2010. truth-out.org/archive/item/93016:lessons-to-be-learned-from-paulo-freire-as-education-is-being-taken-over-by-the-mega-rich

Giroux, Henry. "Rethinking Education as the Practice of Freedom: Paulo Freire and the Promise of Critical Pedagogy." *Truthout*. 1 January 2010. truth-out.org/archive/component/k2/item/87456:rethinking-education-as-the-practice-of-freedom-paulo-freire-and-the-promise-of-critical-pedagogy

Giroux, Henry. *On Critical Pedagogy*. A&C Black, 2011.

Goldrick-Rab, Sara. "Public Higher Education Should Be Universal and Free." *The New York Times.* 20 January 2016. nytimes.com/roomfordebate/2016/01/20/should-college-be-free/public-higher-education-should-be-universal-and-free

Goldsmith, Kenneth. *Uncreative Writing: Managing Language in the Digital Age.* Columbia University Press, 2011.

Greene, Maxine. *Releasing the Imagination: Essays on Education, the Arts, and Social Change.* Jossey-Bass, 1995.

Groom, Jim. "We've been MOOCed." *Bava Tuesdays.* 20 July 2012. bavatuesdays.com/weve-been-mooced

Guest Pryal, Katie Rose. "A Lecturer's Almanac." *Hybrid Pedagogy.* 21 October 2013. hybridpedagogy.org/a-lecturers-almanac

Gutierrez, Karla. "18 Mind-Blowing eLearning Statistics You Need to Know." *Sh!ft Disruptive Learning,* shiftelearning.com/blog/bid/247473/18-Mind-Blowing-eLearning-Statistics-You-Need-To-Know

Harris, Katherine D. "NITLE Digital Pedagogy Seminar." *triproftri,* 3 April 2012, triproftri.wordpress.com/2012/03/27/nitle-digital-pedagogy

Hawthorne, Nathaniel. *The House of the Seven Gables.* James Thomas Fields, 1851.

Hayles, N. Katherine. *Electronic Literature: New Horizons for the Literary.* University of Notre Dame Press, 2008.

Hollis, Leah P. *Bully in the Ivory Tower: How Aggression and Incivility Erode American Higher Education.* Patricia Berkly, 2012.

hooks, bell. *Teaching to Transgress.* Routledge, 1994.

Howard, Rebecca Moore. "Arguing Against Turnitin." *Chenango Metonymy.* 4 May 2013. rmoorehoward.wordpress.com/2013/05/04/arguing-against-turnitin

Howard, Rebecca Moore. "Understanding 'Internet Plagiarism'." *Computers and Composition*, vol. 24, no. 3, 2007, pp. 3-15.

Hunter, Leann, et al. "Digital Humanities Made Me a Better Pedagogue, a Crowdsourced Article." *Hybrid Pedagogy*. 10 July 2012. hybridpedagogy.org/digital-humanities-made-me-a-better-pedagogue-a-crowdsourced-article

Inman Berens, Kathi. "The New Learning is Ancient." *New Media Curious*. 15 January 2013. kathiiberens.com/teaching/philosophy

Inman Berens, Kathi. "Want to 'Save the Humanities'? Pay Adjuncts to Learn Digital Tools." *Disrupting the Digital Humanities*. 5 January 2015. disruptingdh.com/want-to-save-the-humanities-pay-adjuncts-to-learn-digital-tools

@jessifer. "'Sustain innovation by finding the cheapest, fastest, least bureaucratic way to make yourself a perpetual learner.' @CathyNDavidson #katz." 22 February 2013, 11:01 a.m. twitter.com/Jessifer/status/305029626114228224.

Kasulis, Thomas. "Chapter Four: Questioning." *The Art and Craft of Teaching*. Edited by Margaret Morganroth Gullette. Harvard University Press, 1984, pp. 38-48.

Kraft, Tiffany. "Adjunctification: Living in the Margins of Academe." *Hybrid Pedagogy*. 18 November 2013. hybridpedagogy.org/adjunctification-living-in-the-margins-of-academe

Kraidy, Marwan M. *Hybridity: the Cultural Logic of Globalization*. Temple University Press, 2005.

Kruger-Ross, Matthew. "A Plea for Pedagogy." *Hybrid Pedagogy*. 7 August 2013. hybridpedagogy.org/a-plea-for-pedagogy

Marks, Laura U. *Touch: Sensuous Theory and Multisensory Media*. University of Minnesota Press, 2002.

Marraccini, Marisa E. "College Students' Perceptions of Professor Bullying." *Open Access Master's Theses.* Paper 9, 11 April 2013. digitalcommons.uri.edu/theses/9

McKenzie, Lindsay. "'Inclusive Access' Takes Off." *Inside Higher Ed.* 7 November 2017. insidehighered.com/news/2017/11/07/inclusive-access-takes-model-college-textbook-sales

McMillan Cottom, Tressie. "Academic Cowards and Why I Don't Write Anonymously." *tressiemc.* 21 January 2014. tressiemc.com/uncategorized/academic-cowards-and-why-i-dont-write-anonymously

McMillan Cottom, Tressie. "Dude, Where's The Race in Your Class Analysis of HigherEd?" *tressiemc.* 1 January 2014. tressiemc.com/uncategorized/dude-wheres-the-race-in-your-class-analysis-of-highered

McMillan Cottom, Tressie. "Why Free College is Necessary." *Dissent.* Fall 2015, dissentmagazine.org/article/tressie-mcmillan-cottom-why-free-college-necessary. Accessed on 21 August 2018.

Melville, Herman. "Bartleby, the Scrivener: A Story of Wall Street." *The Piazza Tales.* Dix & Edwards, 1856.

Milgram, Stanley. *Obedience to Authority: An Experimental View.* Harper, 2009.

Mod, Craig. "Books in the Age of the iPad." *@craigmod.* March 2010. craigmod.com/journal/ipad_and_books. Accessed on 21 August 2018.

Morris, Sean Michael and Jesse Stommel. "If Freire Made a MOOC: Open Education as Resistance." *Hybrid Pedagogy.* 20 November 2014. hybridpedagogy.org/freire-made-mooc-open-education-resistance

Morris, Sean Michael and Jesse Stommel. "Pedagogies of Scale." *Hybrid Pedagogy.* 12 June 2013. hybridpedagogy.org/pedagogies-of-scale

Morris, Sean Michael, Jesse Stommel, and Pete Rorabaugh. "Beyond Rigor." *Hybrid Pedagogy.* 9 October 2013. hybridpedagogy.org/beyond-rigor

Morris, Sean Michael. "Collegiality as Pedagogy." 15 December 2015. seanmichaelmorris.com/collegiality-as-pedagogy

Morris, Sean Michael. "Critical Digital Pedagogy and Design." 1 May 2017. seanmichaelmorris.com/critical-digital-pedagogy-and-design

Morris, Sean Michael. "Digital Humanities and the Erosion of Inquiry." *Hybrid Pedagogy.* 12 February 2016. hybridpedagogy.org/digital-humanities-erosion-of-inquiry

Morris, Sean Michael. "Instructional Design Vs. Online Pedagogy." 21 April 2014. seanmichaelmorris.com/instructional-design-vs-online-pedagogy

Morris, Sean Michael. "Tobacco and Patchouli: Writing about Teaching." 24 April 2017. seanmichaelmorris.com/tobacco-and-patchouli-writing-about-teaching

Morris, Sean Michael. "What is MOOCification?" *MOOC MOOC.* moocmooc.com/articles_files/What_Is_MOOCification.html. Accessed on 21 August 2018.

Papert, Seymour. *Mindstorms: Children, Computers, and Powerful Ideas.* Basic Books, 1993.

Papert, Seymour. *The Children's Machine: Rethinking School in the Age of the Computer.* Basic Books, 1994.

Patton, Stacey. "Dear Student: It's February and You Still Don't Have Your Textbook?" *Chronicle Vitae.* 6 February 2015. chroniclevitae.com/news/898-dear-student-it-s-february-and-you-still-don-t-have-your-textbook

Patton, Stacey. "Dear Student: No, I Won't Change the Grade You Deserve." *Chronicle Vitae.* 13 February 2013. chroniclevitae.com/news/908-dear-student-no-i-won-t-change-the-grade-you-deserve

Patton, Stacey. "Dear Student: Should Your Granny Die Before the Midterm." *Chronicle Vitae.* 29 January 2015. chroniclevitae.com/

news/886-dear-student-should-your-granny-die-before-the-midterm

Patton, Stacey. "Dear Student: Sorry, You're Too Late to Sign Up for My Class." *Chronicle Vitae.* 27 February 2015. chroniclevitae.com/news/921-dear-student-sorry-you-re-too-late-to-sign-up-for-my-class

Pérez, Annemarie. "Teaching Manifesto." 12 August 2016. citedatthe-crossroads.net/blog/2016/08/12/teaching-manifesto

Pynchon, Thomas. "Is it O.K. to be a Luddite?" *The New York Times.* 28 October 1984. archive.nytimes.com/www.nytimes.com/books/97/05/18/reviews/pynchon-luddite.html

Ramsay, Stephen. "The Hermeneutics of Screwing Around; or What You Do with a Million Books" *Digital Culture Books.* quod.lib.umich.edu/d/dh/12544152.0001.001/1:5/–pastplay-teaching-and-learning-history-with-technology. Accessed on 22 August 2018.

Rathgeber, Brad. "My Trouble with Mark Edmundson's Trouble with Online Education." *Brad's Blog.* 22 July 2012. bradsblog.onlineschool-forgirls.org/post/27782812008/my-trouble-with-mark-edmund-sons-trouble-with

Rheingold, Howard and Laurie Rowell. "An Interview with Howard Rheingold." *eLearn Magazine.* February 2010. elearnmag.acm.org/fea-tured.cfm

Rheingold, Howard. "Participative Pedagogy for a Literacy of Literacies." *Freesouls,* freesouls.cc/essays/03-howard-rheingold-participa-tive-pedagogy-for-a-literacy-of-literacies.html. Accessed on 22 August 2018.

Rheingold, Howard. *Net Smart: How to Thrive Online.* MIT Press, 2014.

Rorabaugh, Pete and Jesse Stommel. "The Four Noble Virtues of Digital Media Citation." *Hybrid Pedagogy.* 25 April 2012. hybridpeda-gogy.org/the-four-noble-virtues-of-digital-media-citation

Rorabaugh, Pete. "Occupy the Digital: Critical Pedagogy and New

Media." *Hybrid Pedagogy*. 6 August 2012. hybridpedagogy.org/occupy-the-digital-critical-pedagogy-and-new-media

Rorabaugh, Pete. "Organic Writing and Digital Media: Seeds and Organs." *Hybrid Pedagogy*. 21 June 2012. hybridpedagogy.org/organic-writing-and-digital-media-seeds-and-organs

Rutter, Michael Patrick. "Harvard and MIT release working papers on open online learning." *The Harvard Gazette*. 21 January 2014. news.harvard.edu/gazette/story/2014/01/harvard-and-mit-release-working-papers-on-open-online-learning

Rybak, Chuck. "Waving the White Flag on Tenured vs. Adjunct." *Sad Iron*. sadiron.com/waving-the-white-flag-on-tenured-vs-adjunct

Sample, Mark. "Intrusive Scaffolding, Obstructed Learning (and MOOCs)." *Sample Reality*. 18 December 2012. samplereality.com/2012/12/18/intrusive-scaffolding-obstructed-learning-and-moocs

Sample, Mark. "Notes Towards a Deformed Humanities." *Sample Reality*. 2 may 2012. samplereality.com/2012/05/02/notes-towards-a-deformed-humanities

Sasser, Tanya. "Digital Writing as Handicraft." *Digital Writing Month*. 6 November 2012. web.archive.org/web/20131223072450/http://www.digitalwritingmonth.com/2012/11/06/digital-writing-as-handicraft

Sasser, Tanya. "Loitering in the Witch's House: My MOOC Experience." *Remixing College English*. 20 July 2012. remixingcollegeenglish.wordpress.com/2012/07/20/loitering-in-the-witchs-house-my-mooc-experience

Schutz, Alfred. *Collected Papers I. The Problem of Social Reality*. Springer Netherlands, 1972.

Shaffer, Kris and Robin Wharton, eds. *Open Music Theory*. openmusictheory.com. Accessed 22 August 2018.

Shaffer, Kris. "A New Way to Do Peer Review." 29 May 2013. pushpullfork.com/a-new-way-to-do-peer-review

Shaull, Richard. "Introduction." *Pedagogy of the Oppressed*. Penguin, 1970.

Shor, Ira and Paulo Freire. *A Pedagogy for Liberation: Dialogues on Transforming Education*. Greenwood Publishing Group, 1987.

Skallerup Bessette, Lee and Jesse Stommel. "A Scholarship of Resistance: Bravery, Contingency, and Higher Education." *Hybrid Pedagogy*. 1 April 2013. hybridpedagogy.org/a-scholarship-of-resistance-bravery-contingency-and-higher-education

Skinner, B. F. *The Technology of Teaching*. Meredith Corporation, 1968.

Small, Gary. *iBrain: Surviving the Technological Alteration of the Modern Mind*. Harper Collins, 2008.

Smith, Anna. "Your Voice in Mine." *Digital Writing Month*. 29 November 2012. web.archive.org/web/20140224032411/http://www.digitalwritingmonth.com/2012/11/29/your-voice-in-mine

Staley, David. "Autonomous Learning and the Future of Higher Education." *The Evolllution*. 14 March 2013. evolllution.com/opinions/autonomous-learning-future-higher-education

Staumsheim, Carl. "Accidental Exposure." *Inside Higher Ed*. 12 November 2014. insidehighered.com/news/2014/11/12/proquest-ends-dissertation-sales-through-amazon

Stein, Gertrude. *Tender Buttons*. Claire Marie, 1914.

Stewart, Bonnie. "Open to Influence: Academic Influence on Twitter, the Short Version." *The Theoryblog*. 10 March 2015. theory.cribchronicles.com/2015/03/10/open-to-influence-academic-influence-on-twitter-the-short-version

Stewart, Bonnie. "What Counts as Academic Influence Online?"*The Theoryblog*. 27 April 2014. theory.cribchronicles.com/2014/04/27/what-counts-as-academic-influence-online

Stommel, Jesse. "The Public Digital Humanities." *Disrupting the Digital Humanities.* 9 January 2015. disruptingdh.com/the-public-digital-humanities

Stommel, Jesse. "The Student 2.0." *Hybrid Pedagogy.* 2 January 2012. hybridpedagogy.org/the-student-2-0

Stommel, Jesse. "Trust, Agency, and Connected Learning." *Hybrid Pedagogy.* 10 November 2014. hybridpedagogy.org/trust-agency-connected-learning

Straumsheim, Carl. "What is Detected?" *Inside Higher Ed.* 14 July 2015. insidehighered.com/news/2015/07/14/turnitin-faces-new-questions-about-efficacy-plagiarism-detection-software

Thacker, Eugene. *In the Dust of this Planet: Horror of Philosophy vol. 1.* John Hunt Publishing, 2011.

"The Student Cyborg & How Technology is Facilitating Education." *Visually.* visual.ly/the-student-cyborg-how-technology-is-facilitating-education. Infographic. Accessed on 22 August 2018.

Thomas, Douglas and John Seely Brown. *A New Culture of Learning.* CreateSpace Independent Publishing, 2011.

Thompson, Clive. "The dumbest generation? No, Twitter is making kids smarter." *The Globe and Mail.* 13 September 2013. theglobeandmail.com/life/how-new-digital-tools-are-making-kids-smarter/article14321886

Thoreau, Henry David. *Walden.* 1854.

Todorov, Tzvetan. *The Fantastic: A Structural Approach to a Literary Genre.* Cornell University Press, 1975.

Vaidhyanathan, Siva. "What's the Matter With MOOCs?" *The Chronicle of Higher Education.* 6 July 2012. chronicle.com/blogs/innovations/whats-the-matter-with-moocs/33289

Watkins, D. "The School of Failure." *Aeon.* 27 April 2015. aeon.co/essays/how-school-grooms-african-americans-for-the-underclass

Watters, Audrey. "Education Technology's Completely Over." *Hack Education.* 7 April 2017. hackeducation.com/2017/04/07/prince

Watters, Audrey. "The Language of MOOCs." *Inside Higher Ed.* 7 June 2012. insidehighered.com/blogs/hack-higher-education/language-moocs

Watters, Audrey. "The Real Reason I Dropped Out of a Ph.D. Program." *Hack Education.* 29 August 2012. hackeducation.com/2012/08/29/the-real-reason-i-dropped-out-of-a-phd-program

Watters, Audrey. "The Web We Need to Give Students." *Bright.* 15 July 2015. brightthemag.com/the-web-we-need-to-give-students-311d97713713

Weinberger, David. *Small Pieces Loosely Joined.* Basic Books, 2003.

Wesch, Michael. "A Vision of Students Today." *YouTube,* uploaded by Michael Wesch, 12 October 2007. youtube.com/watch?v=dGCJ46vyR9o

"What Happens in 60 Seconds on the Internet" *Gizmodo.* 20 June 2011. gizmodo.com/5813875/what-happens-in-60-seconds-on-the-internet.

Wharton, Robin. "Re-Thinking Plagiarism as Unfair Competition." 13 January 2013. robinwharton.com/2013/01/re-thinking-plagiarism-as-unfair-competition-presented-at-cccc-chicago-il-24-march-2006

Wylie, Ian. "Schools Have the Final Word on Plagiarism." *Financial Times.* 8 April 2012. ft.com/content/97a2c816-57ca-11e1-ae89-00144feabdc0

PREVIOUS PUBLICATIONS

Most of the chapters in this collection are revised from previously published work.

"Critical Digital Pedagogy: a Definition" originally appeared on Hybrid Pedagogy in 2014. It was revised and expanded from the version here for an edited collection from University of Chicago Press, *Moocs and Their Afterlives.*

"What is a Pedagogue?" originally appeared on Sean Michael Morris's personal blog in 2014.

"Digital Pedagogy: a Genealogy" originally appeared on *Hybrid Pedagogy* in 2013 as

"Decoding Digital Pedagogy, Pt. 2: (Un)Mapping the Terrain."

"Beyond the LMS" originally appeared on *Hybrid Pedagogy* in 2013.

"Learning is Not a Mechanism" originally appeared on *Hybrid Pedagogy* in 2015. The publication there was adapted from a piece published on *Educating Modern Learners.*

"Teaching in Our Right Minds: Critical Digital Pedagogy and the Response to the New" originally appeared on Sean Michael Morris's personal blog in 2014.

"Is it Okay to Be a Luddite?" originally appeared on *Hybrid Pedagogy* in 2014.

"Winona Ryder and the Internet of Things" originally appeared on *Hybrid Pedagogy* in 2016. The publication there was adapted from a piece published in *Educause Review.*

"Adventures in Unveiling: Critical Pedagogy and Imagination" originally appeared on *Hybrid Pedagogy* in 2018.

"Online Learning: a Manifesto" originally appeared on *Hybrid Pedagogy* in 2012.

"How to Build an Ethical Online Course" originally appeared on *Hybrid Pedagogy* in 2013.

"The Failure of an Online Program" originally appeared on *Hybrid Pedagogy* in 2013.

"A User's Guide to Forking Education" originally appeared on *Hybrid Pedagogy* in 2013.

"The Discussion Forum is Dead; Long Live the Discussion Forum" originally appeared on *Hybrid Pedagogy* in 2013.

"Reading the LMS against the Backdrop of Critical Pedagogy" originally appeared on Sean Michael Morris's personal blog in 2017.

"Why Online Programs Fail, and 5 Things We Can Do About It" originally appeared on *Hybrid Pedagogy* in 2013.

"The March of the MOOCs: Monstrous Open Online Courses" originally appeared on *Hybrid Pedagogy* in 2012.

"On Presence, Video Lectures, and Critical Pedagogy" originally appeared on Sean Michael Morris's personal blog in 2017.

"The Course Hath No Bottom: the 20,000-Person Seminar" originally appeared on *Hybrid Pedagogy* in 2015.

"Critical Instructional Design" originally appeared on Sean Michael Morris's personal blog in 2017.

"Courses, Composition, Hybridity" originally appeared on Sean Michael Morris's personal blog in 2016.

"The Twitter Essay" originally appeared on *Hybrid Pedagogy* in 2012.

"Digital Writing Uprising" originally appeared on *Hybrid Pedagogy* in 2012.

"The Pedagogies of Reading and Not Reading" originally appeared on *Hybrid Pedagogy* in 2014.

"Queequeg's Coffin: A Sermon for the Digital Human" originally appeared on *Hybrid Pedagogy* in 2013.

"Digital Humanities is About Breaking Stuff" originally appeared on *Hybrid Pedagogy* in 2013.

"What is Hybrid Pedagogy?" originally appeared on *Hybrid Pedagogy* in 2012.

"Publishing as Pedagogy" originally appeared on *PhD2Published* in 2012.

"Collaborative Peer Review: Gathering the Academy's Orphans" originally appeared on *Hybrid Pedagogy* in 2013

"Hybrid Pedagogy, Digital Humanities, and the Future of Academic Publishing" originally appeared on *Hybrid Pedagogy* in 2014.

"Call for Editors" originally appeared on *Hybrid Pedagogy* in 2014.

"We May Need to Amputate" originally appeared on *Hybrid Pedagogy* in 2014.

"I Would Prefer Not To" originally appeared on *Hybrid Pedagogy* in 2014.

"Not Enough Voices" originally appeared on *Hybrid Pedagogy* in 2016.

"Vulnerability, Contingency, and Advocacy in Higher Education" originally appeared on Jesse Stommel's personal blog in 2014.

"A Manifesto for Community Colleges, Lifelong Learning, and Autodidacts" originally appeared on *Hybrid Pedagogy* in 2013.

"Free College; Free Training for College Teachers" originally appeared on Jesse Stommel's personal blog in 2016.

"Textbooks, OER, and the Need for Open Pedagogy" originally appeared on Jesse Stommel's personal blog in 2018.

"A Guide for Resisting Edtech: the Case Against Turnitin" originally appeared on *Hybrid Pedagogy* in 2017.

"Dear Chronicle: Why I Will No Longer Write for Vitae" originally appeared on Jesse Stommel's personal blog in 2015.

"Dear Student" originally appeared on Jesse Stommel's personal blog in 2015.

"Wide-awakeness and Critical Imagination" originally appeared on Sean Michael Morris's personal blog in 2018.

"Leaving Wisconsin" originally appeared on Jesse Stommel's personal blog in 2015.

"Epilogue: Hospitality and Agency" originally appeared on Sean Michael Morris's personal blog in 2017.

Printed in Great Britain
by Amazon